Praise for *Why It Matters*

"John White has captured a lifetime of personal and professional practical leadership experiences and delivers *Why It Matters* with the precision of a renowned industrial engineer and the compassion of a most humble servant leader. Personifying all the roles of teacher, coach, mentor, role model, and evaluator, John has captured the reflections of dozens of leaders across the spectrum of politics, business, sports, the military, and academia while revealing their singularly unique styles, and, at the same time, their unforgettable regrets. This fabulous compendium of leadership reflections really does matter, not only for future aspiring leaders who are engaged in the process of becoming successful but also for the rest of us whose opportunity for self-reflection enables us to continue enjoying the journey—the joy of leadership."

—**Martin R. Steele**, Lieutenant General, US Marine Corps (retired)

"*Why It Matters* is more than a leadership book. It is a story of the career of a unique person. John White has served in the trenches as a faculty member, as a Dean of Engineering, as a Presidential Appointee to the National Science Foundation and its Board and as an entrepreneur. The book tells the story of his career—its challenges and its life experiences. It is laced with leadership experiences on his part and on the part of our nation's business, government, nonprofit, and academic leaders. It is presented with the same self-effacing honesty and sense of humor you would confront with a face-to-face conversation. This book is one you will want on your bookshelf."

—**Ray M. Bowen**, President Emeritus, Texas A&M University

"John White hired and mentored me in one of my first leadership positions at Georgia Tech, and his influence on my career as a leader continued beyond the years we worked together. He is not only a leader, he's a keen observer of leadership styles and characteristics. John is always teaching others, using data and goal-driven analyses—and dry humor! I am not surprised that his students find his course one of the best and most demanding, even life-changing."

—**Jean-lou Chameau**, President Emeritus, Caltech

"John White has combined the visionary insights of a proven leader across multiple sectors with the analytical insights of an engineer to write the ultimate practical guide to leadership. Drawing upon his extensive experience in academe, business, government, and nonprofits, John synthesizes and distills lessons drawn from a variety of recognized leaders to take the reader through identifying core principles of leadership and developing leadership attributes by making generous use of examples and anecdotes drawn from his own rich experiences as well as those of many others. John then applies his lessons to the key tasks of leading organizations, and more critically, the people within them and their external stakeholders. John values transparency and allows readers to learn from his mistakes as well as his successes. I heartily recommend this invaluable book to all who aspire to successful servant leadership."

—**Norman L. Fortenberry**, Executive Director,
American Society for Engineering Education

"John White brings over half a century of experience as an educator and leader to *Why It Matters: Reflections on Practical Leadership*, a rich, lively, and detailed examination of all aspects of leadership. While sharing his remarkable personal story, John invites us to explore the words and wisdom of many other leaders who have influenced him over the years, each with a distinctive style, outlook and mission. At the same time, he guides us toward a comprehensive understanding and expression of our own leadership practices and principles. Wherever you are starting from on your leadership journey, you will find in these pages enough inspiration, insight and practical knowledge to make the most of every step along the way."

—**Gary S. May, Chancellor**,
University of California, Davis

"More than once, I heard John White say, 'my goal is to be the leader of the best team, not the best leader of a team.' I love that quote; it is one of my favorite leadership quotes. I once asked him if he created it and he said he wasn't sure (I'm confident he is the original author of this quote). John is humble, but after reading the book I now understand why we need to be cautious about claiming authorship (this point is based on one of many great stories you will enjoy in this book). Wait until you read John McDonnell's story in the book. Then you will understand the importance of transforming an individual sport into a team sport. This book is full of memorable stories that illustrate the leadership concepts that he is explaining. One weekend, when I began reading this book, I had planned to read just a couple of chapters, but I kept going until I had read most of the book in a single day because I was enjoying it and learning important leadership lessons. Now this is one of my favorite books on leadership and I plan on reading it again. Finally, I have observed John for many years, and I've even worked on a project with him, and I can tell you that he is a man of integrity and character who is a true servant leader."

—**Matthew A. Waller**, Dean, Sam M. Walton
College of Business, University of Arkansas

"As a colleague in higher education, I've had the fortunate experience of being inspired by John White's career in leadership at Georgia Tech, the National Science Foundation, and at the University of Arkansas. In *Why It Matters*, John shares reflections not only from his own 'servant leadership' philosophy, but also wisdom from leaders he has studied, built upon, and enhanced over the years. His personal values, leadership style, and community and team-building practices—such as including key members who think differently than you—have contributed to institutional success and transformation from fundraising to advancing national rankings. A lifelong advocate for diversity in engineering and higher education, he offers key insights into organizational cultures. John exemplifies the leadership to turn challenges into opportunities for institutional growth."

—**Henry T. Yang**, Chancellor,
University of California, Santa Barbara

Why It Matters

REFLECTIONS ON PRACTICAL LEADERSHIP

John A. White

GREENLEAF
BOOK GROUP PRESS

Published by Greenleaf Book Group Press
Austin, Texas
www.gbgpress.com

Distributed by Greenleaf Book Group

For ordering information or special discounts for bulk purchases, please contact Greenleaf Book Group at PO Box 91869, Austin, TX 78709, 512.891.6100.

Design and composition by Greenleaf Book Group and Lindsay Starr
Cover design by Greenleaf Book Group and Lindsay Starr
Illustrations and caricatures by Dusty Higgins, Torchbearer Creative, LLC

Publisher's Cataloging-in-Publication data is available.

Print ISBN: 978-1-62634-958-2

eBook ISBN: 978-1-62634-959-9

Part of the Tree Neutral® program, which offsets the number of trees consumed in the production and printing of this book by taking proactive steps, such as planting trees in direct proportion to the number of trees used: www.treeneutral.com

Printed in the United States of America on acid-free paper

22 23 24 25 26 27   10 9 8 7 6 5 4 3 2 1

First Edition

To Mary Lib—the wind beneath my wings.

Contents

III. REFLECTIONS

Foreword

I n less than one paragraph into his book, John White brings forth the eternal and elusive question: Are leaders born, or made? And, as only John can do, he then twists this conundrum into something slightly more tangible: Can leadership be taught or must it be caught? I believe you will arrive at your own answer to this question upon reaching the end of this book. No matter where you fall on that question, there is no doubt that leading, and being a leader, is a choice. It is rarely easy, often filled with disappointments, but that said, it can be one of life's most rewarding experiences. But if you choose to be a leader, then commit to being a good leader; this book can provide important and highly valuable insights to make that a much more likely outcome.

To clarify all biases upfront, I believe, after his mother and father, his wife, Mary Lib, and children, Kim and John III, I am John White, Jr.'s biggest fan. I had the great privilege of being one of John's doctoral students at Georgia Tech. That early mentorship then provided me the blessing of a lifelong relationship landing somewhere between John being my second father and a deeply admired older brother. (I am sure many times John felt whatever our relationship was, it was an onerous challenge, but as in all things, he accepted it with a kind and loving heart!)

I truly had the honor of walking, and watching, from within an arm's reach, John's great and glorious living examples of how a wise and true gentleman journeys through life with amazing grace, compassion, influence, effect, and leadership. No wonder his (potentially) last book to be published is about leadership. So, this bias either makes me one of the most appropriate individuals to provide the initial peek into *Why It Matters: Reflections on Practical Leadership*, or I am completely without balanced insight and judgment. That said, to set this book down now will mean missing out on a revealing, heartfelt, comprehensive, and unique view into leadership that cannot be achieved from any other one source or experience.

Many definitions of leadership, and books on leadership, are constructed from the perspective of leadership as a noun: the ability of, the act of, the art of, or a process of. Any time spent around John White personally, and reading his paragraphs, quotes from other leaders, and examples within this treatise, demonstrate that John is focused on leadership as a verb: the action of leading and being a leader. Ralph Waldo Emerson wrote, "What you <u>do</u> speaks so loudly I cannot hear what you <u>said</u>." To that end, *Why It Matters* is aimed directly at the "doing/being" of effective leadership.

Returning for a moment to the proverbial born/made question, my belief is leaders are born <u>and</u> made. The capacity to lead is based on character traits of courage, self-confidence, a will to persevere in the face of challenge, empathy, and the internal fire to be counted, having your life make a difference. Whether these traits come through genetics passed down through generations or as a by-product of the environment, I believe these are not "taught or acquired" through experience or lecture. But these character traits alone do not make effective leaders. Many of the leaders interviewed as part of John's course at the University of Arkansas on leadership, and then during the process of turning that course into this book, provide, in the end, a comprehensive list of leadership characteristics critical for success. These are developed through knowledge, experience, mentoring, observation, and reflection, being as much about personal growth as professional development. They emerge over time from finding oneself, repetitively, whether by choice or by chance, in the crucible of circumstances where leading others is required to prevail. The more difficult the circumstances, the greater the opportunity to build leadership capabilities and capacity. The lessons contained within this book can, at a minimum, raise your consciousness to the myriad of leadership challenges you will face, and prepare you ahead of those moments of truth.

In Chapter 3, one of my great competitor's CEO, John Roberts of J. B. Hunt, speaks to keeping a list of leadership characteristics (the difference between leaders and bosses) on his desk. I would bet that anyone who takes leading as a serious responsibility will have their own unique leadership list. My list was passed down to me early after becoming CEO, by my dear friend and mentor, Lou Tice. Although Lou has since answered the great roll call in Heaven, I can still hear his voice and see the gleam in his eye as I read through this list:

LEADERS MUST:

1. Be advocates for the ideal.

2. Lead from the power of their ideas and who they are.

3. Make work purposeful.

4. Be courageous.

5. Build efficacy in others.

6. Be gracious under pressure.

7. Protect and direct the culture.

8. Accept criticism gracefully.

9. Market their core values.

10. Have a greater sense of purpose than the moment.

11. Value truth more than loyalty.

12. Value mercy more than justice.

A worthwhile sidebar as you take the journey through *Why It Matters* is to compile your own list, or compare your list, if you have one, of leadership characteristics to serve as your guide.

John White often said, "where you stand depends on where you sit." The point being, an individual's perspectives are usually based on their experiences and current circumstances. Many of us have, or had, careers based in one or two industries, and maybe only a couple of different organizations. What makes John's perspective unique is his leadership experience from a career spanning higher education, government, research, private industry, professional associations, and public company corporate governance. This alone makes his leadership insights brought forward throughout *Why It Matters* both novel and extraordinarily valuable.

In addition to his perspectives, John's expansive career brought him an unbelievable network of relationships, including many who are mentioned in this book. Most of those individuals mentioned also participated with John in his leadership courses at the University of Arkansas. That these individuals traveled considerable distances, often multiple times, to be a part of John's course speaks volumes to the respect, appreciation, and friendship that exists from those lucky enough to be part of John's network forged over a highly successful career. Those highly interactive and engaging classroom experiences are also part of the foundation and structure within this book, representing a double down into the minds and hearts of successful leaders.

As the world becomes more complex, integrated through technology but polarized by ideologies, the need for strong, caring, and highly competent, fully equipped leaders is becoming one of our greatest needs. Unfortunately, leadership is not a commodity, and leaders capable of rising to the escalating challenges of our times are truly in short supply. That puts an ever-growing demand on apostolic efforts from experienced leaders to raise new leaders up behind them. A critical part of leadership development is having role models. *Why It Matters* provides a "rare and raw" view into John's life experiences in leading, as well as a playbook to focus leadership development and dialogue.

A cherished mentor of mine, Ahmed Yehia, passed on a wonderful definition of greatness: "achieving admirable results, with exemplary character." Not only do we need more leaders, we need great leaders. John White is one of my best examples of a great leader, achieving truly admirable and impactful results, with the absolute highest character. Not everyone can be as fortunate as me to have been mentored, and loved, by John White, but with *Why It Matters*, everyone can get a clear view into the wisdom and the heart of a great leader, and that is a priceless opportunity if you have chosen to answer the leadership calling. I am sure your time spent with this book will be highly valuable, with the added benefit of being heartwarming at the same time. I wish you Godspeed.

—Christopher B. Lofgren, Ph.D.
Chairman, US Chamber of Commerce Board of Directors
Retired President and Chief Executive Officer, Schneider National, Inc.

Preface

No doubt, many agree with Dilbert's view of leadership books. So why did I write a book on leadership? Despite the number of existing books, there remains a paucity of exemplary leaders. Clearly, reading a book on leadership will not make you an exemplary leader any more than reading a diet book will cause you to lose weight. A change of behaviors is required for both improvements. But what about the age-old question of whether leaders are born or made? A more fundamental question is whether leadership can be taught or whether it must be caught.

Soon after I stepped down from being chancellor of the University of Arkansas (UA), several faculty colleagues encouraged me to offer a course on leadership. At the time, I'd been an engineering educator for forty-five years, and every course I'd taught consisted of equations. But the thought of sharing with students the lessons I had learned about leadership was enticing. So I made a trip to Blacksburg, Virginia, to meet with one of my mentors, Paul E. Torgersen.

Paul was my department head when I rejoined the Virginia Tech faculty following completion of my doctorate at The Ohio State University. Later, he became my dean and then-president of Virginia Tech. He continued to mentor me during my service as dean of engineering at Georgia Tech and as UA chancellor.

Paul advised me to use Steven B. Sample's *The Contrarian's Guide to Leadership* as a starting point. Drawing heavily on Steve's book and on materials from a similar course taught by Warren Bennis and Steve, I designed Leadership Principles and Practices, a course for seniors and graduate students from all majors. Over a sixteen-week semester, fifteen guest leaders met with the class for the first half of the period. The balance of the time was devoted to discussions of assigned books on leadership and lessons from my leadership journey. Teaching the leadership course turned out to be the highlight of my fifty-six-year career as an educator, and contributed to my receipt of the university's top teaching award.

The guest leaders didn't give presentations; they simply responded to our questions. Students were unprepared for the level of transparency and candor the guest leaders and I provided. Multiple guest leaders openly shed tears as they shared their experiences, holding nothing back.

Over the nine offerings of the course, forty-four guest leaders met with the class, including eleven current or former chief executive officers, two retired board chairs, a cofounder and retired chief financial officer, a former senior vice-chair, a marketing president, three executive vice presidents, a senior vice president, a senior director, two directors of companies, two retired US Navy admirals, a retired US Marine Corps general, a US senator, an Arkansas governor, an Arkansas attorney general, a vice-chair of an international public accounting firm, the leader of a statewide bank, an entrepreneur, a leadership author and consultant, an executive director of a nonprofit legal services organization, and the UA system president, as well as three UA chancellors, a former UA vice chancellor, a UA athletics director, a UA executive associate athletics director, two UA deans, and a UA academic department head. Twenty-nine guest leaders are quoted in this book; their caricatures follow the Preface.

More than 250 students completed the course. Over the nine course offerings, the students said it was the most demanding course they had taken and that it had changed their lives. Each week, during three hours with the students, I felt like we truly caught lightning in a bottle. The class chemistry was unlike anything I had experienced in my other classes. To gain an understanding of how the course was organized, see the sample syllabus posted on https://JohnAWhiteJr.com/WhyItMatters.

The accuracy of Miles's law, "Where you stand depends on where you sit," is obvious when reading leadership books. Sample's experiences as a university president influenced *The Contrarian's Guide to Leadership*, and Jeswald Salacuse's *Leading Leaders* reflects his service as a law school dean. Likewise, Bill George's *Discover Your True North* and Lee Iacocca's *Where Have All the Leaders Gone?* reflect their corporate experiences. Tony Zinni's *Leading the Charge: Leadership Lessons from the Battlefield to the Boardroom* and Jim Mattis's *Call Sign Chaos: Learning to Lead* are shaped by their military experiences. John Maxwell's experiences as a minister color the way he presents material in his numerous books, including *The 21 Irrefutable Laws of Leadership: Follow Them and People Will Follow You*. Experiences gained from years of coaching shape *Wooden on Leadership* by John Wooden and *The Mentor Leader* by Tony Dungy. And historian Doris Kearns Goodwin's governmental service and education are reflected in *Leadership in Turbulent Times*.

My experiences in academia, business, and government have heavily contributed to my views of leadership, but my views have also been shaped by numerous leadership experiences in nonprofit organizations.

Over the years, I learned that leadership matters and, along the way, I also learned much about several leadership matters, pun intended. My most intense learning period occurred during my eleven years as chancellor in the crucible of the University of Arkansas. But I believe I may well have learned more about how to be an exemplary leader since stepping down as UA's chancellor in 2008. Teaching that leadership course taught me more about leadership than I think I had ever learned previously. If I'd only known then what I know now, I would've been a better chairman of SysteCon, the consulting firm I cofounded; a better director of the Material Handling Research Center I founded at Georgia Tech; a better assistant director at the National Science Foundation; a better engineering dean at Georgia Tech; and a better chancellor at the University of Arkansas. I also would've been a more effective leader of nonprofit organizations and a more valuable member of governing boards and advisory boards. I would've even been a far more effective husband, father, grandfather, teacher, friend, and person.

Truly, leadership is a journey. I'm still on it, learning more each year. While it's true you can learn more from bad leaders than from good, I benefitted by learning from both. I have been fortunate to have been able to observe and adopt the best practices of many good leaders, but the bad leaders taught me what *not* to do in certain situations. When students complain about the bad leaders they've had during internships or bad professors they've had, I encourage them to store their experiences in a mental file so they can open it at the right times and avoid making the same mistakes. In fact, a bad professor motivated me to become a good professor; I knew I could do a much better job. An ineffective department head motivated me to change jobs, resulting in increased career opportunities. Dark clouds can have silver linings.

Guest Leaders Gallery

Beebe

Brazzelle

Brown

Buffington

Duke

English

Faubel

Gearhart

Graham

Johnson

Lofgren

Long

McCarthy

McGinnis

McKenna

McMillon

Needy

Peterson

Pincus

Roberts

Rutledge

Simpson

Smith

Steele

Steinmetz

Strode

Sugg

Townsend

White

PART 1

Beginnings

CHAPTER 1

Defining Leadership

The adage "When the going gets tough, the tough get going" was manifested during the COVID-19 pandemic. The fiery furnace created by the virus and its aftermath separated the dross from the gold. People's true natures were revealed. Individuals we may not normally think of as traditional leaders stepped forward in the face of devastation and provided exemplary leadership—nurses, doctors, first responders, neighbors, family members, and friends. At a time of uncertainty, division, and social unrest, many people came together and worked to serve others. Conversely, many people holding leadership positions failed to lead when effective leadership was needed.

Politics, business, war, nonprofit organizations, and athletics are settings in which the need for leadership is most visible. The November 24, 2020, issue of *FOX Sports Insider* focuses on the dynasty of the Dallas Cowboys football team during the 1990s. After addressing its current situation, with a record of three wins and seven losses going into its Thanksgiving game with Washington, the article ends with a quote from Brandon Marshall, linebacker for the 2015 Super Bowl champions, the Denver Broncos, regarding what Dallas must do to become a winning team: "Go get a leader. That's the only thing that's missing on this team. They have the roster, a good coach. They need leadership." Brandon Marshall recognized that leadership matters.

Using the metaphor of a bus, Jim Collins in *Good to Great* emphasizes the need for a leader, the driver of the bus, to assign the right people to the right seats. During the game, two very important Dallas Cowboy players had to leave the metaphorical bus following their injuries. Dallas lost the game. Leadership matters, but so does luck.

In 1978, historian, political scientist, and authority on leadership studies James MacGregor Burns estimated that there were upwards of 130 definitions of the word *leadership*. More than forty years later, the number surely exceeds 200. Instead of endeavoring to enumerate them, I provide a sampling.

In *Leading Leaders*, Jeswald Salacuse defines leadership as "the ability to cause individuals to act willingly in a desired way for the benefit of a group." In *Leadership: Theory and Practice*, Peter Northouse defines it as "a process whereby an individual influences a group of individuals to achieve a common goal." The key words here are *process*, *influences*, and *common goal*. Throughout this book, you'll find that *process* and *influence* are frequently associated with leadership. Northouse's recognition of a common goal is important because leaders can be so focused on achieving what's best for the organization that they lose sight of what's best for their followers. A leader must not overlook the what's-in-it-for-me factor for followers.

In *The Contrarian's Guide to Leadership*, Steven Sample defines leadership in terms of people having identifiable followers they exercise power and authority over. Sample's definition excludes such individuals as Eleanor Roosevelt and Michelle Obama; they had influence but not power or authority. On the other hand, John Maxwell defines it as having influence, which First Ladies Roosevelt and Obama certainly possessed. Supreme Court jurist Ruth Bader Ginsburg exhibited leadership through the power of her votes, actions, and words.

Among the various definitions of leadership, I find Ronald Heifetz's analysis—in *Leadership Without Easy Answers*—informative. To him, leadership is "mobilizing people to tackle problems." He adds, "There seem to be two common denominators of these views: station and influence." Some lead based on position, such as a captain, president, general, and department head. Others lead through the influence they have within a group or team. In contrast to many, Heifetz incorporated values in his definition, thereby eliminating Adolf Hitler, Joseph Stalin, and others. Heifetz's definition implies action. To him, a leader mobilizes people to accomplish a given task.

Harry Truman defines it as "the ability to get [people] to do what they don't want to do and like it." Dwight Eisenhower reportedly said, "I'll tell you what leadership is. It's persuasion and conciliation, and education, and patience." According to Colin Powell, "Leadership is the art of accomplishing more than the science of management says is possible." He also notes, "Leadership is solving problems. The day soldiers stop bringing you their problems is the day you have stopped leading them." Another leader with a military background, General Marty Steele, told the leadership class, "Leadership is about understanding who you are, knowing your strengths and weaknesses, and how to use them with others."

In an interview in *Fortune* magazine, President Bill Clinton said, "Leadership means bringing people together in pursuit of a common cause, developing a plan to achieve it, and staying with it until the goal is achieved."

Clinton's definition includes five essential elements: a common cause, a plan, a goal, persistence, and achievement. Leaders must convince followers that a common cause exists. A plan must be developed with a tangible goal, and persistence is required to ensure the goal is achieved. Without a common cause, followers won't follow. Without a plan, your followers will meander. Without a goal, there will be no means of measuring success. Without persistence, the team won't have sufficient staying power to accomplish the task. Finally, if achievement does not occur, everyone's efforts were for naught.

Clinton pointed out in the same interview that leaders don't have all the answers. Persistence is needed to overcome obstacles, setbacks, and difficulties arising in pursuit of the goal. In *Lincoln on Leadership*, Donald T. Phillips observes, "You may need to be brave enough to admit you were wrong and alter the plan. Then leadership calls for self-confidence, calm, and powers of persuasion to keep spirits high and ensure the team stays on track."

The key to successful leadership is followers. They are the difference between success and failure. Salacuse notes, "The test of leadership is followership." Along the same lines, Maxwell observes, "He who thinks he leads but has no followers is only taking a walk."

In *The Leadership Challenge*, James Kouzes and Barry Posner observe, "Leaders never make extraordinary things happen all by themselves. Leaders mobilize *others* to want to struggle for shared aspirations, and this means that, fundamentally, *leadership is a relationship*. Leadership is a relationship between those who aspire to lead and those who choose to follow. You can't have one without the other."

Among numerous leaders, John McDonnell stands apart. McDonnell coached men's track and field teams at the University of Arkansas. His teams won forty national championships: nineteen in indoor track and field, eleven in cross country, and ten in outdoor track and field. Arguably the greatest coach in any sport, he was named National Coach of the Year thirty times. No other coach in any sport comes close to matching McDonnell's record. To me though, his number of national championships is not what made McDonnell stand out. It was his ability to transform an individual sport into a team sport. McDonnell was adept at getting athletes to think of their team before themselves. In long-distance races, a team member would sacrifice his opportunity to win by setting the pace for others. He instilled a team-first culture within his program.

Isn't that what exemplary leadership is all about—getting everyone to prioritize the team over the self? John Wooden was able to do it in basketball; Vince Lombardi did it in football; both are team sports. However, John McDonnell did it in track and field—an individual sport. No one else in golf, gymnastics, tennis, or any other individual sport has done it to the extent McDonnell did. McDonnell's approach to athletics competitions is needed in all leadership situations: team first!

SERVANT LEADERSHIP

At some point in the late twentieth century, there was a paradigm shift in leadership. Dictator stereotypes gave way to servant stereotypes. During the 1960s, '70s, and '80s, servant leadership became vogue. Fortunately, the paradigm shift occurred before I took on major leadership roles.

Throughout my leadership journey, my goal has been to be a servant leader. Because it's ingrained in me, I mistakenly assumed everyone knew what I meant when I used the term. However, while teaching the leadership class, I discovered my assumption was wrong. At times, I expected students to read my mind. Apparently, this was the case with the subject of servant leadership.

When Admiral Jack Buffington met with the leadership class, he didn't rely on students reading his mind. He was very direct, saying that, as a young officer, "The best leadership advice I was given was to use servant leadership."

Simply stated, servant leadership is serving your followers. When former president and CEO of Tyson Foods, Donald Smith, met with the leadership class, he said, "My job is to serve people who serve people." A student asked how he defined servant leadership; Smith said, "Servant leaders have a humble confidence, are a resource to people being led, value teamwork, never let people think they are superior to the people they lead, never assign work they are not willing to do, and help others reach their potential."

Smith associated three words with servant leadership: heart, head, and habits. Associated with the heart are a person's core values, concern for others, and courage to make decisions. Vision and motivational strategies are attributes of the head. He cited accountability and responsibility as attributes of habits. Smith said that servant leaders must have strong core values, evidence genuine concern for others, be courageous and make tough decisions, have vision, be able to motivate followers, be accountable, and be responsible. They must be selfless leaders.

LEADERSHIP HALLS OF FAME AND SHAME

Over the years, I asked students in my Leadership Principles and Practices course to list four historical leaders they could envision following. Abraham Lincoln was always included in more lists than anyone. Others who consistently received the most votes include Martin Luther King Jr., George Washington, Winston Churchill, and Nelson Mandela. The students had no difficulty naming four exemplary historical leaders. Their most challenging task was deciding who should be left off the list. However, if I had asked for contemporary leaders, I suspect that the students would have struggled to identify four local, state, national, or international leaders they would gladly follow.

How did the United States, during a period of its smallest population, produce leaders such as John Adams, John Quincy Adams, Samuel

Adams, Benjamin Franklin, John Hancock, Alexander Hamilton, Patrick Henry, John Jay, Thomas Jefferson, James Madison, and George Washington? Where have all the leaders gone? Two hundred years from now, will people include anyone alive during the twenty-first century in their Leadership Hall of Fame?

Today, the Democratic and Republican parties have difficulty selecting nominees for the presidential election. Perhaps it's because the American presidency is, as John Dickerson titled his book, *The Hardest Job in the World*. Not only is it hard, but it's surely the most scrutinized. Few are willing to subject themselves to the scrutiny of the media. They follow Harry Truman's advice,  "If you can't stand the heat, you'd better get out of the kitchen."[1] In politics, media scrutiny is so great that few make it into the house, much less as far as the kitchen.

Are our expectations and requirements beyond the capabilities of mere mortals? Have we raised the bar so high that few are able to get over it? Leadership matters, but where are the leaders? Some claim the nation's strongest leaders are in business, not government. Do the facts support the claim?

A record number of people have been added to my Leadership Hall of Shame in the past thirty years. It includes a long list of corporate CEOs, as well as politicians, educators, entertainers, athletes, broadcast executives, religious leaders, and members of the media. Egos, arrogance, greed, envy, ignorance, or sexual indiscretions were at the heart of most entries into the Leadership Hall of Shame.

Iacocca put Enron's Ken Lay, the New York Stock Exchange's Richard Grasso, ExxonMobil's Lee Raymond, and Halliburton, "the world's largest oil and gas services company," in his Hall of Shame. He attributed the downfall of corporate CEOs to the Seven Deadly Sins, calling attention specifically to greed and envy.[2]

The association of greed with corporate CEOs was illustrated by Gordon Gekko, played by Michael Douglas in the 1987 movie *Wall Street*, for which he won an Oscar. Gekko was an inside trader and corporate raider. Among Gekko's comments was "Greed is good. Greed is right. Greed works. Greed clarifies, cuts through and captures the essence of the evolutionary spirit. Greed in all its forms—greed for life, for money, for love, knowledge—has marked the upward surge of mankind."

Hall of Fame football coach Vince Lombardi is credited with saying, "Leadership is not just one quality but, rather, a blend of many qualities, and while no one individual possesses all of the needed talents that go into leadership, each man can develop a combination to make himself a leader" and "Leaders are made, they are not born. They are made by hard effort, which is the price which all of us must pay to achieve any goal that is worthwhile."

LEADERSHIP STYLES

Leaders employ a variety of leadership styles. In *Discover Your True North*, Bill George considers six leadership styles: directive, engaged, coaching, consensus, affiliative, and expert. A leader who uses a directive style gives orders, provides little opportunity for followers to use flexibility and innovation, and relies on rules and compliance, whereas an engaged style motivates followers around shared values and a common purpose. The coaching style of leadership is founded on the development of followers for leadership roles. A consensus style treats followers as equals, encouraging them to participate in decision-making. An affiliative style is subtle, relying on trust in creating harmony. Used in engineering and science, as well as consulting and financial services, an expert style draws on the knowledge and expertise of the followers and the leader.

Because leadership is, as Steven Sample put it, "highly situational and contingent," leaders employ multiple styles, depending on the situation, circumstances, and capabilities of their followers. Leaders who are limited to using a single style will miss opportunities to advance the organization. George notes, "You should adapt your leadership style to the capabilities of your teammates and their readiness to accept greater responsibility." He continues, "In leading, it is important to understand the situation in which you are operating, as well as the performance imperatives, and have the flexibility to maximize your effectiveness *in that situation*."

In *Primal Leadership*, Daniel Goleman and his coauthors consider a slightly different set of six styles, noting, "Typically, the best, most effective leaders act according to one or more of six distinctive approaches to leadership and skillfully switch between the various styles depending on the situation.

"Four of the styles—visionary, coaching, affiliative, and democratic—create the kind of resonance that boosts performance, while two others—pacesetting and commanding—although useful in some very specific situations, should be applied with caution."

In describing the presidential leadership approaches of Abraham Lincoln, Theodore Roosevelt, Franklin Roosevelt, and Lyndon Johnson, Doris Kearns Goodwin categorizes Lincoln's approach as transformational leadership, Theodore Roosevelt's as crisis management, Franklin Roosevelt's as turnaround leadership, and Lyndon Johnson's as visionary leadership. She titles the section addressing their approaches "The Leader and the Times: How They Led," confirming Sample's belief.

As Max De Pree put it in *Leadership Is an Art*, "Many managers are concerned about their style. They wonder whether they are perceived as open or autocratic or participative. As practice is to policy, so style is to belief. Style is merely a consequence of what we believe, of what is in our hearts."

Choosing a leadership style is a personal matter. It depends on the combination of leader, follower, and situation. A leader must be flexible and sensitive to the sensitivities of followers. In addition to style, timing and pace are critically important. A leader's instincts and intuition will serve as guides in selecting the best style for the moment at hand.

Frequently, the students in the leadership class asked our guest speakers to identify their leadership styles. None responded with a single style. As Greg Brown, chairman and CEO of Motorola Solutions, said, "The best leaders do not have one style." John White III, Fortna's president and CEO at the time, reminded the students that "One size does not fit all." After acquiring companies in South Africa, England, and Germany, White said he made adjustments because of the differences in communication styles. "It's important to have a portfolio of leadership styles," he said and reminded the students that "Style is not about the message but how you deliver the message."

EFFECTIVE LEADERSHIP

In *The Effective Executive*, Peter F. Drucker distinguishes between *effectiveness* and *efficiency*. How well you do things right is a measure of your efficiency; how well you do the right things is a measure of your effectiveness. In *Drucker on Leadership: New Lessons from the Father of Modern Management*, William A. Cohen observes, "Drucker noted that the major difference between a manager and a leader is that the manager focuses on doing things right, while the leader focuses on doing the right things. This is not a simple play on words. Of course, you would like a leader who is both efficient (doing things right) and effective (doing the right things), but if it is a choice between the two, and this determines focus, then the leader must focus on getting the right job done, at the expense of efficiency."

Leaders are responsible for ensuring the right things are being done right. Exemplary leadership means more than doing the legal, ethical, and moral thing; it means doing the right thing, and it means doing it all of the time, not just some of the time. Mike Duke, former president and CEO of Walmart, reminded the students it was not enough to simply do what is legal. Your actions must pass legal, ethical, moral, humane, truth, accuracy, reasonability, and front-page tests. Ask how you will feel if what you do is on the front page of newspapers. Pam McGinnis, president of global marketing at Phillips 66, advised them to "prioritize doing the right thing over doing the fun, fast, and easy thing." Blake Strode, executive director of ArchCity Defenders, said, "Ignorance is not an excuse for not doing the right thing." However, as Reynie Rutledge, chairman and CEO of First Security Bancorp, told students, "You always want to do the right thing, but most of the time you don't know what the right thing is."

The COVID pandemic provided ample evidence that not everyone agrees on what the right thing is. Some believed that people should be required to wear masks or be vaccinated; others believed that individuals should decide for themselves. Many occasions will arise when the choices leaders must make are tough, when the right choice isn't obvious. What do you do in such a situation? After consulting with others, after obtaining all the information you can, you make the best decision you can and move on. In the end, you must be able to look yourself in the mirror and say, "I did the best I could."

Jim Collins, in *Good to Great*, reminds us that "good is the enemy of great." By extension, acceptable is the enemy of exceptional, satisfaction is the enemy of optimization, and perfection is the enemy of execution. Let's consider the extensions individually. First, acceptable is the enemy of exceptional for the same reason good is the enemy of great: You settle for less than the best. Don't settle. Strive for exceptional performance.

Second, satisfaction is the enemy of optimization for the same reasons good is the enemy of great and acceptable is the enemy of exceptional: Why would you satisfice when you could optimize? Again, don't settle; strive for optimality.

Third, perfection is the enemy of execution because perfection is never achieved. Striving for perfection can lead to paralysis of analysis. I'm reminded of an engineering design law: At some point in the design of a product, you have to shoot the engineers and get on with production.

Wait a minute! Does this mean there will be times when good isn't the enemy of great, when acceptable isn't the enemy of exceptional, and when satisfaction isn't the enemy of optimization? Yes, there'll be times when good enough is simply good enough. Don't let imperfection become the enemy of good!

Herbert A. Simon, recipient of the Nobel Prize in economics, introduced me to the notion of satisficing, instead of optimizing, in decision-making.[3] Recognizing the intractability of realistic models of many real-world problems, Simon posited that decision-makers can satisfice by finding an optimal solution to a simplified model of the real world or by finding a satisfactory solution to a more realistic model of the real world. Often, the latter is preferred.

Steven Sample captured the notion of satisficing when he stated in *The Contrarian's Guide to Leadership*, "Anything worth doing at all is worth doing just well enough. The tricky job for the leader is deciding what *just well enough* means in each particular situation."

My industrial engineering education taught me there's always a better way. In my advocacy for continuous improvement, it was a struggle for me to decide when enough was enough, to recognize I should eat the elephant a bite at a time and be satisfied with less than the best as an interim solution. Over the years, people who worked with me recognized that I was often pleased but was never satisfied. I knew we could always do better. Fortunately, I was surrounded by people who provided the pragmatic perspective I often lacked.

It also took longer than it should for me to realize that, if you can't sell the best solution to your followers, then it's not the best solution. Without buy-in from your team, your brilliant ideas will never be implemented. Therefore, having followers develop the solution is much preferred to the leader developing it.

In *Leadership Without Easy Answers*, Heifetz categorized problems as those requiring technical solutions and those requiring adaptive solutions. Generally, technical problems are much easier to solve than adaptive problems. Furthermore, adaptive problems are solved more effectively by having people affected by the solution solve them. Adaptive change, as the name implies, requires people to adapt to a new reality, one requiring changes. As Heifetz notes, people don't resist change; they resist loss created by uncertainty. Letting followers create a solution to the problem increases their level of comfort with uncertainty.

Mary Pat McCarthy, retired vice-chair of KPMG LLP, said one way students can determine whether they are effective leaders is to see whether people want to work with them or for them. The cream always rises to the top. People vote with their feet.

White said, "Leadership is not embodied in a title. Leaders are effective if they are inspiring people, making things better, accomplishing great things, and causing people to dream more and think bigger."

As you gravitate from doing to leading, you'll make sacrifices, especially in terms of what you deem acceptable. I am a bit of a perfectionist, so it was hard for me to relinquish control and let others do something when I knew I could do it better. Most, if not all, leaders struggle with letting go. In *How to Lead*, when David M. Rubenstein asked Bill Gates how difficult it was for him to rely on others to code software, Gates replied, "In my career, this evolution of being an individual performer, then a manager, then a manager of managers, and then setting broad strategy—you have to get used to the fact you don't have as much control." Effective leaders don't control; they lead. Many times, they have to get out of the way and let followers solve problems or, as Drucker put it, pursue opportunities.

CHAPTER 2

Beginning Leadership

You never get a second chance to make a first impression. Fortunately, first impressions don't have to be *forever* impressions. However, to recover will take time and energy better invested in making progress. So get off to a good start and avoid losing ground because of foolish missteps.

In *Leadership in Turbulent Times*, Doris Kearns Goodwin notes, "No fixed timetable governs the development of leaders. While Abraham Lincoln, Theodore Roosevelt, and Franklin Roosevelt all possessed inherent leadership capacities, the period of time when they first perceived themselves as leaders and were considered leaders by others occurred at different stages of their growth."

I asked leaders who met with the class when they had first recognized their own leadership abilities. Most said in high school; others said in grammar school or college. A few said they were still waiting!

While serving as Schneider National's president and CEO, Chris Lofgren said he eased into leadership roles by being in situations where "something had to be done and someone had to do it," so he wound up getting people to take action. As a result, he concluded leadership was his calling. He was right. He's an exceptional leader.

In *How to Lead*, David M. Rubenstein says that, when talking to emerging leaders, he tells them life is divided into three phases: preparing for a career, building a career, and receiving the benefits of the achievements occurring during the second phase. Those who succeed during the first phase aren't guaranteed success during the later phases. Being a successful leader during the first twenty-five years of a person's life doesn't guarantee success as a leader in successive phases. He notes how successful leaders are often late bloomers, developing leadership abilities during the second phase of their lives.

My experiences with leaders align with Rubenstein's. However, I think he assigns a higher percentage to "often" than I do. Among the successful leaders I know, more than 75 percent demonstrated leadership abilities before reaching the age of twenty-five. But the important points in Rubenstein's observations are that leadership abilities can be developed later in a person's life than most believe and that having demonstrated leadership abilities at a young age does not guarantee success as a leader later in life.

BEGINNING A NEW LEADERSHIP POSITION

How should you begin a new leadership position? It depends on how you got it. Consider, for example, Lyndon Johnson's presidency, which occurred because his predecessor, John F. Kennedy, was assassinated. Goodwin notes, "This unfolding tragedy presented Lyndon Johnson with extreme danger yet also an unprecedented opportunity for action and judgment."

Not unlike the change of command in a military battle, Johnson had to take control, lead the nation, and assure everyone—his own citizens and other people around the world—that the nation was in capable, qualified hands. He couldn't dawdle; he had to act quickly, decisively, and sensitively. Everything he did would be observed, analyzed, and commented on. Suddenly, he was under a microscope, with everyone watching, judging, weighing, and drawing conclusions about his ability to lead the nation.

After addressing the nation, Johnson's first order of business was to solidify his team. He knew it would be a mistake, as Lincoln had said, "to change horses in midstream," so he approached each member of Kennedy's team, letting them know he needed them and the country needed them, too. He asked them to teach him how to be POTUS. Goodwin notes how his empathy and candor won the day.

Your placement in a leadership position is unlikely to be the result of an assassination. However, we can learn much from how Johnson responded to the situation. You may well succeed someone who was very popular and vacated the position under unfavorable conditions. Different challenges face a person who is promoted from within versus an outside hire.

Promotion from Within

If you are promoted from within, you may end up leading your former supervisor, for example. If there were several contenders for the leadership position, you'll need to answer questions such as whether you want to retain contenders who were not selected and, if so, how.

RETAINING OTHER CANDIDATES

Before Donald Smith accepted an offer to be president and CEO of Tyson Foods, he asked to be paid less than what they offered. He wanted more money awarded to a member of the executive team he deemed to be essential for his success. Smith believed that, if the person wasn't compensated appropriately, he would leave the company. Smith put his money where his mouth was. His strategy resulted in a strong leadership team and success for the firm.

The students asked other CEOs who visited the class how their firms were able to retain highly qualified but unsuccessful internal candidates for the CEO positions. Several said they weren't able to retain them.

When it was time for Jack Welch's successor to be named at General Electric, the two-year process concluded with three finalists: Jeff Immelt, James McNerney, and Robert Nardelli. When Immelt was selected, McNerney left GE to become CEO at 3M, and Nardelli left GE to become Home Depot's CEO; both had successful careers after leaving GE.

Inexplicably, I was nominated for Georgia Tech's presidency in 1987. At the time, I was a regents' professor and director of a research center. Thinking it would be interesting to learn how presidential searches were conducted, I applied for the position, went through the interview process, wasn't selected, and resumed my professorial duties. John Patrick Crecine, selected to be Tech's ninth president, came to Tech from Carnegie Mellon University where he had served as its provost. Soon after Crecine arrived on campus, he invited me to meet with him. In the meeting, Crecine said he knew I was a candidate for the presidency and didn't want me to leave Tech because I wasn't selected. I assured him I wasn't disappointed in not being chosen and conveyed my appreciation for him reaching out to me. Instead of treating me as an adversary, he treated me as a valued colleague.

In 1991 I was selected to be dean of engineering at Georgia Tech after being at the National Science Foundation in Washington, DC, for three years. Upon returning to campus as dean, I knew I faced a challenge. I'd never been director of one of the schools within the college, and several school directors were candidates for the position. So, soon after I became engineering dean, I met privately with individuals who were not selected, let them know I considered them to be valuable members of the team, and assured them I would do everything I could to support them and help them achieve their goals. Things turned out very well. In fact, the person I feared would be my greatest challenge turned out to be an ally and one of my strongest supporters.

Warren Bennis notes in *The Essential Bennis*, "For the leader who has come up through the ranks, one of the toughest [challenges] is how to relate to former peers who now report to you." He goes on to point out, "It's difficult to set boundaries and fine-tune your working relationships with former cronies. . . . Relationships inevitably change when a person is promoted from within the ranks. You may no longer be able to speak openly as you once did, and your friends may feel awkward around you or resent you. They may perceive you as lording your position over them when you're just behaving as a leader should."

Based on others' experiences, I know things won't necessarily go as smoothly as they did for me. Having served on boards of directors when changes occurred at the CEO level, I know many people leave as soon as they can if they aren't selected for the position. However, while serving on their boards of directors, I was impressed with how smoothly leadership transitions occurred at Eastman Chemical and J. B. Hunt Transport Services. Of course, the objective isn't for the transition to go smoothly; it's for the transition to be successful. Frequently, a transition appears to go smoothly, but the successor is unable to provide the leadership needed, and a subsequent change in leadership occurs. Such was the case with GE, when the transition from Jack Welch to Jeffrey R. Immelt appeared to go smoothly—but didn't.

BUILDING NEW RELATIONSHIPS

In addition to dealing with colleagues who weren't selected for the leadership position, you will need to establish new relationships with people you lead. Prior to your selection, if you were hired from within, you were one of the gang. Now, you're the leader. Juggling friendships and leadership responsibilities can be challenging, especially if you have to demote or fire a friend.

One of my department head colleagues remarked that, after his promotion, the faculty members no longer included him when they went to lunch. Another department head continually had lunch with the same faculty members, prompting others to claim he showed favoritism to his "lunch bunch." Avoiding an appearance of favoritism is a challenge for all leaders but especially when someone is promoted within the organization. Although relationships change, it doesn't require the leader to become friendless. It requires forethought and sensitivity from all parties. If people are truly friends, they'll accept the need to have a different relationship at work.

The leader and the leader's friends must respect the need for distance, but so must their followers. Because of confirmation bias, often people see favoritism when it doesn't exist: Because they believe it will occur, they see it. In their case, it's not *seeing is believing*, but *believing is seeing*. A leader and a leader's friends must make efforts to let others know that favoritism doesn't exist. You must endeavor to treat every follower professionally and respectfully.

When Admiral Mike Johnson met with the leadership class, he told the students that you have to maintain a distance between yourself and the people you lead. You can't be one of the guys; you need to be their leader. Admiral Jack Buffington and General Marty Steele delivered the same message when they met with the students.

SITTING IN THE CHAIR

No matter how well you thought you understood the challenges, demands, and breadth of responsibility of a leadership position, once you occupy the position, you'll realize you had no clue. I experienced it, I heard it from my successor, and I've heard it from many leaders who ascended into a leadership position after being in the number-two position for several years.

Mike Duke told the students that, the first time he entered his new office as Walmart's president and CEO, he couldn't bring himself to sit in the CEO's chair. While Duke was sitting in a different chair making notes, his predecessor, Lee Scott, walked into the office. He said that, after succeeding David Glass, he had hesitated in the same way. Scott said it would get easier each day for Duke to occupy the chair, and it did.

Interestingly, when Doug McMillon, Duke's successor, met with the leadership class, a student asked what he had difficulty doing his first day as CEO. McMillon's response was, "Sitting in the CEO's chair."

McMillon shared with me, "Actually, on my first day, I rode with a truck driver and visited stores. On my second day, I couldn't sit in the chair. I was spooked by it. Mike saw me, laughed, and came in encouraging me to walk around the desk a few times and, 'by the end of the day, sit in the chair. Somebody has to do it now because I'm not doing it anymore.'"

No matter how much you prepare, you'll find that sitting in the leader's chair is unlike anything you anticipated. However, like your predecessors, you'll get through it, and you'll make your mark such that your successor will feel the same way about sitting in your chair.

CHANGE FROM WITHIN

Being promoted from within carries another special challenge. Any change you make runs the risk of being interpreted as criticism of your predecessor. Even if your predecessor welcomes the changes you make, some in the organization will take offense to any change. Don't worry about them; they probably won't like anything you do.

After leaving each leadership position I've held, I've made sure to speak positively about changes my successors made, but I've witnessed situations where leaders criticized their successors' modifications. What they didn't see was the disappointment their former followers had in them when they heard the criticisms.

Some leaders take the Farragut approach. In the Battle of Mobile Bay during the Civil War, Admiral David Farragut ordered his ship to advance through a minefield, saying, "Damn the torpedoes, full speed ahead!"[1] Those who take this approach don't care how their predecessors feel about impending changes.

Criticism of a predecessor is much the same. I prefer to praise my predecessors and build on their successes to date. It's impossible to accurately second-guess decisions made by a predecessor, because you can neither turn back the clock and replicate the conditions at the time decisions were made, nor base your decisions on the same set of data and information available to the predecessor when their decisions were made. Criticizing a predecessor, intentionally or unintentionally, serves no useful purpose. It alienates predecessors' supporters and team members. Doing so makes you look small. Tread carefully! A strong foundation is never built on negativity.

Predecessors can undermine or support you; it's best to have their support. Leadership should be focused on the windshield, not the rearview mirror. What you do from this point on matters, not what your predecessor did or didn't do. Many people will fill your ears with uninvited criticisms of your predecessor. Listen, but don't agree! Don't draw conclusions. Give your predecessor the benefit of the doubt. Until you've walked in their moccasins long enough to get athlete's foot, you have no idea what caused them to do or not do certain things. Remember, the same people will be filling your successor's ears with uninvited criticisms about you.

Coming in from Outside

Coming in from outside to lead an organization has special challenges, too. Establishing credibility requires starting afresh. Despite the previous successes resulting in your selection, you are, at best, starting at zero. With some people, you are starting from a negative position, because they didn't want you as their leader, or they wanted someone else, or they're upset about the removal of your predecessor, or they themselves wanted to be selected. Coming in from outside, I faced many of these when I was selected to be UA's chancellor.

It wasn't an easy decision for me to leave Georgia Tech after twenty-two years on its faculty. My plan was to retire after completing my deanship. However, my alma mater came calling. About a dozen years before, I had been contacted about the chancellor position at the University of Arkansas. Bill and Hillary Clinton had nominated me, just as they did this time. Then, I had neither the interest in nor the qualifications for the position.

Ultimately, through the persistence of B. Alan Sugg, the UA System president, and the encouragement of my wife, Mary Lib, I agreed to be a candidate for the chancellorship. My wife's winning argument was if I didn't do it, someday I would regret it.

Unexpectedly, my chancellorship started from a negative position because the search committee chose not to interview a particular internal candidate. His supporters were opposed to my selection. I never understood why I was blamed for him not being interviewed, but I was. Complicating matters, his wife was a member of the Arkansas legislature. In her case, the saying, "Hell hath no fury like a woman scorned," attributed incorrectly to Shakespeare, should have been changed to "Hell hath no fury like a woman whose husband was scorned." She did not pass up any opportunity to create difficulties for me and the university.

The situation reminded me of a story Joe Frank Harris, then the governor of Georgia, shared at a prayer breakfast. He talked about a very effective state senator who lived below the "gnat line." South of Macon, Georgia, he said, gnats were really bothersome, but north of Macon, they weren't. He said the senator didn't let gnats distract him. Between each word, Governor Harris blew out of the corner of his mouth, saying, "The (blow) senator (blow) just (blow) blew (blow) them (blow) away (blow) as (blow) he (blow) worked."

I concluded I should blow this particular gnat away by remaining focused on my goals and objectives for the university. Following Steven Sample's advice, "If a leader must choose between being sensitive to others and being able to stay on course, he should prefer the latter," I stayed on course.

Because I was an engineering professor from Georgia Tech, several faculty members were opposed to my selection. They didn't believe an engineer could be an effective chancellor. Their minds were made up; nothing I did in the following eleven years changed their beliefs. I didn't let it deter me, because I had returned to my undergraduate alma mater to do all I could to elevate the academic reputation of the university. Those who thought I wanted to turn it into a Georgia Tech knew nothing of my roots within the university and the state; they didn't know of my love for the humanities and my parents' belief I'd major in English in college; they didn't know I believed that as UA goes, so goes the State of Arkansas.

While serving as CEO of Walmart, Lee Scott invited me to address a management group. In introducing me, Scott said people in Arkansas were excited about the changes I planned to make until I started making them. If a change affected them, then they were opposed to it. When he thought his job of leading Walmart was difficult, Scott said he thought of me, because it seemed like everyone in the state who attended UA or a Razorback athletics event believed he or she could do a better job than I could.

Scott's comment drew laughter from the audience, but I thought, *You've no idea how true your statement is, Lee.* I'm sure many people in the state could have done the job better than I could, but I was the one who was hired to do it.

The first three years as chancellor were rough. Soon after I started, I met with Scott's predecessor, David Glass. Glass said he supported what I wanted to accomplish at the university, but he thought the strong resistance I'd face would cause me to give up before I accomplished my goals. I remember saying, "David, students can protest me, faculty can vote no-confidence in me, and the press can attack me, but only three votes will make me quit: God's, my wife's, and Alan Sugg's. I came home for a reason, and I'm not going to quit until I've made a difference for Arkansas."

Several years later, I saw David and reminded him of our conversation. He said I didn't need to remind him. On many occasions, he had wondered whether I regretted saying that. I assured him that it strengthened my resolve to continue doing all I could to strengthen the university. Beginnings can be tough! The old saying "If you're up to your elbows in alligators, it's hard to remember your objective is to drain the swamp" often came to mind.

Robert Gates, a former director of the CIA, served as Texas A&M's president during part of my UA chancellorship. When we met in his office, we discussed the challenges a CEO of a public research university faces. While in his fifth year as president, he resigned to become secretary of defense under President George W. Bush and continued to serve for President Barack Obama. Following his governmental service, Gates remarked often that the A&M presidency was his toughest job.

In contrast to promoting a leader from within, when a leader comes from outside, an element of uncertainty is added to the organization. In addition to uncertainty regarding the leader's style and personality, when a leader is brought in from outside, it is to effect significant changes. Such was expected of me. UA's trustees wanted the university's academic reputation and its financial position to improve significantly under my leadership.

I'm sure many things I said and did made the job tougher than it needed to be. With twenty years of hindsight, I could've done many things differently, and should have. However, I'm comforted by knowing I always did what I thought at the time was best for the university and the state.

EARLY DAYS

If your organization needs a wake-up call, I don't recommend the fire-for-effect approach used by the artillery in World War II. Although some believe a leadership change requires a totally new leadership team, I'm not among them. Political elections aside, it would have to be a very unusual situation for a total overhaul of the leadership of an organization to be required. Certainly, if criminal activity occurred or if a culture of dishonesty, sexual harassment, intimidation, or similar problems existed, wholesale changes would be justified, but losing years of institutional memory by removing everyone at the top is a steep price to pay.

Arriving from outside the organization, it takes time to assess the capabilities of the team members you inherit. Returning to Jim Collins's metaphor, it takes time to ensure you have the right people in the right seats in the bus you're driving. The right talent today might not be the right talent for tomorrow. Scale and speed requirements can highlight leadership challenges not obvious when an organization is small.

The harsh reality is the people who got you where you are might not be capable of taking you where you need to go. Or, as Marshall Goldsmith put it, "What got you here won't get you there." Because it occurs so frequently, John Maxwell's first irrefutable leadership law, the law of the lid, is based on recognizing the limits of individuals to take an organization to the next level.

When you arrive from outside the organization, it takes time to learn who you can count on to provide honest, objective feedback. In fact, you might never find them. Expect everyone to have an agenda; if they don't, you're fortunate. As President Ronald Reagan said to the USSR's General Secretary Mikhail Gorbachev during nuclear disarmament negotiations in the mid-1980s, based on a Russian proverb, "Trust, but verify." Seek information from multiple sources. Don't let the organizational chart limit your information network.

In *George Washington on Leadership*, Richard Brookhiser notes, "Washington, as commander in chief and president, solicited the views of a team of associates, either individually or collectively, in councils of war or cabinet meetings. . . . Sometimes, he reached outside his official team to get the input of people lower down in the organization, or outside it altogether."

To get information from various sources, leaders use a variety of techniques. Mike Duke shared with the leadership class that while he served as Walmart's CEO and president, he used diagonal communication to obtain feedback from all levels of the organization so he would know how things were going across the company. Abraham Lincoln used managing by wandering around techniques. General Jim Mattis, as he described in *Call Sign Chaos*, relied on skip-echelon to increase the speed and agility of decision-making. He also used what he called focused telescopes to bypass normal reporting channels and gather information, noting he copied the technique "from Frederick the Great, Wellington, and Rommel, among others."

Pam McGinnis provided the students with wise counsel on how to begin a new job. She said, "Listen for thirty days." When I became chancellor, I should've listened to more people and for a longer period of time. I thought I needed to hurry, because I planned to only be chancellor for five years. Had I known I'd be in the position for eleven years, I could've paced things better.

Had I read *The Essential Bennis* before becoming chancellor, I might have approached things differently during my first year. Bennis notes that a new leader is always on stage and that everything is "fair game for comment, criticism, and interpretation" (or misinterpretation). Bennis points out that a new leader's initial words and deeds receive intense scrutiny and that people will use them to quickly accept or reject the leader. Consequently, he recommends taking a low-key approach when entering a new leadership position. Doing so buys you time to learn more about the strengths, weaknesses, and personalities of your leadership team, as well as the organization's culture and needs. You'll have an opportunity to demonstrate your desire to listen and learn before leading.

Unfortunately, the best advice I received on how to begin a leadership role came to me when I was no longer chancellor. Donald Smith shared that each time he was promoted to a leadership position at Tyson Foods, he met with people in the organization and admitted he didn't know their business as well as they did. Then, he asked three questions: "What are we good at?" "What aren't we good at?" and "If you were king or queen for a day, what would you do to make things better?" Based on their answers, he prepared his agenda. Smith said, "The answer is always in the room."

When I shared Smith's approach with my son, John, he replied, "When I took a new leadership position, I used three ups, three downs, and a magic wand. I asked people to tell me three things we were very good at, three things we were not very good at, and what they would change if they had a magic wand." If I had asked him sooner how he handled transitions, I would've been more effective in my leadership roles.

Finally, be wary of gatekeepers, staff members who manage your calendar and determine who meets with you. They'll have their lists of good and bad people. Gatekeepers often have agendas different from yours. Sometimes they have scores to settle. It took several years for me to learn how to listen to and interpret advice I was receiving. It required listening between and behind the words.

DO YOUR HOMEWORK

Learn as much as you can about the organization you'll lead before your leadership position becomes effective. My selection to be UA chancellor was announced in the spring of 1997; my chancellorship didn't begin until July 1. In the interim, I communicated with UA administrators, alumni, faculty, and staff to learn as much as I could before arriving in the office on July 1.

Because relatively few decisions were made during the summer, Mary Lib and I toured the state with Richard Hudson, then the university's vice chancellor for government and community relations, listening to as many people as we could, learning their aspirations for the university. Based on what we learned, my priorities changed dramatically. I'd planned to emphasize research and graduate studies, but after learning that a majority of the state's high-ability students were leaving the state for undergraduate studies, I concluded we needed to significantly increase the quality and size of the entering freshman classes. My first request of the UA Board of Trustees was to raise admission requirements. We also increased the number of merit-based scholarships.

ON BECOMING A SUCCESSFUL LEADER

In 2017, I was invited to address an academic leadership workshop in Houston on how to become a successful leader. I accepted the invitation but began by informing the audience that I had changed the advertised title. No doubt influenced by *On Becoming a Leader* by Warren Bennis, I titled my presentation "On Becoming a Successful Leader." After inviting anyone to leave who came expecting me to provide a recipe for how to become a successful leader, I said I was still trying to become one.

No one left, so I said the "-ing" in "becoming" is important, because becoming a successful leader is an endless journey. An important key is how you define success and how you define leader. Success is not a destination but a journey, and being a leader is not about a title but about the team. I told them my goal was to be the leader of the best team, not the best leader of a team, and that the focus must be on the team, not the leader.

Years after the Houston conference, I was struck by a statement Ben Reiter made in the acknowledgments section of *Astroball*: "The central lesson I took from the Astros has been the importance of focusing on processes over outcomes." The central lesson I have taken from my leadership journey is the importance of focusing on the *process* of becoming a successful leader, not the *outcome* of being a successful leader. And I have learned the importance of enjoying the journey—the joy of leadership.

John Roberts, president and CEO of J. B. Hunt Transport Services, shared with the leadership class that, not long after being elevated from a position in sales to president of a major business division within the company, he was struggling to establish a new relationship with the members of his leadership team. Becoming very frustrated in an off-site meeting with the team, Roberts said, "I am the president of this division, and you will do what I tell you to do."

As soon as he said it, Roberts thought, *Oh, my Lord, I can't believe that just happened. I can't believe it has come to this.* At a low point in his leadership journey, Roberts recognized it was an admission of failure in leading the group. However, he immediately set about remedying his mistake. The performance of the division escalated; Roberts became viewed within the company as an exemplary leader and was elevated to his current position of president and CEO. Although Roberts did not realize it at the time, the off-site meeting was a defining moment for him and for J. B. Hunt Transport Services.

Because leadership is an unending journey, there is no end to leadership beginnings. Each day brings an opportunity for a new beginning, and each beginning offers opportunities and challenges. Strive to ensure the organization you lead becomes stronger over time. If a leadership vacuum exists, it will be filled.

CHAPTER 3

Leadership Values
and Attributes

L eaders' values guide their actions. When General Marty Steele met with the leadership class, he said, "Never sacrifice your core values to appease colleagues." Given what they learned about his leadership journey, they understood he meant it. He lived it.

Following a presentation I gave in November of 2014 at Oklahoma State University titled "Leadership Matters: An Engineer's Perspective," a professor approached me and said he thought most of what I said had less to do with leadership and more to do with being a good person. I agreed. I also said I believed a necessary condition for a person to be an exemplary leader is for the person's core values to include honesty, integrity, compassion, empathy, and humility.

Although Adolf Hitler and Joseph Stalin might have been successful leaders, they are not included in my (or, hopefully, anyone's) list of exemplary leaders. Being a good person is not a necessary condition for being a successful leader, but it is a necessary condition for being an exemplary leader. Likewise, being a good person is not a sufficient condition for being an exemplary leader. There are many good people in the world but few exemplary leaders.

When I asked my students to identify essential attributes in an exemplary leader, being an effective communicator dominated their responses. Other attributes cited most frequently, in rank order, were confidence, integrity, vision, honesty, delegation, decisiveness, inspiration, humility, and courage. Based on surveys discussed in *The Leadership Challenge*, Kouzes and Posner found that a majority of respondents believed a leader must be honest, forward-looking, competent, and inspiring. Over a five-year period, the same four characteristics consistently received the most votes across the six continents surveyed. Interestingly, of the top four in the survey by Kouzes and Posner, all but "competent" were identified by my students as well.

John Roberts told the students that he considered accountability and inspiration to be essential attributes of a leader. While inspiration was included in the list from the students, accountability was not.

Donald Smith said he believed that common sense and courage are essential. The students cited courage but didn't mention common sense. Smith's inclusion offers the opportunity to emphasize that it isn't all about IQ. Common sense, albeit uncommon, is essential.

What are the ten most important attributes for your leader? How does your list compare with the following one? Interestingly, each attribute appeared on lists from the students in the leadership class.

- Honesty

- Integrity

- Confidence

- Inspiration

- Commitment

- Passion

- Communication

- Decision-making

- Accountability

- Delegation

- Empowerment

- Creativity

- Innovation

- Empathy

REPUTATION

Reputations, which take years to build, can be destroyed in the blink of an eye—or the blink of a lie. If you don't believe me, ask Lance Armstrong, Martha Stewart, former University of Arkansas football coach Bobby Petrino, US Olympic swimmer Ryan Lochte, Tyco's Dennis Kozlowski, Theranos founder Elizabeth Holmes, HealthSouth's Richard Scrushy, scheme namesake Charles Ponzi, Bernie Madoff, or the parents involved in the 2019 college admissions bribery scandal. There is no shortage of people to include in a list of high-profile liars, beginning with the first to earn America's enmity, Benedict Arnold. In many cases, where lies were told or mistakes were made, if an admission and an apology had been offered immediately, the damage would have been minimized. Instead, denials and cover-up attempts led to automatic entry into the Leadership Hall of Shame.

Reputations can be destroyed or severely damaged by more than lies. Consider the impact on the reputation of the Houston Astros after players and staff members conspired to steal catchers' signs and communicate them to batters during the 2018 World Series. Consider the impact on the reputations of Pennsylvania State University, Michigan State University, the Roman Catholic Church, and a host of other organizations when sex-related crimes were uncovered. There are numerous examples of individuals and organizations causing serious damage to their reputations with cheating, criminal activity, and abuses of power.

INTEGRITY AND CHARACTER

How then does one build a good reputation? I believe in a values-based process, with a foundation of integrity and character. In connection with Father's Day, in the June 21, 1998, edition of the *Northwest Arkansas Times*, I was included among individuals asked what life lessons they had learned from their fathers. My response was, "My religious foundation came from the example set by my father; he also taught me to place character and integrity above all else."

Integrity and character are manifested in a person's actions, words, and deeds. A failure of integrity and character will destroy a person's reputation. John Maxwell linked the two concepts in *The 21 Irrefutable Laws of Leadership*: Character makes trust possible, and trust makes leadership possible.

Chris Lofgren said, "Character is more important than reputation." While I agree in principle, in my view, the two are intrinsically linked. Anyone lacking character and integrity will not have a good reputation.

Mike Duke told the students that character and integrity should be in everything they do. He also reminded them that, when it comes to integrity, leaders will be judged by their worst days, not their best or average days. Lofgren reminded them, "There is no right way to do the wrong thing."

In *On Becoming a Leader*, Warren Bennis identifies integrity as a leader's most important characteristic. He emphasizes the need for leaders to repeatedly demonstrate their integrity. Noting that too many leaders fail to recognize that they are being watched all of the time, he writes, "They forgot that something's being legal doesn't mean it's right." Bennis also notes, "Leadership is always about character." He observes that every leader possesses one or more of the following ingredients: a guiding vision, passion, integrity, curiosity, and daring. He also identifies three essential requirements for integrity: self-knowledge, candor, and maturity. Experience matters!

Dwight D. Eisenhower once said, "The supreme quality of leadership is unquestionably integrity. Without it, no real success is possible, no matter whether it is on a section gang, a football field, in an army, or in an office."[1]

When David Rubenstein asked Condoleezza Rice in *How to Lead* about qualities great leaders possess, she placed integrity at the center. She also identified vision as an essential quality, emphasizing the need to see what can be, not just what is. She told Rubenstein that great leaders must be humble. Drawing on lessons her parents taught her, Rice focused on three things: the need to work hard enough to be twice as good as your peers; although you can't control your circumstances, you need to control how you respond to them, so don't be a victim; and don't let anyone else define you—don't let their prejudice affect you.

Character is what forms the nature of a person. It also implies morality and ethical behavior. Hall of Fame basketball coach John Wooden observed in *Wooden on Leadership*, "Ability may get you to the top, but it takes character to keep you there." He looked for character in players he recruited, not players who were characters. For Wooden, character means respecting yourself, respecting others, and respecting the game or business you are involved in. He noted, "Character starts with little things like picking up after oneself, and it ends with big things like not cheating to win."

Wooden added, "I believe who you are inside—what you believe—is important, but what you do means more, much more. Actions trump words, and your values must be visible if they are to have an impact on those you lead or hope to attract as part of your team."

When I asked John Roberts what he looked for in someone he was hiring or promoting, he quickly identified character as the first attribute. He said a person's complete value system must represent someone he could trust and rely on.

Doris Kearns Goodwin pointed to Franklin Delano Roosevelt as an example of a leader whose character and intelligence carried him through difficult times.

Frequently, I've heard character defined as how a person acts when no one is watching. So I appreciated the treatment of the definition in *Dilbert* by Scott Adams.

DILBERT   **BY SCOTT ADAMS**

DILBERT © 2015 Scott Adams, Inc. Used by permission of Andrews McMeel Syndication. All rights reserved.

Coach Vince Lombardi is credited with saying, "Winning is a habit. Watch your thoughts; they become your beliefs. Watch your beliefs;

they become your words. Watch your words; they become your actions. Watch your actions; they become your habits. Watch your habits; they become your character."[2]

Coach Wooden provides the following solid advice to leaders: "Character counts, and values matter. And you, the leader, set the standard for both in your organization." He reminds us too that character is not easily taught and cautions against working with anyone lacking character. He believes not only that actions trump words but also that character trumps ability.

JUDGMENT

In a 2007 *Wall Street Journal* article, Warren Bennis and Noel Tichy say, "After a five-year study of leadership covering virtually every sector of American life, we came to the inescapable conclusion that judgment regularly trumps experience. Our central finding is that judgment is the core, the nucleus of exemplary leadership. With good judgment, little else matters. Without it, nothing else matters."

In their book *Shakespeare in Charge*, Norman Augustine and Kenneth Adelman identify judgment among the most important competencies of an effective leader. Having sound judgment trumps IQ scores. Being smart is one thing, but having good judgment is quite another. Possessing both is much preferred, but if you have to sacrifice one, don't sacrifice judgment.

HUMOR

Another important—if not essential—attribute for effective leadership is a sense of humor. It has served me well, and it has helped me relieve tensions and negotiate some tricky situations. I'm not alone in my belief. John Dickerson notes in *The Hardest Job in the World*, "We should also ask those who want the job"—of president of the United States—"or want to stay in it to tell a joke.... Humor in the face of unrelenting pressure demonstrates equanimity, a crucial attribute of

presidential success. It can also humanize a president, break the ice in tense situations, and win willingness to listen to a president's point of view."

Lincoln's sense of humor was one of his strongest attributes. Doris Kearns Goodwin notes how Lincoln recognized the role humor played with others and for himself. He needed it to survive.

PATIENCE AND FORTITUDE

Two attributes I believe are essential for successful leadership are symbolized by the two marble lions in front of the New York Public Library. New York's mayor, Fiorello LaGuardia, named them Patience and Fortitude. These are attributes New Yorkers needed in order to survive the economic depression during the 1930s. Patience and fortitude are also attributes leaders need, especially during turbulent times. I certainly needed them during my years as UA's chancellor.

PURPOSE AND VISION

When David Rubenstein asked former secretary of state General Colin Powell what makes people great leaders, he said it was important for leaders to understand that they lead followers. He added that leaders need to engage followers in work having purpose and value and that they must provide the inspiration needed for followers to achieve the purpose of their work and provide the resources required to accomplish their tasks successfully.

Rubenstein's interview demonstrated that Powell was very deliberate and purposeful in his leadership. For every job he held, Powell made sure he knew what he was trying to do, as well as the purpose and vision for the job. He answered questions of *why* and *what* regarding each job. Powell said leadership is all about inspiring followers.

TRUST

Trust is a necessity for exemplary leadership. Once it is lost, it's difficult if not impossible to regain. People might say they forgive you for violating their trust, but they will never forget it. Trust is not given. It must be earned.

In *The Five Dysfunctions of a Team*, Patrick Lencioni nails it. The five dysfunctions are the absence of trust, a fear of conflict, a lack of commitment, the avoidance of accountability, and an inattention to results. As Lencioni notes, trust establishes the foundation for a team. Without it, a team crumbles.

General Mattis observed in *Call Sign Chaos*, "Trust is the coin of the realm for creating the harmony, speed, and teamwork to achieve success at the lowest cost." He pointed out that trusting people is important, but letting them know and having them believe you trust them is far more important.

Trust is a function of truth and speed. Communicating good news and bad news quickly and accurately enhances trust. Too many leaders have used carrier pigeons to deliver good news and snails to deliver bad news. Mike Duke told the students in the leadership class they should let bad news travel faster than good news.

When banker Reynie Rutledge met with the leadership class, he said the scariest time in his life was the 2008 recession. He also reminded them, "It takes a heartbeat to lose trust." Trust can be very fragile. It's like a crystal ball you dare not drop. Like Humpty Dumpty, it's unlikely you'll ever be able to restore trust to its original shape and size.

Each time General Steele met with the leadership class, he shared four attributes he deemed essential for exemplary leaders. He said they must

- have the judgment to know what is right and what is wrong,

- have the integrity to do what is right,

- have the character to deal with those who don't do what is right, and

- have the courage to stop those who won't deal with those who don't do what is right.

Trust is a two-way street. If you want people to trust you, then you must trust them. Leaders trust others to perform their duties. Leaders trust but always verify.

BOSSES VERSUS LEADERS

Robert G. Ingersoll, in an 1884 essay, writes, "It is the glory of Lincoln that, having almost absolute power, he never abused it, except upon the side of mercy." Too few leaders possess Lincoln's self-restraint. Instead, power goes to their heads, and they become mere bosses rather than true leaders.

John Roberts keeps a list of the differences between bosses and leaders on his desk. He doesn't know the source of the list, but he has taken its message to heart. When he met with the leadership class, he emphasized the differences: bosses create fear, but leaders instill confidence; bosses affix blame, but leaders correct mistakes; bosses give answers, but leaders ask questions; bosses make work drudgery, but leaders make it interesting; and bosses are interested in themselves, but leaders are interested in the team.

Roberts's last point reminds me of something Greg Brown emphasized when he met with the class: "Be interested, not interesting." Too many leaders try to sell themselves to others when they should invest themselves in others; the best way to become invested is to be interested in them, to learn more about them.

After distinguishing leaders from managers, Bennis lists in *On Becoming a Leader* the differences between them. "I tend to think of the differences between leaders and managers as the differences between those who master the context and those who surrender to it. There are other differences, as well, and they are enormous and crucial."

COURAGE

President and CEO of Walmart International, Judith McKenna, told the leadership students, "Have the courage of your convictions. Let go of fear, and have the courage to take those steps forward."

Courage can come with a price but also with rewards. As Bennis notes, "Good ideas are only made stronger by being challenged. The subordinate who speaks truth to power needs courage and may pay the price for candor. But, by doing so, he or she evinces nothing less than leadership. The willingness to stand up to the bosses may not save the candid individual's job, but it will serve him or her well in another, better organization."

In one of the final scenes in the 1939 movie *The Wizard of Oz*, Dorothy, accompanied by Scarecrow, Cowardly Lion, Tin Man, and her dog, Toto, return victoriously to the Emerald City with the broom of the Wicked Witch of the West. By bringing the broom, they expected that the Wizard of Oz would grant their wishes. After dealing with Scarecrow's request for a brain, the Wizard of Oz turned his attention to Cowardly Lion, saying, "As for you, my fine friend, you are a victim of disorganized thinking. You are under the unfortunate delusion that, simply because you run away from danger, you have no courage. You're confusing courage with wisdom."

Cowardly Lion is not alone in confusing courage with wisdom. Just because a leader doesn't act on a controversial matter doesn't mean the leader lacks courage. Don't judge the lack of action to be a lack of courage; similarly, because a leader acts does not mean the leader is courageous. Many leaders don't categorize themselves as courageous, because they consider the decisions they make to be logical, reasonable, and correct for a given situation. Perhaps others placed in similar situations would be afraid to make the same decisions because they felt they lacked courage. Why is it courageous to do the right thing? I don't consider it courage; I consider it leadership.

When I was in high school, my parents gave me a copy of John F. Kennedy's Pulitzer Prize–winning *Profiles in Courage*. It was mesmerizing and motivating. The opening sentence grabbed me: "This is a book about that most admirable of human virtues—courage." The book held my attention to the end: "In whatever arena of life one may meet the challenge of courage, whatever may be the sacrifices he faces if he follows his conscience—the loss of his friends, his fortune, his contentment, even the esteem of his fellow men—each man must decide for himself the course he will follow."

I wondered how many people I'd come to know during life's journey whose profiles in courage would merit inclusion in a similar book. I also wondered if I'd pass the test, if I'd prove to be courageous when courage was needed. Would I stand up, would I step forward, would I say, "Choose me"?

BEING LEADER VERSUS LEADING

In my address in Houston to faculty members who aspired to be higher education leaders, I advised any who were considering taking on the duties and responsibilities of a department head to wait until they achieved the rank of full professor. Being a department head is the most difficult job in academia; I avoided it. When UA chancellor Joseph Steinmetz met with the leadership class, he confirmed my claim: He served as a department head at Indiana University, and he also found it difficult.

Interestingly, albeit in a different context, similar advice applies to individuals desiring to take on leadership positions in industry. The issue is one of demonstrated competency. In a university, promotion to full professor is a sign of demonstrated competency. Augustine and Adelman note in *Shakespeare in Charge*, "Basic competence is so fundamental to leadership that it's all too often forgotten."

Competence was included among the top four characteristics in the Kouzes and Posner survey. Lee Iacocca also included competence in his "Nine Cs of Leadership"—curiosity, creativity, communication skills, character, courage, conviction, charisma, competence, and common sense. General Mattis included it in his three Cs of leadership fundamentals—competence, caring, and conviction.

When David Rubenstein asked Eric Schmidt, former chairman of Google/Alphabet, if he thought people were born leaders or if they become effective leaders through training and education, Schmidt indicated he thought it was a combination of innate skills and learning. But, he added something less frequently cited by leaders: exceling at something (competency). He said it is no longer sufficient for a person to be a generalist, saying that it is important for leaders to be very good at something and that they can learn other things over time. He summarized his views regarding what it takes to become an effective leader by saying, "Discipline, hard work, and loving what you do will get you very far."

In *The Contrarian's Guide to Leadership*, Sample titled chapter 10 "Being President versus Doing President." Many people think they want to *be* president, but very few want to *do* president. The former think it's easy to *be* and *do* president. They're mistaken. They think the position is glamorous, just as those who don't travel frequently believe airplane travel, staying in hotels, and living out of suitcases are glamorous. People who want to *be* and not *do* president are attracted by the title, the accompanying aura, perks, power, and prestige of the position—all of which vanish or lose their significance all too soon.

Two days shy of one hundred days into his term as president, Donald Trump said, "I loved my previous job. I had so many things going. This is more work than in my previous life. I thought it would be easier."[3] But you don't have to be POTUS to learn that leadership, simply stated, is hard work. Generally, leadership is a 24/7/365.25 (including leap years—oops! Just revealed my engineering precision).

Anyone wanting to be president, Bill Clinton told Rubenstein, must realize that it's about the people, not themselves. Too many people, because of arrogance, forget. He added that leaders want to be able to say the organizations they led are better off and the people impacted by those organizations have a better future. Clinton said, "The most important thing is to be humble, to listen, to realize everybody's got a story—all the things I learned as a kid."

In addressing the question of why anyone would really want to be a leader, Rubenstein gave three reasons: Lives can improve because of changes leaders create; by growing leaders, leaders can multiply the number of lives improved; and leaders can experience feelings of accomplishment and achievement through their impact on the lives of others.

To Rubenstein's list, based on my experiences, I can add a fourth reason: guilt (the gift that keeps on giving). Others believed I'd be more effective than other candidates for leadership positions. As a result, in several instances, I took on leadership positions reluctantly, but once I was in the position, I did it to the best of my ability. If I didn't do it and the organization suffered as a result, I'd feel guilty. Guilt can be a powerful motivator.

When asked if he would have been more effective if he had been older when he became president, Clinton told Rubenstein that, in some ways, he thought so, but not in other ways. I identified with his response when he said, "Sometimes you get a bunch done because you're too dumb to know you can't do it." What we accomplished during my tenures as engineering dean and chancellor certainly qualified.

Doing leadership means influencing, inspiring, visioning, daring to differ, dreaming, succeeding in spite of others, refusing to fail, communicating, empowering, innovating, teaming, learning, deciding, and serving people. It also means hiring, assessing, developing, praising, disciplining, rewarding, compensating, motivating, promoting, demoting, replacing, retiring, and firing people. Leadership is not limited to a job title; it's everyone's job. Leadership is facing challenges, facing facts, and taking risks.

Leadership is hard work! Drucker stated correctly, "Leadership is a foul-weather job." James Carville and Paul Begala point out in *Buck Up, Suck Up . . . and Come Back When You Foul Up: 12 Winning Secrets from the War Room*, "Hard work can make up for a lot—lack of innate genius, grating interpersonal skills, even ugly scars and tattoos. But without a strong work ethic, even the geniuses, the charmers and the folks with flawless skin wind up losers." So, if you are not prepared to work hard, avoid being a leader. Not only is leadership hard work, but it's also needed most when a crisis occurs.

Do you really want to be a leader? If so, why?

Leadership is a contact sport and a team sport. It's not a popularity contest. It requires enduring criticism, possibly being the subject of attacks by the press, peers, and competitors, biting your lip, and staying the course.

Winston Churchill said, "Never give in— never, never, never, never, in nothing great or small, large or petty, never give in except to convictions of honour and good sense."

During the most difficult periods of my chancellorship, I could count on Lewis Epley, who chaired UA's board of trustees when I was appointed, to call me or send me an email. Each email included Churchill's quote.

 Epley challenged me to stay the course. His support and encouragement were timely, effective, and appreciated.

A friend and colleague, John R. Canada, told me that in the spring of 1963, I said I'd like to be a university president. I have no memory of saying it, but the conversation apparently occurred as we walked back to our offices after hearing T. Marshall Hahn, Virginia Tech's newly inaugurated president, share an inspirational vision for the university with the faculty. Over the following twenty to twenty-five years, I never entertained the idea of holding an administrative position within a university, so I must've said that to John because I thought it sounded like a neat job to have. Even if I truly had an interest in becoming a university president at that point, my thoughts would have shifted to becoming an eminent professor as I learned what the president actually did.

While I no longer focused on holding an administrative position, my desire to lead didn't diminish. As a result, I focused on being a leader within my profession and became quite active in the industrial engineering professional society, resulting in my presidency of the Institute of Industrial Engineers in 1983 and 1984. The presidency of the professional society led to my selection to chair the American Association of Engineering Societies. In turn, the broad support I received from engineering societies led to my selection to lead the Engineering Directorate at the National Science Foundation (NSF). My leadership experience at NSF led to my deanship at Georgia Tech. Other leadership opportunities occurred within my church and within my college, where I led a multidisciplinary research center. Also, in 1977, I cofounded SysteCon and served as its chairman until its acquisition by Coopers & Lybrand in 1984.

Over my career, I've known many people who wanted to be president of this or that organization because it would look good on their résumés or for the perks and prestige associated with the position.

I've also seen how disillusioned they were when they found out things weren't all they thought they would be, how challenging and difficult the position of president was, and how quickly the applause and accolades dissipated.

In contrast, my leadership journey, like that of so many others, has not been influenced by titles and perks associated with positions. Instead of a title, it has been about having opportunities to make positive differences for people and organizations.

ETHICAL BEHAVIOR

Leaders frequently have to decide between doing what benefits them personally and doing what is right. The answer is to always do what is right. The situation arises so frequently that Coleman Peterson, the former head of human resources for Walmart, advised the students to know what they are *not* willing to do and to stick to it. It's important for you to live your values. An ethical dilemma is a golden opportunity to do so.

Melinda Faubel, director of external affairs for AT&T Arkansas, shared a time when a finalist for a job borrowed a phone during an interview, called her boss, and told him she would not be at work that afternoon because she was ill—needless to say, she was not hired.

Mike Duke told the students he learned how to deal with ethical dilemmas from his first boss, John Weitnauer, who was CEO for Richway Discount Stores. While Duke was meeting with Weitnauer, he received a telephone call from a supplier of gasoline for the store's retail pumps. This was during a period of gasoline shortage in the 1970s, and retailers were having difficulty meeting demand. The sales person said he would provide Richway with all the gasoline they needed if Weitnauer gave him an expensive tennis racket sold in its stores. Weitnauer thanked him for calling and said Richway did not do business that way; then, he asked the sales person to have his boss call and explain to Weitnauer why their company chose to do business this way. Duke said Weitnauer never received the requested call, but he communicated very clearly how a leader handles an ethical dilemma.

Several years later, I had an opportunity to work with Weitnauer. He was a client for SysteCon. He retained us to design an automated distribution center for Richway. Weitnauer is one of the most respected leaders in Atlanta. When Duke shared his story with the class, it confirmed everything I'd heard about Weitnauer.

Duke advised the students to "know what is right and what is wrong before you are ever confronted with a situation calling on you to decide what action to take. In this way, you will not have to give the situation any thought. You will know immediately how to respond."

Pam McGinnis said, "Don't ever let someone tell you to do something unethical."

Ethical dilemmas in business typically involve small things, not multimillion dollar briberies. The danger is that you can easily justify letting something slide by because it's not a big deal. However, gradually, over time, small things become medium things, then bigger things. The best approach is to nip them in the bud—say no to the small things and never consider compromising your values and damaging your reputation. In the leadership class, Donald Smith said, "Use situational leadership, not situational ethics."

It's also important to not be perceived as having done the wrong thing. People who see you doing something can draw incorrect conclusions. For example, let's say Company X is a major supplier to your company. It offers you tickets to the Super Bowl, including seats in its skybox. You decline because you know you wouldn't be offered the tickets if you didn't hold your current leadership position. You know it's not about you; it's about your position. Then, you attend the Super Bowl using tickets you purchased. Should you stop by and visit with people in the skybox? If you do, people who see you will assume you are a guest and that Company X is rewarding you for doing business with it. I would save the networking for another venue. Perceptions matter!

LEADERSHIP'S SECRET SAUCE: LISTENING, LEARNING, AND LOVING

When asked what makes great leadership, Sir Richard Branson, founder of the Virgin Group, replied in Rubenstein's *How to Lead*, "Being a really good listener is one of the most key things." He added, "Another key thing is loving people—a genuine love of everybody and looking for the best in people." When asked what the key ingredient is to being a successful leader, Branson said, "Surrounding yourself with great people. Learning to delegate early on—not trying to do everything yourself. Making sure you've got the kind of people who are praising the team around them, not criticizing them. And having people who are willing to really innovate, be bold, and create something that everybody who works for the company can be really proud of."

When Virginia Rometty, IBM's former chairman, president, and CEO, was asked by Rubenstein what positioned her for success, she credited being a constant learner. She admitted she didn't know everything, but she had a strong desire to learn. She viewed every situation as a learning opportunity. Being curious, she looked for evidence of curiosity in people she hired.

Listening and learning are two of the key ingredients in exemplary leadership's secret sauce. General Mattis pointed out in his book that he did the following: "In keeping with George Washington's approach to leadership, I would listen, learn, and help, then lead."

Listening isn't the same as agreeing or balloting. If you listen to ten people, and eight say you should do *this*, but two say you should do *that*, don't conclude that you must do *this*. In *The Contrarian's Guide to Leadership*, Sample shares an instance in which Abraham Lincoln's cabinet voted on an issue he favored. After counting the votes, "Lincoln announced, 'One aye and seven nays. The ayes have it!'"

Obviously, you should ignore votes infrequently. Voting and then ignoring the results will damage the morale of followers. In general, don't take a vote if you aren't going to support the majority. Likewise, don't ask a question if your mind is made up and you're going to ignore the answer. Perhaps you think taking votes and asking questions is participatory leadership; it isn't if they are meaningless. Your team members will see through your smoke screen. At the same time, if your mind is made up and you don't listen, then you might be missing the opportunity to reevaluate and obtain a better result.

When leaders follow Lincoln's example and go in a different direction, coaching moments occur. After listening to why your followers voted as they did, you can explain why you are opposed to the majority opinion or preference. In doing so, you will provide your followers with opportunities to be heard and will let them know the rationale behind your decisions. Generally, you will have a greater breadth of knowledge and understanding of ramifications of a decision than will your followers. Leaders should seize every opportunity to expand followers' knowledge and understanding. Listen, learn, love, and lead.

PART 2

Leadership Matters

CHAPTER 4

Communication

Abraham Lincoln, Franklin Roosevelt, and John F. Kennedy are mentioned frequently for their communication abilities, and Ronald Reagan is commonly referred to as the Great Communicator. Among James Carville's and Paul Begala's twelve winning secrets from the war room is to know how to communicate. Communication is essential for effective leadership.

Although my students identified being an effective communicator as an attribute essential to being an exemplary leader, many leaders struggle with communicating effectively. However, even if you're not an effective speaker or you don't have great writing skills, it's still possible to communicate effectively. Let your actions speak for you. Followers will trust and respect you and will overlook faults you might have in speaking or writing.

The most frequent complaint I've heard about leaders is a *lack* of communication, as opposed to *poor* communication. Too many leaders seem to believe their followers are mind readers. Let your followers know your hopes, dreams, aspirations, delights, and expectations. And, at times, privately let them know your frustrations and disappointments.

Jeswald Salacuse notes in *Leading Leaders*, "The essence of all leadership lies in compelling communication." Walmart's Judith McKenna told our leadership students, "The biggest challenges of leadership are communication and motivating others." Donald T. Phillips observes in *Lincoln on Leadership*, "Every leader must realize that the power to motivate followers resides almost solely in the ability to communicate effectively." He points out that one-on-one conversation is far more effective than speaking to a large group. In addition, informal chats allow a leader to feel the pulse of the organization. He adds, "*Loyalty* is more often won through such personal contact than in any other way."

In his autobiography, Lee Iacocca said, "The only way you can motivate people is to communicate with them."

Donald Smith told the leadership students, "Everything counts and everything communicates." He added, "The key to leading is communication, and the key to communication is to keep your message plain and simple." He reminded them, "Ambiguity breeds mediocrity; clarity breeds excellence."

Soon after Smith was assigned to a position at Tyson Foods headquarters, chairman and CEO Don Tyson stopped by Smith's desk to welcome him and ask how things were going. After a couple of minutes, while Smith was going into great detail about his work, Tyson walked away without saying a word. Smith was stunned and wondered what he'd done wrong. He shared with his supervisor what happened and received some very valuable advice: When Tyson stops by again, have your message distilled into a single sentence. If he wants to know more, let him ask for more. The advice was simple: Be succinct. Often, when lower-ranked people meet with top-ranked people, they try to demonstrate the depth and breadth of their knowledge; in doing so, they diminish their effectiveness, and instead of making a positive impression they do the opposite.

Every day, when Smith came to the office, he was ready with his sentence. Weeks went by before Tyson dropped into the department again and asked Smith what was happening with his work. Delighted with his second chance, Smith shared his sentence. Tyson said, "That's interesting," and asked Smith for more details. After about thirty minutes of conversation, Tyson thanked Smith for the update and encouraged him to keep pursuing what he was doing. Thereafter, when Smith came to the office, he was always ready with his sentence.

The greatest challenge in communication is ensuring that the message being sent is the message being received. A frequent mistake is believing we're great communicators. It's been the case for me. Too often, I've expected people to read my mind. A majority of the mistakes in my leadership journey have been failures to communicate accurately.

In communicating to a large group, a small group, or a single person, frame your message and deliver it effectively. The effectiveness of your delivery is measured by how well it's received. Communication is a two-way street. Unfortunately, some people always have their send buttons activated and seem to not even have a receive button.

SILENT COMMUNICATION

People use both verbal and nonverbal methods to communicate. The former include speaking and writing; the latter include actions and body language. Among nonverbal methods is silence. Lincoln was known for his speaking ability; however, he chose to remain silent during much of the 1860 presidential campaign. Donald T. Phillips writes, "On June 19, 1860, he wrote to a friend: 'In my present position . . . by the lessons of the past, and the united voice of all discreet friends, I am neither [to] write or speak a word for the public.' Less than a month later, he told a group: 'It has been my purpose, since I have been placed in my present position, to make no speeches. . . . Kindly let me be silent.'"

Saying nothing or ignoring a question sends a message, although there is no assurance it will be interpreted correctly. Likewise, frowns, smiles, and a stoic countenance can communicate. As James C. Humes notes in *Speak Like Churchill, Stand Like Lincoln*, "Silent signals can register even louder than speech."

Although I might not say a word, Mary Lib says she can tell when I'm upset because my ears turn red. Walmart's Doug McMillon indicated that members of his leadership team can tell when he is getting frustrated because he sighs. Another leader who met with the leadership class provided two examples of body language communicating when she was bored, frustrated, or upset: She rubbed her hands together and had "fiery eyes." What's your tell when you're upset?

Rolling your eyes, sighing, tapping your foot, yawning, and a host of things can communicate feelings, and each can be misunderstood. Early in my career, my leader appeared to have a health disorder, because each time I met with him to discuss something of great interest or concern to me, his eyes rolled back, and he fell asleep. Instead of concluding he had no interest in my concern, I concluded he was having a bad day. Perhaps I was mistaken.

When you're having a bad day, don't let it show. When you're angry or upset, it's advisable to remain silent. Lincoln's approach to dealing with criticism was quite simple: He wrote detailed letters to his antagonists, defending himself, venting his anger and frustration, and then didn't send them. As Donald T. Phillips notes, "He felt better for having stated his case but did not want any of his angry or emotional remarks made public." Today, instead of writing harsh letters and not sending them, we can type a harsh email, text message, or tweet and not send it. Just be careful not to press send before gaining control of your emotions.

Exemplary leaders recognize the wisdom of being "quick to listen, slow to speak, and slow to become angry."[1] Listen carefully, and take time to process what you hear before speaking. It will lessen the likelihood of anger entering the picture.

MIXED MESSAGES

Regardless of how you deliver them, avoid sending mixed messages. As my son, John, told the leadership students, "There's nothing more frustrating than mixed messages." Noting the pains Lincoln took to be consistent in communicating, Phillips writes, again in *Lincoln on Leadership*, "Nothing frustrates subordinates more than receiving mixed messages. No matter what the method of communication—memos, discussions, phone calls, etc.—to lead effectively, you must be clear and confident in what you have to say, and then you must follow through."

As on most university campuses, underage drinking was a front-burner issue when I became UA's chancellor, especially with football season and tailgating on the horizon. There were student deaths related to alcohol consumption on multiple campuses. Universities across the nation were attempting to deal with the issue.

I decided to address it head-on. It didn't take long to get people's attention, including students and the media. On August 24, 1998, we unveiled an anti-alcohol program called "Be Vocal, Be Visible, Be Visionary." Working with community and student-government leaders, we sent a letter to parents requesting they discuss alcohol abuse with students before they left for college campuses in a couple of weeks.

To avoid sending a mixed message, my positions on the subject of alcoholic beverages on campus were twofold: enforce laws and be consistent. Apart from the minimum drinking age, there was a state law prohibiting open containers in public spaces, which included tailgating areas.

The football stadium had a number of private boxes in which alcohol was permitted. Because boxes are rented, they were deemed private spaces. For tailgating, officers were asked to remind people to not have open containers visible. The same rules applied to the basketball arena, which included private boxes.

To be consistent, if alcohol is permitted in private boxes, shouldn't it be permitted in residence hall rooms and rooms in fraternity and sorority houses? Treating room rentals the same as box rentals led to a consistent message: Alcohol was permitted in leased rooms for students of legal age. Our attempts to avoid mixed messages led to some interesting press coverage, including a cartoon in the *Arkansas Democrat-Gazette*.

Despite our attempts to avoid mixed messages, we weren't perfect. When we were made aware of inconsistencies, we attempted to rectify them. We endeavored to be consistent and to have our actions mirror our words. Saying one thing and doing another destroys trust. As Phoenix advised Achilles in the *Iliad*, "Be both a speaker of words and a doer of deeds."

MEDIUM AND CHANNEL

You must decide how best to deliver your message, be it publicly by way of a speech or a presentation, or one-on-one. Depending on the size and locations of the audience, telecommunications alternatives might be required. Also, depending on the message, communicating both verbally and in writing might be appropriate.

While serving as UA's chancellor, I delivered annual state-of-the-university addresses, using different media. Initially, I spoke in an auditorium to a variety of stakeholders, then a video of the speech was later posted on the university's website. I also used birthday cards to communicate certain messages, and I sent semiannual letters to stakeholders, which were printed in newspapers.

The appropriate communication medium and channel depend on the message, its urgency, and the audience. Regardless of the choice, not everyone will receive it. Not unlike a minister delivering a sermon about the importance of attending services, those most in need of a message won't receive it. It's necessary to communicate, communicate, communicate and to use a variety of media and communication channels.

LISTENING

A key component of communication is listening. Because you're the leader, many will want to hear what you have to say on every issue, but you must listen before you speak. In a meeting with your followers, be the first to listen and the last to speak. Pam McGinnis admitted to the leadership class that she had to realize "they don't always want to hear from you. Shut your mouth, and listen to other people."

Numerous leaders reminded the students that they needed to be exceptional listeners. There's a reason you have one mouth and two ears; listen more than you speak. To enhance communication quality, Blake Strode advised the students to "Start with curiosity; start with questions, and really listen to the answers." Walmart's Mike Duke seldom gave orders; instead, he asked questions. After listening to the responses, he asked more questions and listened to the responses. Turning a deaf ear to responses is a sure-fire way to lose the support of your followers.

The guest leaders consistently cited listening as an essential ability. Motorola's Greg Brown told the leadership students that, in meetings, he talks 5 percent of the time and spends the rest of the time listening. He reminded them "Leaders should speak less and speak last."

After stepping down as UA's chancellor, I took six months to prepare for my return to a full-time faculty position. In the meantime, Kim LaScola Needy arrived to be the department head. Not long after I returned to campus she came to my office to discuss something. Needy said that while I considered myself just one of the faculty, I was not. Junior members of the faculty were not speaking up in the meeting until they heard my position on issues. She said she would like for me to speak last. I readily agreed and suggested I sit to her right in the conference room and for her to go around the table clockwise, which meant I'd be the last person called on to speak. The system worked. The experience reminded me you never see yourself as others see you. I was also reminded of the need to have people around you who'll be honest and objective in helping you see yourself through the eyes of others. Needy was and continues to be such a person for me. She's an exemplary leader.

What we see can bias what we hear. In *Leadership in 100 Quotes*, Charles Phillips notes, "Good communication skills are often stated as a requirement for leadership positions, and listening well is a key component of communicating. Yet none of us should take listening for granted; for one thing, people with really good concentration are rarer than we might think."

Reading between the Lines

Leaders need to read between the lines when they listen. Judith McKenna told the students to pay as close attention to what people *aren't* saying as to what they are. By avoiding blind spots and watching carefully, you can hear the message more clearly. As we discussed earlier, body language can communicate more powerfully than words. Watch the body language of the speaker, as well as of the people who aren't speaking. As Yogi Berra said in *The Yogi Book*, "You can observe a lot by watching." Although many might dismiss what Berra said because it's funny, there is wisdom behind his words.

Listening is not the same as hearing. It's not easy for some people to listen. In *Leading Leaders*, Salacuse notes, "One of the reasons that some people find it hard to listen is that their minds process information much faster than others can speak."

Active Listening

Coleman Peterson told the students they need to be *active listeners*— to listen carefully, then repeat or summarize what the speaker said. In *Personal Coaching for Results*, Lou Tice notes, "I've heard it said that in any person-to-person communication, there are at least six people involved: The person you believe yourself to be, the other person's beliefs about who you are, the person you think the other person believes you are, and the three corresponding perceptions that apply to the other person." Tice also observes, "Active listening certainly involves [the] use of critical thinking skills, such as recalling related issues, questioning, agreeing, disagreeing, and reaching logical conclusions. But its *primary* purpose is to understand the meaning of the message *from the speaker's point of view*."

In *The Speed of Trust*, Stephen Covey notes that listening first means "not only to really *listen* (to genuinely seek to understand another person's thoughts, feelings, experience, and point of view) but to do it *first* (before you try to diagnose, influence, or prescribe)." Covey writes, "Some people say that to listen first is inefficient, that it takes too much time. I couldn't disagree more. . . . This behavior . . . has an almost unparalleled positive impact in establishing trust, and on speed and cost."

Carville and Begala emphasize that being a good listener is "harder than it sounds. If you're successful, ambitious, driven, intelligent . . . it's probably difficult to listen to someone else. When we say listen, we don't mean reload or catch your breath or plan your next bons mots. . . . Really listen. Engage your partner nonverbally, visually, and intellectually."

Carville and Begala cite Bill Clinton as an extraordinary listener. They worked on his presidential campaign and observed firsthand his ability to make people feel heard. Mary Lib and I observed it numerous times. When you talk to Clinton, you have his undivided attention. His eyes are focused on your eyes; they don't wander toward someone else during the conversation. His message is clearly "I am listening to you," and he really is. Even years later, he can recall specific conversations he had with you.

The students believed I could remember everything, but, of course, I couldn't. However, at times, I am a very good listener. Upon returning from a meeting on February 28, 2002, with Nolan Richardson to deliver

the message that we were removing him as UA men's basketball coach, UA legal counsel Scott Varady gave me a recording device and asked me to record everything I remembered from the meeting. UA men's athletics director Frank Broyles, also in the meeting, was asked to do the same. The next day, we gave the recorders to UA staff to be transcribed. My recollections were thirteen pages in length; Broyles's were three pages. When the transcriptions were given to Richardson's lawyer, he requested a copy of the tape of the meeting. We told him the meeting wasn't taped, but I don't think he believed us. All we did was record everything we remembered.

During the trial, Richardson's attorney asked me a question. Following several comments among the attorneys and the judge, I asked him to repeat. Saying he thought I had this great memory, based on my recollection of the meeting with Richardson, he asked why I couldn't remember his question. I said his question wasn't memorable, but my meeting with Richardson was. I don't know why, but I can recall some things verbatim but not others. Mary Lib believes I have selective memory. I swear I'm not consciously choosing to not remember things she says.

Naive Listening

Tom Peters and Nancy Austin introduced me to naive listening in *A Passion for Excellence*. Naive listening is listening to the ultimate customer, not just those who report directly to you. They shared an example from Milliken & Company, a textile company based in Spartanburg, South Carolina, at the time led by Roger Milliken and Tom Malone, people I knew and respected.

Milliken's marketing director shared with Peters his experience after working two weeks on the night shift of the housekeeping staff for a major hospital. The manager learned firsthand while scrubbing floors and cleaning carpets the strengths and limitations of Milliken's products and performed naive listening with people using their products.

He found the experience invaluable and planned on doing it with more customers. For managing by wandering around to be successful, you must wander into the right places and perform naive listening. You must be strategic in where you wander and keep your ears and eyes open.

At SysteCon, this happened quite frequently, where listening to workers on the factory floor led to ideas for improvement I would not have thought of. Donald Smith's approach at Tyson Foods was quite similar. He asked people he was leading his three questions: What are we good at, what aren't we good at, and, if you were in charge, what would you change? Naive listening requires setting aside preconceived ideas and biases and really listening without an agenda.

DEALING WITH NESTORS

Referring to an obscure character in Shakespeare's *Troilus and Cressida*, Augustine and Adelman point out in *Shakespeare in Charge* that Nestor talked a lot but said little. He was elderly and respected, so people put up with him. He said the same things repeatedly and would use a hundred words to convey a thought when twenty or fewer would do. They note, "To another's nugget of thought, Nestor adds neither depth nor

breadth. When everything's already been said, he keeps on saying it."
Most organizations seem to have a Nestor.

The Pareto principle, or the 80-20 rule, applies to many things, including people who ask questions, but it seems at times more like a 95-5 rule: 95 percent of the questions are asked by 5 percent of the people.

Taking Action

Keep in mind Peter Drucker's advice from *Managing the Nonprofit Organization*: "Make sure to listen—but also make sure to take action on what you hear and learn." Listening and not acting is guaranteed to dampen inputs in the future. It's also a way to destroy trust in a leader. Turning a deaf ear, repeatedly, to people who are providing you with information they believe is important for the organization will cause you to lose credibility with your followers.

SPEAKING

As Hamlet said, "Words, words, words." Words matter, and the spoken word usually matters more than the written word. Sample notes in *The Contrarian's Guide to Leadership*, "Words are the primary stock-in-trade of leadership, and all leaders use them to attract, hold, inspire, and galvanize their followers." Speaking is preferred to writing, and speaking face-to-face is better than by phone. Speaking via video conferencing is better than a phone call, because you can still read the other person's body language.

Speaking one-on-one is preferable to speaking to groups. However, time constraints might preclude one-on-one communication with everyone who needs to hear your message. Regardless of how you choose to speak, you must know your message and know your audience.

Before speaking, make sure what you want to say needs to be said. As my son advised me, "If it'll make you feel good to say it, don't say it." Next, if the message needs to be said, does it need to be said by you? Might it be more effective to have someone else say it? Finally, if it needs to be said, is this the best time to say it? Timing is critical in delivering messages, especially when delivered verbally.

Know Your Audience

Admiral Jack Buffington told the leadership students to "never talk down to people. Adjust your conversation to your audience." It took me far too long to learn that my choice of words should be based on the person I'm addressing. I believed the shortest distance between two people was straight talk, but being blunt can be off-putting for some. I needed to shape my speech to fit my audience.

Early in my chancellorship, I met with a UA trustee who said he couldn't figure out how I was able to get away with the harsh things I was saying publicly about the state's education system and support for higher education. He said anyone else would have been run out of the state by then. He concluded that people accepted me because I grew up in Arkansas and they recognized I cared deeply for the state. He said he thought they understood that my comments were heartfelt and reflected a genuine concern for a brighter future for all Arkansans. Reflecting on what he said, I tried to tone down my rhetoric. However, I still made missteps as my passion for excellence in higher education outpaced my ability to articulate what needed to occur.

Choosing words carefully applies when speaking to individuals and to a larger audience. Judith McKenna reminded the students that words matter and encouraged them to "Shape your message around your audience."

Most of the mistakes in my leadership journey have been communication mistakes resulting from words spoken, not written. If I could have a do-over as chancellor, I'd more carefully choose words that conveyed my aspirations, desires, dreams, thoughts, and hopes for the state and the University of Arkansas. Often, I was too quick with a quip and spoke without thinking about the effect my words would have. Words I spoke caused far more trouble for me than decisions on budgetary, personnel, policy, or operational matters.

Over my career, I've given thousands of presentations to large and small audiences. You would think I would've figured out how to avoid inserting my foot in my mouth by now. My only explanation—not an excuse—is that I occasionally activate mouth before activating brain. When it occurs, it's a product of frustration, not calculation.

In a presentation I gave to the Fayetteville Chamber of Commerce on July 20, 2000, I criticized the effectiveness of the northwest Arkansas legislative delegation in securing increased support for the University of Arkansas. In retrospect, I shouldn't have vented my frustration. Also, I was inaccurate. My frustration was with one legislator, not the whole delegation. I should've followed my son's advice; I shouldn't have said what I did. Leaders shouldn't choose their words based on how they make them feel but based on how they make others feel. Three weeks later, I appeared before a legislative committee to explain my ill-chosen words. Several legislators had a field day with my visit, as did the press.

Permission granted by *Arkansas Democrat-Gazette*. All rights reserved.

Get to the Point

Greg Brown told the students that, when asked a question, they should "start with the answer." Chip Heath and Dan Heath point out in *Made to Stick*, "People are tempted to tell you everything, with perfect accuracy, right up-front, when they should be giving you just enough info to be useful, then a little more, then a little more."

Distilling your message, reducing it to its core, is essential when communicating, especially with busy people. Heath and Heath observe, "To strip an idea down to its core, we must be masters of exclusion. We must relentlessly prioritize. Saying something short is not the mission; sound bites are not the ideal. Proverbs are the ideal. We must create ideas that are both simple *and* profound. The golden rule is the ultimate model of simplicity: a one-sentence statement so profound that an individual could spend a lifetime learning to follow it."

They add, "We know that sentences are better than paragraphs. Two bullet points are better than five. Easy words are better than hard words. It's a bandwidth issue: The more we reduce the amount of information in an idea, the stickier it will be."

Judith McKenna advised the students to "Keep messages unbelievably simple." She said she writes what she plans to say, then she "distills, distills, distills." She advised the students to "Prepare! Prepare! Prepare!" before giving a speech. She spends hours shaping, sharpening, simplifying, and preparing her message. She distills her message to its core.

Donald T. Phillips observes, "Today's leaders would do well to embody Lincoln's simple, straightforward approach, especially when sending complex messages that can be easily misread. Messages are more often 'heard' when the communicator is honest, sincere, and succinct. In other words, say what you mean, and mean what you say."

Your followers need to be able to trust what you say. Think before you speak. Recognize that your words matter. Your goal is for your followers to say about you what Henry V said to the archbishop of Canterbury: "We will hear, note, and believe in heart that what you speak is in your conscience washed as pure as sin with baptism." The trust of your followers is priceless.

Repetition

Carville and Begala offer six rules for successful communication: Tell a story, be brief, be emotional, be unique, be relevant, and repeat your message relentlessly. The importance of repetition is emphasized by Patrick Lencioni in *The Advantage*, where he writes, "I've heard claims that employees won't believe what leaders are communicating to them until they've heard it seven times. Whether the real number is five, seven, or seventy-seven, the point is that people are skeptical about what they're being told unless they hear it consistently over time."

Over and over, the guest leaders meeting with the leadership class cited the need for repetition in conveying messages. You'll grow tired saying the same thing, but if you want people to internalize and, indeed, accept your message, say it over and over and over and over and over and over and over again.

By repeating your message, you'll accept it and model it.

The Power of the Pause

My father used to say, "Those who speak well speak a lot." Indeed, practice is essential, and there are techniques you can practice to improve the effectiveness of your speech. After giving the commencement address at my granddaughter Emma's high school graduation, my son remarked on my use of the "power of the pause." I've used it for so many years that I don't even recognize I'm doing it. Along with twenty other power techniques, Humes covers the power of pausing in *Speak Like Churchill, Stand Like Lincoln*.

Humes observes, "When you pause, you sound sincere, as if you're trying to come up with the right words to express your thoughts." No doubt, my use of a pause while speaking is a result of my years of teaching college students. If I noticed students were having difficulty paying attention, I would pause. Invariably, heads raised, and all eyes focused on me. I didn't need to say, "Pay attention!" Likewise, when I paused while giving a speech, the focus and level of attentiveness in the audience increased. Humes notes how "Pregnant pauses can turn even familiar words or phrases into compelling communication."

Adaptability, Preparation, and Confidence

Students have asked how I'm able to stand in front of thousands of people and give a speech. My response is that I don't think about speaking to thousands but about talking to individuals. I focus on one person in the audience and pretend I'm only speaking to that person, then I turn to another person and repeat the process. I'm not nervous because I'm confident. I've done my homework. Importantly, I speak from my heart. I let the audience know how much I care, and I endeavor to show my passion for the subject.

Storytelling

No doubt, my views regarding the power of stories are influenced by my reliance on them in my teaching and writing. Upon returning full-time to the UA faculty, I regularly received the Resident Raconteur Award from students in the department. As a child, I loved listening to stories—a love that carried over to making up and telling stories to our children and reading stories to them.

Mike Duke told the leadership students, "Communicating through storytelling is very effective." His views were shared by his colleague, Judith McKenna; she told the students, "The single hardest thing is communicating, telling a story, and taking people with you. It's incredibly valuable. You have to simplify. You have to explain the why."

Author and historian Doris Kearns Goodwin was asked in a 2018 article for *Fast Company* about the most important lesson business leaders can take from the presidents she's studied. She responded, "If I were to pick one, it would be the ability to speak to audiences with stories. . . . Clarity, simplicity, humor—these people were experts."

Carville and Begala note, "Facts tell, but stories sell." They certainly helped me sell prospective clients on retaining SysteCon to design distribution centers, sell students on attending UA, and convince donors to support UA financially. During my first semester as UA's chancellor, I was walking across campus when a faculty member called out to me. He wanted to introduce me to someone. It was a woman with her son. It was obvious the parents, both UA alumni, wanted their son to attend UA. It was also equally obvious he had no interest in doing so. So I asked, "Where do you want to go?"

"Vanderbilt!" he said.

I responded, "Vanderbilt is a fine university. You'll get a great education. But you can also get a great education here. I did! In fact, I never had to take a second seat to anyone in graduate school because of the fine education I received.

"Vanderbilt is going to be excellent with you or without you. If you come here, you can be a part of something exciting. You can contribute to making the University of Arkansas great. We're going to become great, with you or without you. If it's without you, it'll take a bit longer. I don't know what you are looking for, but you can make a difference here. Good luck. Take care of yourself."

Several weeks later, I received a note from the young man. He said he was coming to UA because he didn't think I would say what I did if I didn't mean it and he didn't want to miss out on our journey. He had a great UA experience. He was a cheerleader and did very well academically. His parents were thrilled, as was I.

At a recruitment event in Little Rock, I shared the story of my conversation with the young man. At the time, I didn't know how the story would end, but one student who wasn't planning on attending UA was in the audience. Years later, he said my story convinced him to enroll. He was UA's student body president before he graduated.

Heath and Heath ask, "How do we get people to act on our ideas? We tell stories." They observe, "For our ideas to endure, we must generate *interest* and *curiosity*." Six principles form the foundation for their book: simplicity, unexpectedness, concreteness, credibility, emotions, and stories. They point out, "The first problem of communication is getting people's attention. Some communicators have the authority to demand attention. . . . Most of the time, though, we can't demand attention; we must attract it." According to Heath and Heath, "Surprise gets our attention," and "Interest keeps our attention." Those are the essence of a good story.

Just as communication is a two-way street, so are stories. While stories are a powerful tool for leaders to use in communicating with followers, hearing stories from followers is an equally powerful way for leaders to get to know their followers. Blake Strode advised the leadership students, "Give people the opportunity to tell their stories directly." Everyone has a story. Listen to it! Learn from it! Stories communicate! Stories matter!

Humor

With few exceptions, my stories contain messages I want to deliver. Occasionally, I'll tell a joke, but there is a message behind my jokes as well. Stories appear in every chapter in this book. Stories are the MVPs in my writing, speaking, and teaching.

People have divergent views about including jokes in a speech. Erich Bloch, while serving as director of the National Science Foundation, advised me to never inject humor into my presentations. Although I respected and admired him immensely, I couldn't bring myself to eliminate humor. It's in my DNA. I continued to include jokes and was pleased to see Bloch in the audience laughing as spontaneously and loudly as anyone.

Leaders shouldn't be comedians, though. The jokes I tell serve a purpose in the speech. They reinforce the message. As Humes points out, "A joke for its own sake—without much relevance to the speech that follows—insults the audience."

Never tell a joke you wouldn't tell to your mother, grandchildren, or minister. Also, match your rhetoric with the situation. There are places and times when humor is not appropriate. General Marty Steele made it clear to leadership students he didn't tolerate ethnic, homophobic, racial, gender-based, nationality-based, or jokes of any type putting anyone down. "In combat," he said, "you don't want to have doubts about fellow marines having your back." Think before you quip. Engage brain before mouth.

People approached me years after hearing me give a speech and shared what they remembered. Nearly always it was a joke or a story. If a picture is worth a thousand words, then I believe a joke or story can be worth at least a thousand pictures. Consider the following: A young man was driving his new sports car on a curvy road. Putting the convertible through its paces, racing around the curves, he was met by another convertible driven by a young woman. As he pulled his car back into its lane, the woman passed him and yelled, "Pig!" *How dare she!* he thought. He turned and shouted at her, "Sow!" rounded the curve, hit the pig in the middle of the road, totaled his car, and killed himself.

I use this story to underscore the importance of listening. If we truly listen openly, with new attitudes, people will provide information we dare not interpret using old, antiquated thinking. If we do, it can lead to our destruction.

WRITING

Communicating in writing is almost a lost art, especially if you limit writing to handwritten communication. Perhaps for this reason, a handwritten note carries special significance. I wrote a brief message on a birthday card for each person in the Engineering Directorate at the National Science Foundation. I also did this while serving as the engineering dean at Georgia Tech. While serving as UA's chancellor, I used a variety of approaches to effect one-to-one contact with a wide range of people, such as adding a personal note when a standard letter was being sent to a large number of people.

Plagiarism

Because of criticism levied against the writing abilities of college graduates, colleges are giving greater emphasis to writing and requiring students to write much more. This has created a new challenge in grading students' writing—plagiarism. The ready availability of online sources makes it easy for a student to obtain content provided by others. In response, professors rely on specialized software to identify plagiarized material in work submitted by students.

Plagiarism is not limited to students. I was asked to address the UA community as part of the interview process for the chancellor position and to share my vision for the university. In thinking about the vision statement, I decided to use "The model land-grant university of the twenty-first century." Although I knew what I meant, few in the audience did. Over time, I realized we needed to draft a vision statement by engaging a wide range of stakeholders. The resulting vision statement was "A nationally competitive, student-centered research university serving Arkansas and the world."

Years after my interview for the chancellor position, in going through files I accumulated while serving as Georgia Tech's engineering dean, I found a publication from Virginia Tech titled "The Model Land-Grant University of the Twenty-First Century." I was stunned! I thought I came up with the vision statement on my own. I had no idea I'd stored the phrase from Virginia Tech someplace in my brain. Machiavelli's quote regarding fortune being "the arbiter of one-half of our actions, but she still leaves us to direct the other half, or perhaps a little less," swirled in my thoughts. I was very fortunate no one connected my vision statement with Virginia Tech's. It could've cost me my reputation; it could've cost me my job. My experience showed plagiarism can occur unintentionally, but the damage it can do is very real, whatever the original motivation.

Putting It in Writing

Do you want a written record of the message you're delivering? As chancellor of a public university in which nearly everything in writing is subject to a Freedom of Information Act request, I had to think twice about putting things in writing. This applied not only to letters but also to email. If we were analyzing options, before creating a written record, we had to consider how we would feel if they were on the front page of newspapers.

One instance in which it proved to be beneficial to put it in writing was my letter to Nolan Richardson following a renewal of his contract. In a meeting with him, I asked if he was happy. When he said he was, I said it was very important for his happiness to be obvious to people across the state, because how he felt about the school had significant influence on parents and whether or not they encouraged their children to attend the university. I said a lot of what I hoped to accomplish depended on him being happy. After he said he understood and affirmed his positive feelings, I returned to my office and prepared a letter to him, repeating what we discussed, including his affirmation of happiness. Following our decision to terminate his employment as men's basketball coach and during the ensuing court battles, my letter to Richardson proved instrumental in our defense against his suit. It was referred to within the UA legal team as my "Be Happy" letter. Putting it in writing mattered!

During his second presidency of The Ohio State University, I visited E. Gordon Gee and shared my experiences in teaching the leadership class. Prompted by the discussion, Gee shared a memo he had prepared and shared with his leadership team at OSU. The contents of Gee's "Rules of Engagement" are available at https://JohnAWhiteJr.com/WhyItMatters.

Gee emphasized the need for members of his leadership team to hire and retain extraordinary people and to be fully themselves. He also identified nine general operating principles he believed to be necessary for success: They will work as one, a unified team; they will trust one another; they will value conflict; they will collaborate; they will make timely decisions; they will hold each other accountable; they will manage to the middle; they will manage their gatekeepers; and they will keep score. Putting it in writing left little to chance; no member of the leadership team should be uncertain about how to function effectively within Gee's team.

OTHER COMMUNICATION CHANNELS

When face-to-face communication is not feasible, video can be an effective way for a leader to communicate. Video conferencing can be an effective means of achieving face-to-face communication within the leadership team. Email, text messages, blogs, tweets, podcasts, and other channels are available. Again, the choice of which to use depends on the audience and the message. It also depends on you. You need to be comfortable with the medium and channel you use. Given the explosion of communication channels available, leaders should not make the mistake of believing they know everything they need to know about communication. Now, more than ever, having a communications professional on your team is essential. I was fortunate in having a savvy group supporting me when I was UA's chancellor. Even so, I still managed to mess things up—but not as much as I would if I hadn't had them by my side.

In *Open Leadership*, Charlene Li makes the case for leaders to become more open with followers and stakeholders. The case is much stronger today than when the book was published in 2010. One effect of the COVID pandemic is that significantly more people are online, using social media, and sharing information. Now, every organization must incorporate social media in its communication strategy and plans.

Barack Obama's use of social media in his campaign for the US presidency was a major factor in his election. As Jennifer Aaker and Victoria Chang note, "Many factors contributed to his success, but a major one was the way Obama and his Chicago-based campaign team used social media and technology as an integral part of their campaign strategy, not only to raise money, but also more importantly, to develop a groundswell of empowered volunteers who felt that they could make a difference."[2]

Eight years later, the power of Twitter was demonstrated by Donald Trump in his 2016 election. Not only did Trump use Twitter in his campaign, but it was also his principal means of communicating during his presidential term. The difference in Trump's communication style and that of his predecessors was striking.

When I consulted Charlotte Brakmann, my granddaughter, about using social media to communicate with followers, she reminded me to be consistent and to engage. She recommended consistency in the choice of color schemes, fonts, and tones. She also reminded me of the rule of seven: It takes seven impressions with a brand before people act. The same applies for leaders delivering messages. Repeat, repeat, repeat, repeat, repeat, repeat! (Six repetitions equals seven deliveries!)

Brakmann also said you cannot post a message and walk away. Social media algorithms, coupled with the ever-changing social media space, necessitate users interact with followers, respond to comments, and maintain a dialogue. If you won't commit to the long haul, either don't begin or rely on a surrogate. If you choose the latter, stay on top of it, because you might be surprised at what your surrogate communicates on your behalf.

Finally, if you choose to ride on the social media bandwagon, make sure someone doesn't make mischief for you. You don't want to find out in the middle of a business meeting that a Zoom cat filter has been installed on your computer.

Know your audience. Use the communication channels that will be most effective in reaching them. To reach a broader cross-section of students than we would with other communication channels, we used podcasts. Over a two-year period, three UA colleagues and I interviewed a wide range of leaders and created a podcast series on values-based leadership: *LeadershipWWEB*.[3]

Because of the diversity of communication channels, leaders need a diverse set of advisors when it comes to choosing the channel for a particular message. If your advisors are mirror images of you (not just in appearance, but in all dimensions of diversity), your decisions are unlikely to reach the broad cross-section of followers you must reach. If you rely on doing it the same way you always have, don't be surprised if the vast majority of your followers miss your message. In delivering a message, the best choice doesn't depend solely on you; it also depends on your followers. If you ignore the best way to communicate with them, they'll never hear your message.

So, how do you decide which channels to use? The better you know your audience, the more effective your choice of channels. Don't be a Lone Ranger. Listen to your advisors, experiment, collect data, and keep trying. Realize that no matter what you do, you won't reach some people.

COMMUNICATION STRATEGY AND PLAN

Depending on the message being communicated, you may need to develop a communication strategy. When the governing board approved splitting Motorola into Motorola Mobility and Motorola Solutions, it was necessary to develop a strategy regarding the message and its recipients. A communication plan was needed to guide how the message would be communicated to various stakeholders. Many people were engaged in delivering the message, which required much more than a press conference or press release. Legal, public relations, finance, marketing, sales, human resources, and other advisors were enlisted to shape the strategy and execute the plan.

You need a variety of communication plans, including but not limited to a crisis management plan. When a murder/suicide occurred on the UA campus on the first day of classes in 2000, we had a crisis management plan. It kicked in immediately, and we followed it. Crises aside, for any significant message leaders deliver, they need to have a communications plan to ensure nothing falls through the cracks. No matter how effective you believe your delivery of a message might be, if you realize afterward that you forgot to do something, your view of its effectiveness will change dramatically. "Why didn't I think of that?" is no substitute for not having a plan. Likewise, "I hope we touched all the bases" won't suffice. Hope is not a plan.

Instead of relying on a mental checklist, document the communications plan—all the things to be done, all the people to be informed, and all the questions and objections you and your team can imagine will result. Clearly state your message's goals and objectives. Have as many people as feasible review the message and plan. Listen to the feedback, and decide what changes to make, if any.

While there is value in having a generic communications plan, how you communicate a particular message is likely to differ in some respects from how you communicated other messages. Instead of using a cookie-cutter approach, design or modify the communications plan to fit your message. In addition to preparing the message, identify the audience, decide who'll deliver it, select the communication channels, establish a timeline, determine how you're going to measure the effectiveness of the delivery and impact of your message, measure its effectiveness, perform an audit of the communication process afterward, and revise the plan accordingly.

Leaders must play to their strengths. Leaders who possess weak communication skills must ensure their teams include people who are effective communicators. If a leader is more effective in one-on-one communications, leverage the leader's strength by doing such things as video recording one-on-one conversations and distributing them broadly within the organization.

CHAPTER 5

Leadership Paradoxes

I n a high school English class, I learned a paradox is a contradiction. A few years later, I learned two words used together having or seeming to have contradictory meanings is an oxymoron. However, I did not associate paradoxes with leadership until I read *Lincoln on Leadership*. Later, I learned some people mistakenly believe servant leadership is an oxymoron.

Identifying Abraham Lincoln as a "master of paradox," Donald T. Phillips observes that "'paradox' is a most appropriate description for not only Lincoln the man but Lincoln the leader. There were, in fact, numerous paradoxes in Lincoln's leadership style." Phillips notes that Lincoln was charismatic, yet unassuming; consistent, yet flexible; a victim of slander, yet immensely popular; trusting and compassionate, yet demanding and tough; a risk taker, yet patient and calculating.

In *Good to Great*, Jim Collins defines a Level 5 Executive as someone who "builds enduring greatness through a paradoxical blend of personal humility and professional will."

Reflecting on my leadership and what I've observed in other leaders, I've identified twenty leadership paradoxes not cited by Phillips. Perhaps you'll identify others.

LEADING AND SERVING

A common misperception about leadership is that everyone serves the leader, as if you're the drum major of a marching band parading in front of followers or John leading the Lost Boys in Disney's *Peter Pan*, singing "Following the Leader."

An exemplary leader serves. Servant leadership is not an oxymoron; it's a powerful way to lead. A.P.J. Abdul Kalam, the eleventh president of India, is a prime example. When he was elected president, he refused to live in the stately mansion but remained in his modest apartment. He set aside personal riches and devoted himself to helping the helpless in India. His popularity was global. When he visited the University of Arkansas, people came from as far away as Atlanta to hear him speak.

Kalam was one of the humblest leaders I've met. Donald Smith is another. So are Mike Duke and Chris Lofgren. Their servant leadership is captured in their attitude as well as their acts. It is a combination of little things they do to send the message of how much they care for the people they lead. They place others before self.

CONSISTENCY AND UNPREDICTABILITY

Consistency is one of my core values. Although I've endeavored to be consistent, many times I chose a different path. Examples of my consistency include two personnel changes I made while serving as chancellor—replacing a dean and a coach. My decisions were based on words they spoke. Even though they were spoken in different settings, they worked against what I was trying to achieve in advancing the university. Having replaced the dean, when the coach made what I considered to be an equivalent mistake, I knew what I had to do in order to be consistent. To do otherwise would suggest I had different requirements for academic leaders than athletic leaders. This wasn't a message I wanted to send and would be inconsistent with my attempts to make the University of Arkansas as nationally competitive in its academic fields as it had been on its athletic fields.

A downside to consistency is predictability. Predictability can lead to complacency in an organization, and complacency can lead to stagnation. To avoid stagnation, leaders take advantage of Newton's first law of motion and apply force to ensure an organization continues to move, advance, and improve. Forces for change occur naturally from within the organization and from external sources. Self-motivated individuals don't need force applied to them. For others, it might become necessary to introduce tension in the organization. Chris Lofgren told the students, "Leadership is about creating a safe place for tensions to exist."

In *Leadership Without Easy Answers*, Heifetz notes a key responsibility of a leader is regulating the level of tension and stress within the organization. He observes that "eliminating the stress altogether eliminates the impetus for adaptive work. The strategic risk is to maintain a level of tension that mobilizes people."

In *Leadership on the Line*, Heifetz and Marty Linsky note, "You can constructively raise the temperature and the tension in two ways. First, bring attention to the hard issues, and keep it focused there. Second, let people feel the weight of responsibility for tackling those issues. . . . People can stand only so much change at any one time." The work associated with effecting change must be paced. They note that the work of pacing "can be ethically complicated because it can involve withholding information, if not outright deception," which brings us to the paradox of having integrity and being deceptive.

INTEGRITY AND DECEPTION

Integrity is essential for an exemplary leader, yet there are many instances in which you must be deceptive. Machiavelli rightly notes, "Everyone sees what you appear to be, few really know what you are." If you are in the middle of chaos and wonder how you will get through the day, it's essential to appear undaunted and in control. Leaders live in fish bowls; people watch what you do and draw conclusions. If you are upset, don't show it.

Donald Smith, not long into his tenure as president and CEO of Tyson Foods, was sitting at his desk one morning when a member of his executive team asked, "Are we selling the company?"

Stunned, Smith responded, "Absolutely not!"

"Everyone is saying we are," the team member said. "You walked by the receptionist without speaking when you arrived this morning." Although Smith was having a bad day, he learned he needed to put a smile on his face when he walked across campus.

When I asked Mike Duke, then-president and CEO of Walmart, if he ever had to be deceptive, he responded affirmatively and recalled the difficulties he faced when deciding whether to recommend selling Walmart's operations in Germany. Duke likened his situation to that of a duck swimming on a pond. To an outside observer, the duck appears to be quiet and serene, but it is paddling like crazy underneath the water.

After posing the same question to my son, John, while he was serving as president and CEO of Fortna, he, too, responded affirmatively and added that your team members "cannot see you sweat!" Remaining calm and composed are critically important.

During World War II, General Dwight D. Eisenhower recorded in his diary an angry exchange he'd had with General George C. Marshall. After sleeping on it, the next morning he tore out the page and replaced it with "Anger cannot win. It cannot even think clearly." Eisenhower's quote reminds us to never make a decision when angry or upset. Likewise, never send a text message or email to someone while angry.

The Greek mathematician Pythagoras is credited with saying, "In anger we should refrain from both speech and action." Good advice!

Your temperament can prove to be the difference between success and failure.

This is not to say leaders can never appear angry or upset. Lashing out at people or situations sends a message that you're out of control. If you must show anger, it should be controlled and purposeful.

Although I seldom became angry, when I did, I tried to hide it. During my first month as UA's chancellor, I noticed the car I was driving needed to be refueled. I pulled off the highway at the next exit. There were no gasoline stations in sight in either direction; I chose to turn right at the intersection. When I got to the next intersection, I saw a Phillips 66 station, pulled into it, and filled the tank.

When I went into the station and handed my credit card to the young lady behind the counter, she looked at me and asked, "Are you the new chancellor at the University of Arkansas?" I replied affirmatively, and she said, "I have been reading in the newspaper you want the best and brightest students in Arkansas to come to UA. What do I need to do to receive a scholarship?"

I asked for her contact information and learned her name was Haley Sims. I told her she would be hearing from someone in our recruiting office. I was thrilled! It seemed like word was getting around, and she wouldn't have asked me about a scholarship if she hadn't believed she was one of the best and brightest students in the state.

I contacted the head of recruiting and passed on her contact information. Two weeks later, I was driving on the same highway and stopped at the station, hoping to chat with Haley. When I went inside, I didn't see her. I asked an elderly woman if Haley was working that day.

She replied, "No, she isn't going to be here today. You are Chancellor White, aren't you? I am Haley's grandmother. We are so excited you talked to her, because Duke has been in contact with her for several years, and we are so worried she might decide to go to Duke and not come back to Arkansas."

I asked if Haley had heard from the University of Arkansas. Haley's grandmother said she had not yet heard anything, but they were hoping she would receive good news soon. I said she would.

When I got back in the car, I was not happy. After taking a few minutes to collect myself, I called the head of recruiting and said I was at the station and had just learned Haley Sims had not heard from the recruiting office. I said I was going to return to the station the next day, and if Haley had not heard from anyone, there would be changes within the recruiting office. I didn't shout. But I'm sure my level of disappointment and frustration was communicated by the tone of my voice.

The next day, I stopped by the station. When I went inside, there she was—with a big smile on her face. "Haley, have you heard from the university?"

She replied, "I got a phone call last night. In fact, the person who called me used to be my babysitter." Haley was valedictorian of her high school. She received a Chancellor's Scholarship from the University of Arkansas, graduated, and attended medical school. Currently, Dr. Haley Sims Vo lives in northwest Arkansas, is married to a UA alumnus, and has three children. Often, I think of Haley and wonder what would have happened if, instead of turning right, I had turned left at the intersection that summer afternoon.

Shakespeare put it well: "All the world's a stage, and all the men and women merely players." Exemplary leaders are thespians; they not only lead but also play the role of leader, especially when things are not going well. Does this mean they lack integrity? No! Smith, Duke, White, and Wooden are models of integrity, but at times they had to pretend to have no worries or concerns. They gained a greater appreciation for another Shakespeare quote, "Uneasy lies the head that wears a crown."

There are many instances when leaders can't bare all and let everyone know what they're thinking, when secrecy is essential. Consider a publicly traded corporation contemplating a divestiture or acquisition, or an athletics director contemplating a coaching change. Consider a team leader weighing a change of employment. In each instance, the final decision might be to do nothing. What would be the impact on the team if these potential changes had been made public?

Being open when it was necessary to keep a secret was one of the greatest leadership challenges I faced while serving as UA's chancellor. As it was a public university, with few exceptions I was required under the Freedom of Information Act to share information with the media. Documents and electronic files were subject to release. Fortunately, thoughts were not included. However, that did not prevent reporters from asking if I was thinking about making a specific personnel change. My only options were "No comment!" and "No!" Of the two, the former is a slippery slope, because many interpret "No comment!" to mean "Yes!" so I followed the advice of a friend, who said he was 100 percent supportive of his direct reports until he decided to remove them from their positions. He treated it as a binary decision: 100 percent for or 100 percent against.

FLEXIBILITY AND INFLEXIBILITY

Being flexible is an important leadership trait. However, there are times when an exemplary leader should be inflexible. The challenge in choosing when to be inflexible is a function not only of the subject but also of the circumstances. A successful leader in one organization will not necessarily be successful in another; likewise, having successfully led an organization twenty years ago doesn't necessarily mean you would be successful leading the same organization today. A leader's style must fit the situation or occasion. Timing matters. A leader's actions must be timed correctly. Ecclesiastes 3:1 states, "There is a time for everything, and a season for every activity under the heavens."

There is a time to be flexible and a time to be inflexible. The key is knowing when. You don't want to be so flexible that you develop a reputation for flip-flopping on key issues. The important thing is to listen, learn, love, and lead. Don't turn a deaf ear to criticism. Don't refuse to listen to opposing views. Don't turn a blind eye to what's happening. Don't make up your mind too quickly. Don't rely too much on instinct and intuition.

TRUSTING AND VERIFYING

Ronald Reagan referred to the Russian proverb so often during nuclear disarmament negotiations in the mid-1980s that Mikhail Gorbachev responded, "You repeat that at every meeting."

Reagan answered, "I like it."

"Trust but verify" has since taken on a life of its own, having been repeated by numerous US politicians during international negotiations.[1] It has also been applied to investment planning[2] and self-managed teams.[3]

When you delegate tasks to others, it's important to follow up to ensure they're being completed as intended. The verification process is not an indication of distrust but a recognition that while authority can be delegated, accountability and responsibility cannot. Ultimately, the leader is accountable and responsible. President Truman's "The buck stops here" sign reminded him he was ultimately responsible for the decisions he made. Unlike some of his successors, Truman understood he was responsible for his actions and the actions of those he led.

DECIDING AND DELEGATING

As the leader, you're ultimately responsible for decisions you and your team members make, but the most important decision you will make is *who* should make the decision, followed closely by *when* to make it.

When David Rubenstein, in his book *How to Lead*, asked Sir Richard Branson, founder of the Virgin Group, what the key ingredients are in becoming a business leader, Branson identified assembling a team of great people and learning to delegate. He emphasized the importance of having people with the right attitude: people who are energy givers not energy takers, who are encouragers not discouragers, who are praisers not criticizers. Branson noted the importance of having people on your team who are innovative, bold, and striving to create things that will instill pride in everyone in the company.

When Rubenstein asked Ken Griffin, founder and CEO of Citadel and the securities trading firm Citadel Services, how he was so successful, Griffin said because of the business he was in, he had learned to delegate. He said the keys to his success were trusting and delegating to competent people.

Delegation is a force multiplier. Building leadership is among a leader's primary responsibilities. An essential task is developing decision-making abilities within members of the team by delegating decisions when feasible.

When you delegate, you have to be prepared for decisions different from those you would have made. As Donald Smith shared with the students, "You have to be willing to accept the best efforts of team members, even when you know you could do better." This is an integral part of leadership development within your team.

Authority can be delegated, but responsibility cannot. You are responsible for what your team members do. When delegating, it is essential you stay informed. However, remember "noses in and fingers out" when delegating. If you delegate authority and second guess or guide every decision, you undermine the person you've delegated it to.

The act of delegation sends a message that you don't decide everything, that you trust others to decide. Who you delegate authority to also sends a message. People will examine your actions carefully. Delegation bestows power and prestige. The person will be viewed by some as the anointed one, the golden child, the heir apparent. So choose carefully, and delineate the limits of authority in the delegation.

Often, I heard, "Chancellor White said . . ." on subjects I'd never considered. People you delegate authority to might believe they know how you think and what you want on a range of topics. If so, believing they're acting on your behalf, they can be prone to speak for you and say things you don't support.

Many believe delegation is a two-way street. It isn't. Many try to delegate upward, to shift their load to the leader's shoulders. I tried doing so multiple times, unsuccessfully.

DEMANDING AND EMPATHETIC

If you asked the students I've taught and the people I've led if I was demanding, they'd say, "Yes!" I agree. I was and still am. I have lofty expectations. I set high standards. However, I don't demand more of others than I demand of myself. Perhaps some believed I was a perfectionist. If so, they confused a pursuit of perfection with a pursuit of continuous improvement.

My focus on achieving excellence was fueled by a series of books on the subject: *In Search of Excellence* (1982), *Managing for Excellence* (1984), *Creating Excellence* (1984), and *A Passion for Excellence* (1985). However, it began much earlier. As an undergraduate industrial engineering student in the late 1950s and early 1960s, it was drilled into me that there is always a better way. From the pioneering work of Frank and Lillian Gilbreth and Frederick W. Taylor, I was infected with the continuous improvement virus. It impacted me personally and professionally.

There were times I expected members of the leadership team to read my mind. To overcome this tendency, I verbalized and documented my expectations. In the first meeting with vice chancellors following my appointment, I shared a list of commitments I was making to them and a list of commitments I expected them to make to me. Several things appeared on both lists: being open and honest; communicating professionally (no vulgarity); making the University of Arkansas a better place for students, staff, and faculty; and, most importantly, having fun. My list included a commitment to protect them from outside influences and distractions—to have their backs. On their list were *keep me informed* and *ask for help when you need it*.

Those who worked with me recognized I was often pleased but never satisfied. During my first year as Georgia Tech's engineering dean, I held a retreat with the directors of the various schools within the college where I posted the following five-year goals:

- Double the number of bachelor's degrees to women.

- Double the number of bachelor's degrees to underrepresented minorities (African Americans, Latinos, and others).

- Double the number of women faculty members.

- Double the number of underrepresented minority faculty members.

- Double the number of doctorates granted.

- Double externally funded research.

- Triple the number of members of the National Academy of Engineering.

- Be ranked among the top five graduate engineering programs by *U.S. News and World Report.*

All but two school directors laughed. The two who didn't were Jean-lou Chameau and John J. Jarvis. I recruited Jean-lou from Purdue to lead the civil engineering school; John was a friend and faculty colleague in the industrial and systems engineering school. No doubt, Jean-lou was so new on the job that he didn't feel comfortable laughing, and John probably felt like I needed a friend in court.

Instead of being put off by the laughter, I was pleased so many felt comfortable expressing themselves so openly. After all, I'd been a member of the Georgia Tech faculty for sixteen years prior to becoming the engineering dean. Also, at least three of the school directors were candidates for the dean's position.

I also understood why they laughed. If the roles had been reversed, I might have laughed too. Because a large proportion of Georgia Tech's undergraduate engineering students participated in the cooperative education program, it took an average of more than five years to receive the bachelor's degree; the school directors argued it would be impossible to double the number in five years. Georgia Tech's undergraduate engineering program was the nation's largest, as measured by student enrollment, and it awarded more bachelor's degrees to women than any other engineering program. Likewise, with the exceptions of North Carolina A&T University and the University of Puerto Rico at Mayaguez, Georgia Tech awarded more engineering degrees to underrepresented minorities than any other US university. Finally, at the time, Georgia Tech was ranked eleventh among graduate engineering programs by *U.S. News and World Report*; the school directors believed improving six positions in the ranking in a five-year period was unattainable.

Despite their objections, I persisted. To accelerate increasing the number of undergraduate women, I declared one year the "year of the woman engineer." Each time we met, I asked the school directors to report on what they'd done since we last met to achieve the college's goal. None of them wanted to say, "Nothing!" Soon, they were actively engaged in increasing the number of women in their programs. By benchmarking top-rated programs in their disciplines and reporting their results annually, they soon realized that doubling doctorates and research funding were necessary to be nationally competitive. Three years leading the Engineering Directorate at the National Science Foundation had equipped me to set high standards. I knew what was possible because I knew what *the best* engineering programs were doing. I also relied on each school director's competitive spirit to ensure each program continued making progress.

Five years later, when the rankings were published in the summer of 1996, Georgia Tech was ranked fifth by *U.S. News and World Report.* I received a phone call from Michael E. Thomas, Georgia Tech's provost, congratulating me on achieving our five-year goal.

I responded, "Mike, if the school directors had done what I recommended regarding GRE requirements for entering graduate students, we would've been ranked third."

He replied, "Can't you be satisfied with achieving your goal?"

I said, "Not when it's within our reach to be the top-rated public university." I said I didn't believe we could move past MIT and Stanford, but we could move past UC-Berkeley and Illinois.

I left Georgia Tech the following summer to become UA's chancellor. Two months later, when the *U.S. News and World Report* rankings were published, I received another phone call from Thomas. Georgia Tech was ranked third. We'd done it!

We didn't achieve all our goals in the five-year period. We increased the number of bachelor's degrees to women by 84 percent, the number of bachelor's degrees to African Americans by 74 percent, the number of degrees to Hispanics and Latinos by 73 percent, the number of women faculty members by 80 percent, and the number of underrepresented faculty members by 50 percent. We more than doubled the number of doctorates awarded and the amount of externally funded research and more than tripled the number of members of the National Academy of Engineering.

After becoming chancellor, I spent a year gathering information and learning the strengths and weaknesses of the university, after which I created a benchmark set of universities and developed a progress report for UA. The benchmark set consisted of fifty-four national public universities, including the University of Arkansas. The progress report included twenty-two performance measures and numerical goals to be achieved by 2010. As with the stretch goals at Georgia Tech, we didn't achieve all our 2010 goals, but we made significant progress.

Donald Smith told the leadership class, "It's important to never be satisfied." John Roberts, with a smile on his face in response to a question about how he is able to motivate people to excel when things are going well, told the students he was "always angry." Mike Duke said it was okay to have twenty-second celebrations of successes, but they had to face reality: The competitors weren't easing up.

The underlying theme of Jim Collins's book *Good to Great* is that good is the enemy of great. It is difficult to transform a good organization into a great one. It is even more challenging to sustain greatness. Complacency sets in.

Regardless of whether you are striving to transform an organization from good to great or to sustain greatness, you must be demanding while also being empathetic.

In *Call Sign Chaos*, General Jim Mattis writes, "State your flat-ass rules, and stick to them." The rules should be known by everyone, but he advises against letting passion dominate humility and compassion. The essential battle for leaders to win is the hearts of people they lead.

VULNERABLE AND RESILIENT

Many leaders of my generation believe you should never let your vulnerability show. They believe leaders need to be tough, that leaders shouldn't cry, and that leaders should never tell their followers they love them. They don't believe their humanity should ever show. When I told the students in my classes I loved them, many were surprised; some were shocked, and, sadly, a few were hearing those words for the first time. Letting your humanity and vulnerability show can create strong bonds with those you lead. Don't fake it, though. Your followers will see right through you.

Chris Lofgren is a big bear of a man. He comes across to many as stern, all business, and unapproachable. Sometimes when he walked through Schneider National's offices, some avoided looking at him; they seemed scared of him. When he agreed to participate in a charity fundraiser, "Dancing with Our Stars," things changed. Almost immediately, people started greeting him and reacting to him differently.

One of the greatest challenges leaders face is seeing themselves as others see them, learning what others think of them. Lofgren became human by dancing the foxtrot with Jamie Keyzer. He had no idea how he was perceived by people he didn't know personally. Dancing revealed this imposing grizzly bear to be a fun-loving teddy bear in disguise.

Pam McGinnis told the students she was willing to be vulnerable. She said, "Don't be afraid to ask dumb questions."

Being strong enough to expose your vulnerability to your followers is one thing. Showing vulnerability to your competition or to outsiders is quite another. People want to be led by someone who is resilient and able to handle attacks, who can withstand the storm, deal with criticism, and appear undaunted in the face of devastating conditions. People want leaders to be strong and unwavering when the going gets tough.

On September 14, 2001, three days after the terrorist attack, President George W. Bush was preparing to speak at the National Day of Prayer and Remembrance service at the National Cathedral. Condoleezza Rice shared in *No Higher Honor*, "Just before the President spoke, the magnificent mezzo-soprano Denyce Graves sang the Lord's Prayer. I didn't see how the President would get through his remarks without breaking down. At the Cabinet meeting preceding the  service, he had been emotional. Colin Powell seated next to him as the secretary of state always is, passed him a note that said, in essence, 'Dear Mr. President, don't break down at the service.' The President, relating this to the Cabinet, said that he would be okay. He was right. He delivered his remarks sensitively but was completely in control. I thought to myself that I could never have done that."

HUMOROUS AND SERIOUS

A powerful weapon in a leader's arsenal is a sense of humor. However, it must be deployed strategically. Churchill's humor, Lincoln's humor, and Reagan's humor served them well, as did the sense of humor of many other effective leaders.

It is especially important for leaders to be able to laugh at themselves. As Harry Truman noted, "Any man who has had the job I've had and didn't have a sense of humor wouldn't still be here." It is even more important for leaders to not laugh at others. Laughing *with* is okay, but laughing *at* is not.

As valuable as a sense of humor is, there are times when it can get you in trouble. During the interview process for UA's chancellor position, I was asked to give a public lecture and share my vision for the University of Arkansas. After walking to the podium in the center of the stage, I pulled a water bottle from beneath the podium and held it up. I said it reminded me of a story I'd heard of a candidate interviewing for a chancellor position at a major land-grant university.

The candidate picked up a dusty bottle from the bottom shelf of the podium and removed the cap. Immediately, a genie appeared and thanked the person for freeing it. The genie granted the candidate one of three wishes: be the handsomest or most beautiful person in the world, be the richest person in the world, or be the wisest person in the world.

Since the candidate was in the middle of the interview process for a university leadership position, the candidate said, "I choose wisdom."

"So shall it be," replied the genie, and waved a wand over the candidate.

Immediately, the candidate exclaimed, "I should have taken the money."

The joke was a success. Timing was everything. When another candidate gave his public lecture in the same auditorium several weeks later, he told the same joke, which didn't go over nearly as well. He had no idea a previous candidate had told the same joke. He was the victim of poor timing.

FAIR AND UNEQUAL

It took me longer than it should have to realize not everyone wants to be led in the same way I want to be led. No two people are the same, even so-called identical twins. People respond differently to different leadership styles. Some want to be given an assignment and left alone to complete it; others want to be given detailed instructions. Some respond best to a carrot, others to a stick, and some to a carrot the size of a stick. Leaders need to know the people they lead, what motivates and what differentiates them.

The notion of equality is pervasive in society. People claim they want to be treated equally, but I believe they really want to be treated fairly, which doesn't mean the same thing. Equal pay for equal performance? Of course! But everyone shouldn't be led in the same way. I'm a proponent of small teams, with someone who knows each member's strengths and weaknesses leading each team.

My successor to the UA chancellorship, David Gearhart, told the leadership class he wanted to be remembered as someone who treats people fairly. Shouldn't that be every leader's desire? The challenge, of course, is the vast differences among the people being led.

PEOPLE AND RESULTS

Don't be surprised if a time comes when the people you lead wonder if you care more about results than about them. You must care for both. If you don't produce results, it won't matter how much you value people, you won't be their leader much longer. Likewise, if all you care about is results, then you're likely to find yourself leading a parade of one—yourself. You can see it in all team-based performances—when the leader loses the support of the team, things go downhill rapidly.

There'll be times when you must be demanding, when everyone on the team must work harder and longer than reasonable and achieving results becomes Job One. However, those times must yield to times when people understand they, truly, are Job One. Results matter, but people matter more.

Donald Smith told the students, "I'm not paid to be popular. I'm paid to be profitable." On another occasion, he said, "I don't get paid for the work I do. I get paid for the work I get done." He was expected to deliver results—and he did. During his tenure as CEO, the stock more than quadrupled in seven years.[4] At the same time, Smith was considered by Tyson employees to be a people-centered CEO. They knew he cared about them, and they obviously cared about him.

Be demanding, not demeaning. Anyone who puts others down reveals insecurities and fails the first test of an exemplary leader: caring for the team.

STEADY AND DISRUPTIVE

Be wary of enjoying what you believe are steady-state conditions. While you're relaxing and contemplating a steady state, your competitors are strategizing how to knock you off your perch. And you might not even know who your competitors are. New entrants arrive in the arena seemingly daily. If a company isn't a disruptor, it's likely a candidate for disruption. If you don't believe me, ask the shareholders of Blockbuster. Its leadership declined an opportunity in 2000 to acquire Netflix for $50 million, believing Netflix's business plan of providing movies online was unachievable.[5] Blockbuster filed for bankruptcy in 2010.

Think about all of the great companies that no longer exist or have been acquired by other companies, including Circuit City and Gillette, both listed in *Good to Great*. Fortune's Top Ten Most Admired Companies in 2020 were Apple, Amazon, Microsoft, Walt Disney, Berkshire Hathaway, Starbucks, Alphabet, JPMorgan Chase, Costco Wholesale, and Salesforce. Excluding Berkshire Hathaway, JPMorgan Chase, and Walt Disney, when were the others first publicly traded? Apple (1980), Amazon (1997), Microsoft (1986), Starbucks (1992),

Alphabet or Google (2004), Costco Wholesale (1985), and Salesforce (2004). Apple is the oldest of the group.

Now, look at Fortune's top ten for 2003: Wal-Mart Stores, Southwest Airlines, Berkshire Hathaway, Dell, General Electric, Johnson & Johnson, Microsoft, Federal Express, Starbucks, and Procter & Gamble. Fortune's 2013 list looked more like the 2020 list: Apple, Google, Amazon, Coca-Cola, Starbucks, IBM, Southwest Airlines, Berkshire Hathaway, Walt Disney, and Federal Express. Only Berkshire Hathaway and Starbucks were in the top ten in 2003, 2013, and 2020. Things can and do change quickly.

It takes strong leadership to move from good to great. It takes stronger leadership to sustain greatness, especially in a climate of disruption. In previous years, all organizations have had to face the possibility of disruption. In 2020, COVID-19 challenged leadership like never before. It impacted every organization and individual, not just businesses. Apex Parks Group, CMX Cinemas, FoodFirst Global Holdings, Gold's Gym, JCPenney, J. Crew, Neiman Marcus, and John Varvatos were among companies filing for bankruptcy during the first five months of 2020.

There are also times when you must be disruptive internally. You must control the level of tension within the organization while being disruptive. You must be capable of holding two conflicting thoughts simultaneously: protect and grow the legacy business and launch a new business to compete with the legacy business.

EMPOWERING AND CONTROLLING

I've worked for or observed leaders who controlled everything, as well as leaders who controlled very little. The latter empowered team members to make decisions to operate with considerable autonomy. But as with most things in leadership, it is not *either/or* but *and*. As a leader, you need to know the strengths and weaknesses of the people you lead and determine who can be empowered and who must be controlled. Likewise, there will be times when someone you empower to do certain things must be controlled when it comes to other things. Such judgments are based on the levels of risk involved. As a leader, you must know when to empower and when to control.

INTROVERTED AND EXTROVERTED

It is interesting how many highly successful leaders are introverts, at least as measured by the Myers–Briggs personality assessment tool. But when you're around them, you would think they're extroverts. When the students asked the leaders about their personality type, several responded that they were introverts pretending to be extroverts. They rose to the occasion; they responded to the demands of the moment. To the list of paradoxes we can add having an introverted leader function like an extrovert. At various points during my career, I vacillated between being assessed as an introvert and an extrovert.

RISK AVERSE AND RISK TAKING

Although my natural instincts are to be risk averse, I knew I had to be willing to take risks. Likewise, I needed to recognize when a situation called for me to be risk averse. John Roberts told the students in the leadership class he was a risk taker, but he would not bet the company when making a decision. He knew when to be risk averse.

A student asked my son if he was a risk taker. He said he was, but he took calculated risks. He reminded the students that if you don't take risks, you won't be able to stay in business, much less grow it. The key is knowing when to take risks and which risks to take.

Leaders must create a climate for risk taking. If the leader is risk averse, followers will be less willing to take risks. General Mattis observes in *Call Sign Chaos*, "You can never allow your enthusiasm to exceed your unit's capabilities, but my assessment was governed by the principle of calculated risk." If you want your followers to take risks, you must reward them for doing so, and you must not punish people for making mistakes if they are taking reasonable risks. Of course, the key word is *reasonable*. If leaders don't tolerate mistakes, they'll be left with a collection of risk-averse individuals on their teams.

Endogenous risks are generated within an organization, whereas *exogenous* risks are generated outside it. The risks Roberts, White, and Mattis referenced are endogenous. To cultivate an environment that encourages followers to take calculated risks, you must consider likelihood and impact.

Exogenous risks are a different matter. Leaders must prepare the organization to defend against and react to such risks. An example of exogenous risks receiving considerable attention is cyber risk. John Chambers, former executive chairman and CEO of Cisco Systems, said, "There are two types of companies: those who have been hacked, and those who don't yet know they have been hacked." Condoleezza Rice and Amy Zegart note in *Political Risk* that "most cyber victims will not know for months that they have been breached: The typical time between a cyber penetration and its detection is 205 days."

FACT-BASED AND INTUITION-BASED DECISIONS

On December 4, 1770, while defending British soldiers being tried for the Boston Massacre, John Adams said, "Facts are stubborn things, and whatever may be our wishes, our inclinations, or the dictates of our passion, they cannot alter the state of facts and evidence."

Early in my career, I took great pride in being a data-based decision-maker.

John J. Jarvis, a colleague from Georgia Tech, was quoted as having said, "White has an analytical mind and a knack for numbers. . . . He's a data freak. He will spend forever—all night, every night—going on the Web, finding all kinds of data and putting it in charts."[6]

Jarvis was exaggerating. However, if asked, I suspect Kathy Van Laningham, UA's former vice provost for planning, would side with

Jarvis. When I was chancellor, she and her team understood me well. They were always ready with data to support my presentations and meetings with university stakeholders.

Why do some leaders choose to ignore facts when making decisions? My perspective was colored by being a fan of the 1950s radio and television series *Dragnet*, starring its creator, Jack Webb, as Los Angeles police detective Sergeant Joe Friday. As evidence of how one can misremember things, when I think of Joe Friday, I hear him saying, "Just the facts, ma'am." so it was quite a shock when I learned he never said it.[7] Just as Sherlock Holmes never said, "Elementary, my dear Watson," at least not in books written by Sir Arthur Conan Doyle.[8] However, Doyle did put these words in the mouth of Sherlock Holmes: "Some facts should be suppressed, or, at least, a just sense of proportion should be observed in treating them," and "Facts are better than theories, after all."[9]

Shelley Simpson, J. B. Hunt's executive vice president of people and human resources and chief commercial officer, told the students to start with the facts. A major issue regarding facts and data is that they do not necessarily provide the information needed for decision-making. Data engineers and scientists face the challenge of producing information from data, from facts.

DILBERT   **BY SCOTT ADAMS**

YOUR DATA SHOWS YOUR PROTOTYPE DID NOT INCREASE SPEED OVER THE EXISTING SYSTEM.

NO, THE DATA PROVES THE PROTOTYPE IS FASTER THAN THE OLD SYSTEM.

I'M LOOKING AT THE DATA RIGHT NOW, AND IT CLEARLY SHOWS FAILURE.

IT LOOKS THAT WAY TO YOU BECAUSE YOU PREDICTED IT WOULD FAIL. YOU'RE SEEING WHAT YOU WANT TO SEE.

MAYBE IT ONLY LOOKS TO YOU AS IF IT WORKED BECAUSE YOU PREDICTED IT WOULD WORK.

SO... WE'RE BOTH LOOKING AT EXACTLY THE SAME DATA AND REACHING OPPOSITE CONCLUSIONS?

IF I THOUGHT DATA WOULD INFLUENCE MY DECISIONS, I WOULDN'T LET YOU GATHER IT.

GIVE ME A MINUTE TO REASSESS MY ENTIRE EXISTENCE.

You must interpret data correctly if data are to inform decision-making. Sherlock Holmes understood "there is nothing more deceptive than an obvious fact."[10] Be careful. Separate fact from fiction.

Astroball, by Ben Reiter, added an element to the data analytics approach used by the Oakland Athletics: integrating fact-based and intuition-based decision-making in the Houston Astros selections for the major league baseball draft. Reiter observes, "A superlative analytics department might get you halfway up the mountain. It was an intangible—the elusive but discoverable qualities of persistence and adaptability—that got you to the top."

I like what John Roberts said on the subject: "First, I make sure we have relied on data analytics to reduce the number of alternatives to a set of finalists. Then, I rely on my intuition and the experience and intuition of my leadership team." He said that often, nonquantifiable aspects of the alternatives tipped the balance in the final choice.

While leaders making risk-based and intuition-based decisions may seem like a paradox, it often isn't. It isn't an *either/or* situation; it's an *and* situation. The best decisions quite likely involve both facts and intuition.

When queried by the leadership class about the percentage of decisions they made based on data, information, or facts versus gut feel or intuition, the visiting leaders gave answers varying from 50 to 70 percent of decisions being based on facts. In recent years, given the emergence of data analytics tools, the percentage of business decisions based on facts has risen significantly. Shelley Simpson said, "I love numbers. I'm a numbers junkie. Numbers are my language." John Roberts said, "Show me the data. Data will take you where you need to go . . . but bad data is worse than no data. Look at the numbers, but play to your heart."

When I assess my leadership decisions, I realize I placed greater reliance on intuition in the latter years of my chancellorship. I also recall how one leader responded when I asked what changes the leader would have made if given the chance to do it over again: "I would have trusted my intuition more!"

DIRECT AND SUBTLE

There are situations when a leader must be direct and situations when a leader must be subtle. Likewise, there are individuals who require directness and others who respond better to subtlety. A leader must select the communication style to fit the occasion and to fit the person.

In some instances, directness is the only option. Consider what Churchill said: "If you have an important point to make, don't try to be subtle or clever. Use a pile driver." Perhaps you know leaders who believed directness was the only way to communicate with followers. I certainly do, and I wondered at the time how much more effective they would have been if they had tailored their communication style to their audience.

A LONG-TERM AND A SHORT-TERM FOCUS

Many corporate leaders are pressured to make decisions based on quarterly financial results, while military leaders and first responders are often faced with making instantaneous decisions. Even when extenuating circumstances appear to dictate the need for short-term decision-making, a leader must consider the long-term implications.

Short-term sacrifices might be needed to deliver long-term results. The trade-off between long-term and short-term decision-making may well prove to be the most challenging paradox a leader faces. It is not an easy choice; if it were, it would not be left to the leader to make it.

When David Rubenstein asked Apple's CEO, Tim Cook, how much attention he paid to analyst remarks about quarterly earnings, he said they were not influential and that Apple's leadership was focused on the long term.

Similarly, when Rubenstein asked PepsiCo's then-chairman and CEO, Indra Nooyi, how she reacted when an activist investor recommended

Pepsi spin off its Frito-Lay business, she said her job wasn't keeping an activist happy but to manage the company for the next generation. Because of the significant number of shares of PepsiCo stock she owned, she wouldn't do anything to jeopardize shareholder value. Nooyi listened to everybody. If anyone had a great idea, she welcomed it. She also had the full support of her governing board, who were aligned with a long-term strategy for the company.

DETAILS AND THE BIG PICTURE

Leaders must be able to navigate between being detail-oriented and keeping an eye on the big picture. F. Scott Fitzgerald notes in his 1936 essay "The Crack-Up," "The test of a first-rate intelligence is the ability to hold two opposed ideas in the mind at the same time, and still retain the ability to function." Leaders must have the ability to think and act paradoxically, with their actions dependent on the situation. The key words in Fitzgerald's quote are *at the same time.* Leaders must see the big picture and the details simultaneously; they must be acutely aware of both. The same challenge exists with the paradox of being steady and disruptive.

After noting the effectiveness of Shakespeare's Henry V, who paid attention to details, Augustine and Adelman write in *Shakespeare in Charge*, "While displaying great courage and gazing far off for vision, a corporate leader must also look closely at critical small factors."

In *Leadership on the Line*, Heifetz and Linsky use the metaphor of a balcony to capture the ability of a leader to maintain big picture and detail perspectives simultaneously. They note, "Seeing the whole picture requires standing back and watching even as you take part in the action being observed. But taking a balcony perspective is tough to do when you're engaged on the dance floor, being pushed and pulled by the flow of events and also engaged in some of the pushing and pulling yourself."

ANSWERING AND QUESTIONING

Many believe leaders must have all the answers. In reality, exemplary leaders have all the questions. Likewise, too many leaders believe they are the smartest people in the room; if they are, they have the wrong people in the room. Leaders need to assemble a team of people who are strong where the leader is weak and knowledgeable where the leader lacks knowledge.

Chris Lofgren shared with the leadership students, "As you advance in leadership positions, it is less important for you to have answers and more important for you to have questions."

Many leaders who met with the leadership class agreed that the ability to listen trumps the ability to speak. Exemplary leaders ask questions and then listen carefully to the answers. Furthermore, their listening involves their ears and their eyes. They read body language and notice the words spoken, as well as the words not spoken. Importantly, they remember what they hear and see.

Paul T. Eaton was a retired professor when I joined the Georgia Tech faculty. He could be cranky and contentious. I believe he intentionally retained his heavy German accent, even though he'd been in the US for more than fifty years when we met. Anytime someone greeted him and asked how he was doing, his answer was always the same: "Lousy!" Most people didn't listen to him; their responses were "That's good," so he was startled when, after asking how he was doing and hearing his response, I said, "I'm sorry. Is there anything I can do for you?" We became close friends. Many people laughed when I shared this story during my remarks at his funeral, because they remembered the sparkle in his eye when he said, "Lousy!" He was always testing people to see if they were listening.

When asked a question, a leader has a choice: Answer it, decline to answer it, or deflect it. An effective way to deflect a question is to ask another question. Notice how often leaders answer a question with a question. It doesn't mean you don't know the answer. You might prefer to use the question as a learning opportunity within the team. If one team member asks you a question, turn and ask another member what the answer is. Discuss it, and see if a consensus answer emerges.

Mike Duke told the leadership students he seldom gave orders. Instead, he asked questions. To illustrate his approach, he told them about a telephone call he received on December 23. A grandmother had left a message expressing her disappointment in her local Walmart store in Florida not having a doll she ordered and paid for. It was to be available that day for her to pick up. The woman was distraught and begged Duke to help her get the doll before Christmas. Duke recognized the doll was likely the granddaughter's only Christmas present.

Duke is a fan of the Disney organization and its founder. Walt Disney advocated an "all-out recovery" when a theme-park customer was disappointed. Disney knew a dissatisfied customer would negatively affect many other potential customers. Duke shared Disney's approach with Walmart's leadership team and encouraged his associates to use it.

After listening to the message and thinking about how to handle it, Duke called the manager of the store in Florida and shared the message on his answering machine. Then, instead of telling the manager how to respond, Duke asked, "What do you think we should do?" When the manager said he would locate the doll at another store and get it to the grandmother, Duke asked, "Is there anything else we should do?" The manager paused and said, "I get it. We'll do an all-out recovery. I'll take care of it."

On Christmas Day, the grandmother called Duke and thanked him for everything. Not only did the manager have someone drive to a store in Alabama and pick up the doll, but he also delivered the doll, along with other gifts and a full Christmas dinner for the family. The grandmother said it was the best Christmas they ever had.

Asking questions, not giving answers, can be an effective tool for a leader. And using an all-out recovery can pay dividends.

In your leadership journey, you'll be confronted with situations in which you act in seemingly contradictory ways. Not to worry. You'll simply be facing paradoxes naturally accompanying leadership. Don't be surprised if your journey is filled with ups and downs, fits and starts, and pauses. It will not be a linear journey. The twenty leadership paradoxes discussed here aren't exhaustive. Your leadership journey will differ from mine, and it's likely you'll generate a different set of paradoxes.

CHAPTER 6

Balance

I n *Oh, The Places You'll Go*, Dr. Seuss writes, "Step with care and great tact and remember that life's a great balancing act." This is good leadership advice as well. Achieving and maintaining balance is arguably the most important thing a leader does. Like a tightrope walker performing without a net, balance is essential for a leader's success.

Achieving balance isn't easy, and what constitutes balance is generally in the eye of the beholder. Importantly, for our purposes, balance doesn't mean weighing things equally. For example, if a leader must balance A and B, it might be appropriate to assign a weight of 90 percent to A and 10 percent to B. Too often, when the word *balance* is used, people think of a scale in which weight on the right side must equal the left. However, depending on the issue, the scale might be balanced appropriately without the two sides being level.

We also can't balance the same way at every instance. Seldom will a leader be able to maintain the same balance over time. Instead of achieving instantaneous and perpetual balance, our goal is to motivate leaders to achieve appropriate balance in multiple areas over time.

BALANCING FAMILY AND CAREER

The need to balance family and career is not limited to leaders. This is a challenge for all career-oriented individuals. If I hadn't known this sooner, I would've learned it from teaching millennials. The most frequently asked question of the guest leaders visiting the leadership class was how they balanced family and career. A CEO of a major corporation responded, "It cost me my first marriage." Another CEO said, "I am the poster child for how *not* to balance family and career. Don't use me as your role model. No success at work is worth failure at home." Two days later, he was in divorce court for the second time.

Nearly every leader meeting with the class said it's a challenge to balance family and career. Several, however, shared how they maintained a healthy relationship with family members while being effective at work. They emphasized the importance of being there for moments that matter to family members and prioritizing family over career. Chris Lofgren reminded the students, "Your work will never love you back!" Mike Duke told them, "Healthy families lead to healthy executives." John Roberts said, "You are going to do a better job if your personal life is right."

Judith McKenna told the leadership students, "On work/life balance, everyone must find his or her unique way. Never judge people who have made decisions different from yours. When you see someone whose life balance seems out of sync, ask how you can help. . . . There are different times in your life where your balance has to be different and you have to recognize what and when they are."

When John Roberts realized he needed to be proactive regarding responsibilities at home and at work, he asked his wife to share with his executive assistant dates and times of important events for their children; after they were placed on his calendar, he treated them like a business commitment. In fact, when he shared this the first time with the students in the class, he turned to me and said, "I will not be here later than 7:00 p.m. My son is playing in a baseball game, and I'm going to be at the game." And he was!

Early in his career, Roberts staked out his claim to family being a higher priority than work. He and his family were vacationing at the beach when he received a phone call from the CEO informing him a plane was on its way to pick him up and transport him to Atlanta, because he was being promoted to president of one of the company's major divisions. Roberts told the CEO he needed to discuss the promotion with his wife before he would agree to accept it. After discussing the situation with her, he called the CEO and said they agreed he should get on the plane (which had already landed and was awaiting him). Because the only clothes with him were chosen for vacationing at the beach, after arriving in Atlanta, Roberts purchased clothes for his first meeting with the team he would lead.

Roberts always takes phone calls from his wife, no matter what he might be doing. He reminded the students that if someone is not happy at home, it's unlikely the person will be productive at work. Roberts has prioritized family over work throughout his career, and he encouraged his team members to do the same. Often, he arrived very early at his office, left during the day to attend family events, and returned to the office to work late into the night. This was a common practice among the leaders who visited the class.

Greg Brown only missed one of his son's 215 basketball games, and that was because the game was rescheduled to a time that conflicted with a meeting he had with Israeli prime minister Ariel Sharon. Brown told the students he considered rescheduling his meeting with Sharon, but his staff persuaded him otherwise.

Admittedly, not everyone is in a position to do what Roberts and

Brown did. Military officers who met with the leadership class were deployed overseas and unable to be physically present when their children had significant events. Fortunately, technology is available that allows for leaders' family members to see and hear them.

Donald Smith responded to a student's question about how he balanced family and career by saying, "I don't! I rebalance." Smith said there are times when the demands of business are so intense you have to sacrifice being with your family, so he and his wife made sure their children understood the sacrifices every member of the family made in order for Smith to be successful at work. He and his wife were able to build memories, not mansions. They took their children on extensive vacations during which Smith was totally invested in his family.

Leaders whose jobs require extensive travel are faced with a particular challenge. My son, John, has been a consultant since 1992. Many years, he was on the road or in the air an average of four days a week. He built up over three million miles with Delta Air Lines. Having acquired firms in England, Germany, and South Africa, his travel was not limited to the US. There were times when he was away from family for weeks at a time. But in spite of his travel, his family unit is one to be envied. How did he do it?

Of course, he gives most of the credit to his wife, Julie. His parents agree! However, several things he did produced strong relationships with Julie; his daughter, Emma; and his son, Austin. Mindful of the need to have quality time with each family member, he schedules date nights with Julie and fun times with Emma and Austin. White makes sure his family members are on his calendar and consciously makes memories with his children. He makes sure to communicate with each family member regularly. He and Julie talk at least once every day; his inability to do this with his children is more a function of their availability than his—collegians!

Emma loves the theater, so White takes her on trips to New York to attend Broadway productions. Austin loves to hunt, so he takes him on hunting trips in the US, Argentina, and South Africa. As a family, they take trips to Europe and go on safaris in Africa. White is process oriented and considers balancing family and career an important process to be managed. When a student asked how he balanced family and career, he responded, "I'm not perfect at it." Where Donald Smith referred to his approach as rebalancing, White called his *harmonizing*. He said, "When I'm home, I'm home."

Greg Brown, John Roberts, Donald Smith, and John White III had something in common: Their wives didn't work outside the home. They had a partner who carried the bulk of the load of caring for children. The same was true for me. Mary Lib deserves the credit for the successes of our daughter, son, and me. Many family units are not structured this way.

When children are involved and both parents work outside the home, balance becomes doubly important and challenging. Not only must each parent balance work and home responsibilities, but they must balance distributing work at home. In olden times, perhaps a couple of decades or more ago, it was common that husbands did the work outside the home while the wives did the work inside the home. Today, the responsibilities of partners depend more on the individual situation each faces. With increasing opportunities for women and glass ceilings being shattered in numerous organizations, more men are choosing to work from home and care for their children. New opportunities are spawning new solutions to old problems.

Mary Pat McCarthy told the leadership class her husband gave up his career in banking to become an at-home dad. They concluded it was the best solution for their family when they adopted three children.

While interviewing Marillyn Hewson, former chairman, president, and CEO for Lockheed Martin, David Rubenstein learned that her husband retired and became an at-home dad when their sons were three and six and she was relocated from Marietta, Georgia, to Fort Worth, Texas. What was planned to be a one-year experiment turned into the best long-term solution for their family.

One guest leader met with the leadership class accompanied by her husband and three children. Her husband is a civil engineer; he supports her career by working from home and taking care of their children.

I frequently assigned a Harvard Business School case study for students to analyze and discuss. The Alex Montana case study provided an opportunity for the students to focus on balancing family and career. It always resulted in a lively discussion. The views of the students differed, generally along gender lines. Below is an abstract for the case study:

> Alex Montana sat at his desk pondering the career decision before him. Alex was director of the North American division of ESH Manufacturing, a $4.6 billion, Cleveland-based company with operations on three continents. ESH's CEO had just offered Montana a promotion to global vice-president. Normally, Montana would have jumped at such an opportunity, but he worried about its impact on his already strained personal life. Since his last promotion, he had trouble balancing an increasingly demanding workload with his responsibilities to his wife and daughter at home. Montana felt pressure to accept the promotion. His boss expected him to accept; in fact, his boss had emphasized that he had no second choice. He had always dreamed of making it big in the business world. Success in this new role could put him in the running for COO and, eventually, CEO. But at what cost?[1]

Complicating Alex's situation, his wife, Maria, was pregnant and counting on Alex being available to assist with their daughter, who was struggling with epilepsy. Maria cofounded an architectural firm, which was quite successful, and postponed her professional pursuits because of their daughter's health condition, but she was anxious to reengage in the firm. Finally, the global VP position required extensive international travel. What should Alex do?

After lengthy discussions, the students coalesced around two options: either decline the promotion and risk being fired or accept the promotion and find a way to handle the situation at home. Interestingly, the male students tended to favor Alex declining the promotion, but the female students tended to favor Alex accepting the promotion.

Shelley Simpson, who faced similar choices early in her career, met with the students just prior to their discussion of the case study, but none of the students thought of using her solution. When Simpson was pregnant with her second child, she and her husband decided to employ a relative as a nanny for their children. For them, when it came to who would continue working, it was not *either/or* but *and*, or *both*. Simpson's career flourished.

Simpson makes sure she is there for her children's special moments. She also expects people on her leadership team to do the same for their children. To the leadership class, she said, "Be there for your people in their major life moments."

Too often, people tend to pose problems as binary choices and ignore the possibility of other options. Chris Lofgren told the leadership class he loved to turn *either/or* choices into *and* solutions. Basically, Lofgren tasked people with finding a way to have your cake and eat it, too. When it comes to family and career, don't think of it as a binary choice; look for ways to achieve both.

Several guest leaders emphasized the need for the students to go into work situations with their eyes wide open. Some organizations are family friendly, and others are not. They encouraged the students to avoid putting themselves in positions where they won't be able to achieve their desired balance in family and career. They also encouraged them to involve family members in making decisions regarding the balance of family and career.

Adriana Lopez Graham told the students that, when she was responsible for international IT for Tyson Foods, she had always explained to her children her reason for traveling to another country: helping provide food for hungry children in the specific country. When friends asked her children why their mother was not attending an event at school, they'd say, "Mommy is feeding children in [insert name of country]." They were proud of what she was doing; they felt their sacrifice was helping others. Family members of military leaders react similarly when a parent's assignment prevents attendance at children's events.

BALANCE IN ACTION

Issues requiring balance must be dealt with simultaneously, requiring the leader to be a juggler on a tightrope.

Emotions

Balancing emotions doesn't mean being emotionless. It means controlling your emotions and using them to increase your effectiveness. General Mattis notes in *Call Sign Chaos*, "A commander has to compartmentalize his emotions and remain focused on the mission. You must decide, act, and move on." Showing emotions can be valuable in the right situation and under the right circumstances. Coming across as uncaring and unsympathetic won't serve you well. Likewise, your passion can energize followers and convey your commitment and the importance of the task at hand.

Psychologist Paul Eckman identified six basic emotions: anger, happiness, sadness, fear, disgust, and surprise.[2] Leaders experience all of these emotions, as well as many combinations.[3] The challenge is in displaying a balance. Your expression, body language, tone of voice, and actions communicate your emotions, intentionally or unintentionally.

When you show disappointment, satisfaction, excitement, love, contentment, joy, contempt, or pride in achievement, it can affect the morale of followers. It's challenging for followers to be productive when you appear constantly disappointed. If you've worked for someone who is never pleased with what you do, you understand fully the power a leader's emotions can have on a worker's performance. Likewise, working for a person who's affirming can yield positive performance. Being balanced is vital.

Balance highs and lows. Celebrate successes but don't go overboard, and don't lose sight of the long-term objective. Likewise, don't throw a pity party when failures occur or when things don't go the way you want. Hall of Fame collegiate basketball coach John Wooden didn't want his players to make a big deal out of winning a game because he wanted them to send signals to opponents that winning was expected.

As the authors of *Primal Leadership* note, emotions are contagious, and the most contagious emotional signal is a smile. There are times when a leader needs to wear a smile even when there is every reason not to. Laughter and smiles can impact resonance significantly among followers. So, as Donald Smith was told by one of his colleagues at Tyson Foods, "Screw a smile on your face, regardless of how you feel."

Short Term and Long Term

A continuing challenge is balancing what is best for the organization in the short term and what's best for the long term. The challenge exists for all organizations, but it can be acute for publicly traded businesses. Depending on the mix of investors' objectives, significant pressure can exist for a CEO to maximize short-term profits. However, every CEO knows an adherence to such a policy will lead to difficulties down the road and, for many firms, it will occur sooner rather than later. However, ignoring short-term profits while pursuing long-term profits is likely to result in disaster. Why? Because there is more uncertainty (and less accuracy) in long-term forecasts than in short-term forecasts. Furthermore, a lengthy sequence of poor short-term profits can prevent the firm from existing long term. Balance is needed.

Peter Drucker notes in *Managing the Nonprofit Organization* that balancing the short- and long-range requirements of an organization is one of the leader's key tasks. This entails paying attention to details and the big picture. He likens it to paddling a canoe. If the right and left hands aren't balanced, you'll wind up going in a circle or following a zigzag course. Drucker also notes the need for leaders to balance concerns for the organization with concerns for individuals, as well as balancing caution with risk and acting quickly with acting slowly.

The essential question for a CEO is how much weight to give the short term versus the long term. The answer, as usual, is that it depends! It depends on the firm's mission, strategy, the mix of investors, the overall economy, and the governing board. In general, it's important to be consistent; mixed messages regarding short-term versus long-term priorities are not welcomed by the investment community.

Dwight D. Eisenhower asked in his 1961 address to the Century Association, "Who can define for us with accuracy the difference between the long and short term? Especially whenever our affairs seem to be in crisis, we are almost compelled to give our first attention to the urgent present rather than to the important future."

Named for him, the Eisenhower matrix can help balance time spent on important and urgent (short term) matters with important but not urgent (long term) matters and to delegate responsibilities for dealing with unimportant matters.

	URGENT	NOT URGENT
IMPORTANT	Q1: ACT	Q2: PLAN (SCHEDULE)
NOT IMPORTANT	Q3: DELEGATE	Q4: DELETE

The Eisenhower matrix.

Eisenhower used the matrix as a tool to manage his time as a leader in the military and as POTUS. Quoting an unnamed university president, Eisenhower said, "'I have two kinds of problems, the urgent and the important. The urgent are not important, and the important are never urgent.'" From my years as chancellor, I understand perfectly what the unnamed university president meant.

Chris Lofgren reminded the students about the importance of knowing what is important, a concept that had been passed down to him by his father. Following it is vital when using the Eisenhower matrix. Everyone is given 24 hours in a day. Some spend their time; effective leaders invest theirs. Focusing on the majors not the minors, being discerning, and maximizing the return on your investment of time and attention are essential.

Predictability and Unpredictability

Several guest leaders, as well as authors of leadership books, have emphasized the need to avoid predictability. In *Beware Those Who Ask for Feedback: And Other Organizational Constants*, Richard Moran advises leaders to "get people's attention occasionally by doing something out of character. Don't be 100 percent predictable." *Keep them guessing* is a message delivered by many, but your followers still need to be confident and comfortable; they can't be worried all the time about impending surprises. A leader should be predictable at least 95 percent of the time. But unpredictable actions should occur at unpredictable times. A leader is responsible for maintaining tension in the organization at an acceptable level. Being unpredictable is one way a leader can increase tension.

Transparency and Secrecy

A leader must decide how much information to share with the leadership team, the overall organization, and the public. The decision depends on the kind of information being shared. The leadership team should not expect a leader to share everything with them. Information should always be shared on a need-to-know basis. I've been in situations where a leader overshared information in the name of transparency and in others in which critical information was withheld from the leadership team. Such approaches cause the team members to lose trust in the leader.

Information sharing can be quite complicated. There will be times when one or two members of the team need to know something, but the other members don't. When the leader shares information with those who need to know, a level of trust must exist among them to ensure the information isn't shared outside the group. If trust is violated, broader issues will develop.

Internal and External

Leaders deal with internal and external demands. As UA's chancellor, I had to address the needs of a broad range of constituents, including students, faculty, staff, alumni, trustees, elected and appointed governmental leaders, business and community leaders, sports fans, and media representatives. Effectively balancing internal and external demands was a constant challenge for me and for my scheduler.

Because some leaders are better equipped to deal with internal demands, they delegate the responsibility of dealing with external demands, but you should never *ignore* them. The same is true when you're externally focused: You must still pay attention to internal demands. Determining the correct balance of attention is a dynamic process. The correct balance today might not be the correct balance tomorrow or next month.

To avoid always greasing the squeaky wheel, someone must monitor the time a leader spends dealing with internal and external demands. If you cannot rely on an assistant to monitor you, then you must monitor yourself. A disciplined approach is required. There are some balls a leader must not drop.

The Eisenhower matrix facilitates balancing internal and external demands by assigning demands to appropriate quadrants. Both internal and external demands must be included to ensure that nothing falls through the cracks.

Deciding and Delegating

As a leader, you should neither make every decision nor delegate every decision. There are certain decisions only you should make, especially those affecting personnel who report directly to you and those affecting the future of the organization. Leaders of schools and universities had to make the difficult decision of how to respond to COVID-19. I was relieved I wasn't UA's chancellor during the pandemic, but if I'd been in the position, I would've made the decision I thought was in the best interest of the students. It's the kind of decision a leader cannot and should not delegate.

Other decisions should be delegated. As General Mattis learned, it's critical for leaders to "delegate decision-making authority or face paralyzing chaos."

My preference is for decisions to be made within the organization at points closest to their impact. However, you should always be aware of the decisions being made.

To avoid predictability, you should occasionally make a decision you would normally delegate and delegate a decision you would normally make. The latter provides an opportunity to develop leadership strengths within the organization.

Speaking and Listening

Because you're the leader, many will want to hear what you have to say on any and every issue, but you must listen before you speak. In a meeting with your followers, be the first to listen and last to speak. Donald Smith told the leadership class, "The answer is always in the room." He listened to what people said about how to strengthen and improve the company. Smith believed people who are engaged with the issue have greater insight and understanding of what is happening and what needs to change. If the leader is the expert in the room, they haven't built an effective team.

Standing Firm and Yielding

There is a fine line between determination and stubbornness. I crossed the line too many times in my career. Knowing we can always improve, I didn't want to settle for less than our best in anything. Big victories didn't offset small defeats; I wanted to win every time. There was a period in my career when it was my way or the highway, the White way or the wrong way. I was so stupid. Why did it take me so long to grow up and get on track to become the kind of leader I was meant to be?

I had to learn to accept losing small battles in order to win the big ones. Too often, I found myself majoring in the minors. I finally realized that insisting on perfection in everything can be aggravating and demoralizing to followers who believe what they've done is good enough. It took years for me to finally accept that I should be satisfied with a 90 percent solution. The only way I could make myself do so was by promising to come back later for the remaining 10 percent. Because more pressing things always come up, I seldom returned to obtain the remaining 10 percent.

There are many things on which I am unyielding. Issues of integrity and inclusiveness, treating people with dignity, having zero tolerance for sexual harassment, opposing bullies, and living my core values are examples where I simply will not yield. For these, it really is my way or the highway. These are the hills I'm prepared to die on.

Being chancellor of a publicly supported university meant we received numerous Freedom of Information Act requests. In fact, we received so many we had to hire more attorneys. On two occasions,

I refused to provide the information requested by media representatives, resulting in court battles.

When the Walton Family Charitable Support Foundation made its $300 million UA gift, legislators questioned the promises we had made. We also received a media request for a copy of our proposal. We refused, were sued, and prevailed in arguing that the proposal contained proprietary information and that its release would be beneficial to our competitors.

I was also sued because I wouldn't release information related to our football coach. Controversies arose on a matter involving a football player, the head coach, the assistant coaches, the head coach's wife, parents, and fans. Frankly, it was a mess and required far more time and attention than it should have. Not only did I have to appear in court, where we prevailed, but I also had to appear before the Arkansas Supreme Court, where we also prevailed. My court appearances could have been avoided if I'd shared with the media how the matter was investigated and who performed the investigation. Because I concluded doing so would violate the privacy protection of UA employees, I refused.

Qualitative and Quantitative

In decision-making, instinct, gut-feeling, and insights are qualitative while data, facts, predictions, and forecasts are quantitative. In support of instinct-based decisions, Ralph Waldo Emerson writes in his essay on intellect, "Trust [your] instinct to the end. . . . It shall ripen into truth, and you shall know why you believe."

For those who pride themselves on being quantitative decision-makers, it can be a struggle to step away from the data and decide qualitatively. It took longer than it should have for me to recognize I needed to balance qualitative and quantitative decision-making.

As Rubenstein describes in *How to Lead*, Jeff Bezos, Amazon's founder and executive chairman, observed, "When you can make a decision with analysis, you should do so. But it turns out in life that your most important decisions are always made with instinct, intuition, taste, heart."

Pam McGinnis said she relied on data and her inner voice. If the topic was one she knew more about, she listened to her inner voice; if the topic was one she didn't know much about, she relied on data.

It's easy to collect data. It's much tougher to interpret it correctly. To avoid drowning in data, think first and collect second. Capture the tails of the distribution, the rare events, the outliers. Don't base decisions on averages, because average situations seldom occur. At the same time, treat exceptions as exceptions. Remember, data are only visible in your rearview mirror; you need to look through the windshield to make decisions for the future. Objectively decide whether the past is indicative of the future. If not, you need to estimate future requirements.

Analysis must be balanced with intuition. No mathematical model can accurately predict the future.

In *Political Risk*, Rice and Zegart identify four types of information: indisputable facts, information that is knowable and known by the organization, information that is knowable but unknown to the organization, and information that is not knowable to anyone. They add, "Low-probability/high-impact events are especially tricky. It is always harder to anticipate unusual events than typical ones." COVID-19 is a perfect example. In balancing analysis and intuition, keep in mind that unexpected events can turn everything upside down. The key to achieving perfect balance is perfect judgment.

Breadth and Depth

To what extent should leaders become involved in the details of work performed by their followers? Once again, it depends! You must balance focusing on the big picture (breadth) and focusing on the little picture (depth).

Mike Duke likened himself to a pelican flying high above the ocean but quickly diving into the water to catch an unsuspecting fish. He outlined three benefits of working this way: It reminded Walmart associates to remain focused on the details in their areas of responsibility. It allowed him to keep up with the details of the business. And it provided an opportunity for him to get to know people working at various organizational levels. As a bonus, it also provided examples he could use when speaking to associates at other locations. Duke shared several examples with the students, including meeting with an unhappy Walmart truck driver, meeting with a waste disposal company to resolve an issue, and meeting with a Walmart supplier when the procurement person was late arriving for an appointment. Duke understood that little things can become big things if they aren't dealt with sooner rather than later.

Regarding oversight of the National Science Foundation, Frank Rhodes, president of Cornell University and chairman of the National Science Board at the time, told board members, "You are responsible for keeping your nose in and your fingers out." As a general rule, the same applies to leadership roles, although there are times when you must get directly involved. Doing it too much is micromanaging; doing it too little is a sign of indifference. Trust, but verify. The buck stops with you.

While serving as UA's chancellor, I encouraged aggressive recruitment of the brightest high school students in the state. The recruitment staff prepared a promotional piece, and they were about to send it to high schools throughout the state. I asked to see a copy before it was sent. On the cover, it stated UA was the state's "penultimate" university. The staff person who prepared it did not know *penultimate* means next to last. Even worse, no one caught it before hundreds of copies were printed. *Penultimate* was changed to *preeminent* before it was distributed. Imagine the repercussions if the original publication had been mailed. Details matter.

When Adriana Lopez Graham was a graduate assistant working in my office, she showed me slides she had prepared for me to use in a meeting with presidents and chancellors in the Southeastern Conference. I asked why two pie charts on one slide were different sizes. She looked at them and said she thought they were the same size. I asked her to measure them. She was shocked to find they were, indeed, different sizes. Each time she met with the leadership class, she used the pie charts to emphasize the importance of a leader being willing to become involved in details.

If you're not careful, you can become bogged down in details. Little things mean a lot. If they're not dealt with, they can become huge things. Details matter.

Permission and Forgiveness

Very few leaders have complete freedom to do whatever they want. Failure has repercussions. When faced with a risky decision, will you ask for permission before acting or ask for forgiveness afterward? Even though I tend to be a conservative decision-maker, I often chose to ask for forgiveness, not permission.

Based on my tour of the state during the summer of 1997, I concluded we needed to raise UA's admission requirements and aggressively recruit the best and brightest students in the state. Other than the Sturgis Fellowship, which was limited to no more than six awarded to freshmen each year, the Chancellor's Scholarship was the most lucrative scholarship offered by the university. Forty-one were awarded to entering freshmen in 1997. At the time, each Chancellor's Scholarship paid $8,000 toward a student's education, which covered tuition, fees, and room and board.

I asked the recruitment staff how many students would come if we announced that any Arkansas student who scored at least 30 on the ACT and had at least a 3.00 grade point average would receive a Chancellor's Scholarship. They said we could recruit no more than 150, so we made the announcement and budgeted for 150 Chancellor's Scholarships for fall semester of 1998.

In November of 1997, the recruitment staff informed me we needed to stop awarding Chancellor's Scholarships because more than 150 had accepted the offer for 1998. Instead of checking with the UA System president, I told the staff to keep recruiting. If we were going to have a crisis, I wanted it to be a financial crisis, not a crisis of integrity from not honoring our commitment. I asked how many freshmen would qualify for the scholarship. Although the staff were reluctant to provide a number, they assured me it wouldn't be more than 300. I added 10 percent to their estimate and approached the Walton Family Charitable Support Foundation, requesting $1.5 million to support Chancellor's Scholarships. After I explained why we needed it, they approved the request, which resulted in a huge sigh of relief from me.

We blew by 330 and landed at 492 Chancellor's Scholars in the freshman class of 1998. The 1,100 percent increase made all the difference for the university. In a meeting with faculty, a young humanities professor said he didn't approve of a lot of things I did, but he totally supported my recruitment of the freshman class. He said that, in previous years, when he'd asked a question on the first day of classes, no hands were raised, but this semester, thirty hands went up. I'm sure many of his colleagues didn't support what he said next: He was willing to forego a salary increase in order for us to continue recruiting such outstanding students.

The Chancellor's Scholars in 1998 began the transformation I envisioned for UA and the State of Arkansas. Based on what happened in other states, I believed what was good for a state's land-grant university redounded to the benefit of the entire state.

If you always ask for permission, the organization won't advance as rapidly; you have a better understanding of the ramifications of taking action than will the person whose permission you need. Fortunately, my relationship with my leader, B. Alan Sugg, was strong. I knew Sugg had my back if I messed up, but I didn't want to put him in the position of having to defend me too frequently. I had to be judicious in opting to ask for forgiveness. Achieving the right balance is essential.

Amplification and Attenuation

In an undergraduate electrical circuits course, I learned, as the name implies, that an amplifier increases the power of an electrical signal. An attenuator, the opposite of an amplifier, reduces or dampens the power of an electronic signal. Team members receive signals from multiple sources, and some can be disruptive to their work. It can be challenging to keep the team focused on their goals and objectives. There are times to increase the pace and times to reduce it. Achieving the right pace is critical when effecting significant change within an organization. You must balance being an amplifier and an attenuator.

Jeff Bezos described his role at Amazon as its chief slowdown officer. When a decision is highly consequential, it's necessary to take the time to make the right one because it's likely irreversible.[4]

Balancing amplification and attenuation is not unlike balancing encouragement and discouragement. In achieving the right balance, you must be attentive to negative impacts of discouragement. Slowing progress without losing your team's enthusiasm requires that you communicate *why* the pace needs to be slowed.

Life

Leaders devote themselves to taking care of their followers but often forget to take care of themselves. Just as it's important to have a balanced diet, it's important to have a balanced life. Too many leaders ignore their health. They fail to undergo annual physical examinations; they don't exercise regularly; they don't set aside time for relaxation, sleep, entertainment, and meditation. If you aren't healthy physically, mentally, emotionally, and spiritually, you're unlikely to be effective.

Don't let your job title be your identity. After serving as chancellor, I took a six-month sabbatical to prepare to resume being a full-time professor. Having served as an administrator twenty years (three years at the National Science Foundation, six years as Georgia Tech's engineering dean, and eleven years as chancellor), I needed to refresh myself in the subject areas I'd be teaching.

During this time, a Georgia Tech colleague asked what I missed most about being chancellor. I replied instantly, "Nothing!" My colleague laughed, and I said, "All of my thinking has been on what awaits me, not where I've been."

I wasn't kidding. I was going to be teaching two graduate courses. I tend to focus on the windshield, not the rearview mirror. My chancellor chapter was closed; I was already focusing on my upcoming professor chapter.

Several months later, the same colleague said he'd thought I would say what I had, but he'd wanted another colleague who was with him to hear it. After retiring, his colleague hadn't been able to stop dwelling on the past. Every day, he called his former executive assistant and asked for a report on what was going on at Tech. He was still identifying himself with his former position.

By this time, I had a better answer to my friend's question. I told him there were three things I missed about being chancellor: I didn't have a bathroom adjoining my office. When I wanted to go to Little Rock, I couldn't hop on the university plane; I had to drive. And I had to shovel my driveway when it snowed. I didn't miss the job of chancellor. I missed people I had worked and associated with. For me, it's always about people.

In the last session of the leadership class, I reminded the students they would be juggling many balls throughout their life journeys. Several balls are made of rubber, and a few are made of crystal. Philip Lader, cofounder of Renaissance Weekend, explained at the event that it's okay to drop rubber balls, but you dare not drop crystal balls. Crystal balls are health, relationships, faith, core values, and other truly important things in life; rubber balls are job titles, salaries, awards, zip codes, and other status symbols. In the long term, rubber balls are far less significant than crystal balls. Crystal balls cannot be put back together again if you drop them. It's critically important to hold on to the crystal balls by having a balanced life.

POLARITIES

Leaders must constantly balance a host of responsibilities. It's important to achieve balance while multitasking and multiprocessing, which can be challenging.

As F. Scott Fitzgerald notes, "The test of a first-rate intelligence is the ability to hold two opposed ideas in mind at the same time and still retain the ability to function." Psychologists call this state *cognitive dissonance.* Dealing with paradoxes and conflicting ideas comes with the territory of being a leader. Conflicts will always exist in organizations, resulting in tensions between or among different entities. An example is a retailer wishing to increase profits and cut prices or Amazon wanting to increase profits but offer free two-day shipping.

When David Rubenstein asked Jeff Bezos about Amazon Prime's free shipping feature, he credited a junior software engineer with the idea. When the finance team analyzed the financial impact, it was shocking. His team recognized the economic impact of a customer purchasing a single, inexpensive item and receiving free two-day shipping. However, relying on heart and intuition, they chose to take a leap of faith and adopt free shipping. Bezos said, "All good decisions have to be made that way."

Chris Lofgren reminded the students that polarities like these are often presented to leaders as *either/or* propositions: "We can do this *or* we can do that." He emphasized the importance of finding a way to do both. If you can't, he said, then polarities are "not a problem to be solved but opposing tensions to be balanced and managed." Amazon was able to offer two-day delivery and increase profits; it was not *either/or* but *and.*

Lofgren's focus on polarities echoes the findings in *Built to Last,* in which Jim Collins and Jerry Porras analyzed the habits of a number of companies they labeled as highly visionary. They identified "a key aspect of highly visionary companies: They do not oppress themselves with what we call the 'Tyranny of the OR'—the rational view that cannot easily accept paradox, that cannot live with two seemingly contradictory forces or ideas at the same time. . . . Highly visionary companies liberate themselves with the 'Genius of the AND'—the ability to embrace both extremes of a number of dimensions at the same time."

Soon after becoming chancellor in 1997, I realized UA was either undersized or overscoped. In comparisons with other land-grant universities, UA had more degree programs per enrolled student. In a report to the UA Faculty Senate, I noted that the scope of our offerings was too broad for the number of students currently enrolled. I said, "For the University to become more efficient and effective, either the number of programs must be reduced or the size of the student body must be significantly increased."

Anyone experienced in higher education administration knows that reducing degree programs is a huge and challenging undertaking. Also, as the state's land-grant university, I believed it was inappropriate for us to reduce the scope of our mission. I opted to employ a two-pronged strategy to increase enrollment: increasing tuition and increasing admission requirements. Many people, including trustees and legislators, thought this was the opposite of what we should be doing. They believed increasing tuition or admission requirements would decrease enrollment and that doing both would be even worse. On July 20, 2000, at a meeting of the Fayetteville Chamber of Commerce, I'd said that asking for more education funding is an absolute joke. On August 10, 2000, I was summoned to appear before the Joint Performance Review Committee of the Arkansas Legislature and explain my remarks.

An article describing the session noted, "Rep. Mike Hathorn, D-Huntsville, spent more than 30 minutes criticizing White, even after he apologized." Later, the article stated, "Hathorn said he didn't understand how the university could raise standards and increase tuition while raising enrollment at the same time."[5]

Obtaining UA Board of Trustees approval to increase tuition was not easy, but it was much easier than obtaining its approval to increase admission requirements. This was unexpected, because I told the trustees in my final interview that I'd be making such a request. The vote was seven in favor and three opposed. B. Alan Sugg, president of the UA System and a nonvoting board member, took the unusual step of speaking directly to the board on the issue.

Permission granted by *Arkansas Democrat-Gazette*. All rights reserved.

"In my seven and a half years as president of the UA System," Sugg said, "never . . . has any issue been debated like this issue has been debated."[6] Little did he know what lay ahead for him and UA trustees. During my interview, I said I was a change agent. Maybe they didn't believe me. It wouldn't take long for them to learn I was very serious. Many more changes awaited them.

But the results speak for themselves. Overall enrollment was 14,384 when I arrived in 1997. Five years later, it was 16,035. Ten years later, it was 18,648. The enrollment in 2020 was 27,549. We avoided the Tyranny of the OR and embraced the Genius of the AND.

CHAPTER 7

Direction

Although leaders have many responsibilities, the most important is establishing or articulating a sense of direction for the organization. Importantly, the leader does not determine the direction but helps determine it. To be effective, determining the direction must be a team effort.

The following terms are used frequently by leaders: *purpose, vision, mission, goals, objectives, strategies, tactics, core values,* and *strategic planning.* At least once a decade, we scramble to adopt a new term. Although the terms differ, a few are treated interchangeably, such as *purpose* and *mission,* and *goals* and *objectives.*

Too often, excluding *planning,* the terms used by CEOs are treated as labels or buzz words with no expectation that people know or care what they mean, how they relate, or how they're defined by the organization. Posters in hallways and offices soon become invisible to the people walking past them. More important than words on paper are the leader's actions. If your words are inconsistent with your actions, then they're meaningless.

I've found many of these terms valuable in my leadership journey. Depending on the situation, they've established a framework for effecting change. At other times, they helped me educate stakeholders about the organization's depth, breadth, and reach. But, more than anything, they helped me maintain focus and discipline. Because the busyness of the day could consume me, I needed reminders of what I was doing, why I was doing it, who I was doing it for, and where we were striving to go. These terms were a roadmap and a scorecard. I believe my example influenced others to use them in the same way.

As Yogi Berra said in *The Yogi Book*, "You've got to be careful if you don't know where you're going 'cause you might not get there."

PURPOSE

Before you can provide direction for a trip, you need to know its destination. And, before sharing the destination, you need to address why you're taking the trip. Answering *why* establishes the trip's purpose. The same applies to establishing directions for an organization: Start with why.

Albeit intangible, an organization's purpose is an idealized goal. Like perfection, it's never achieved but is worth pursuing. Preparing a purpose statement might seem silly, a waste of time. After all, everyone knows why your organization exists, don't they? Actually, you'd be surprised how little agreement there is within the organization. A purpose statement gives meaning to people's work each day, why they spend more waking hours at work than at home. It can help their family members understand and accept time spent at work. It helps people know the difference they make in the lives of others. It's a reminder that it's not all about the money.

Consider the following purpose statements. Harley-Davidson's is "Fulfill dreams of personal freedom." Whole Foods Market seeks to "Nourish people and the planet." General Mills lives by this statement: "We serve the world by making food people love." Tyson Foods believes in "Raising the world's expectations for how much good food can do." And Disneyland sets about "Creating happiness for others."

Hewlett-Packard cofounder David Packard articulated HP's purpose in 1960, telling a training group, "Purpose (which should last at least 100 years) should not be confused with specific goals or business strategies (which should change many times in 100 years). Whereas you might achieve a goal or complete a strategy, you cannot fulfill a purpose."

Purpose is a two-sided coin. Organizational purpose is on one side; leadership purpose is on the other. Bill George notes in *Discover Your True North*, "Gaining alignment around a purpose is the greatest challenge leaders face."

VISION

The importance of vision for an organization has been known for millennia as indicated by Proverbs 29:18, "Where there is no vision, the people perish." Salacuse notes in *Leading Leaders*, "The creation of an effective strategy begins first with providing the company with a strategic vision, and the source of that vision is inevitably top management, if not the CEO alone."

Collins and Porras note, "To pursue the vision means to create organizational and strategic alignment to preserve the core ideology and stimulate progress toward the envisioned future. Alignment brings the vision to life, translating it from good intentions to concrete reality."

In a speech he delivered in Moscow in the USSR in 1988, President

Reagan said, "To grasp and hold a vision, that is the very essence of successful leadership."[1] In many ways, a leader having imagination is more important than the leader being a visionary. Leaders need to be able to imagine how things will work out if personnel, organizational, budgetary, and a host of other changes occur. If a leader cannot imagine a better future for the organization, there is little hope for success.

President George H. W. Bush admitted he was not a visionary. His "the vision thing" quote is associated with him even more often than "read my lips." Many claim Bush was not an effective leader. Is being visionary a necessary condition for being effective? No! Effective leaders create a common vision for an organization by engaging members of the organization. Indeed, if the resulting vision is the product of a team effort, rather than solely one person's vision, it's more likely to gain support and traction within the organization.

George H. W. Bush didn't have grand plans for the nation, but he accomplished much. Just as Truman followed Roosevelt, Bush followed Reagan. In both cases, the styles and personalities of the successor and predecessor differed significantly. No doubt, history will judge Bush's presidency more positively than his contemporaries did during and immediately following his presidency.

In the cases of Roosevelt–Truman and Reagan–Bush, it was a vice president succeeding a president. Frequently, the pendulum does not swing but jerks, with significant changes in personalities in presidential successions. Consider the personality differences in the following presidential successions: Eisenhower, Kennedy, Johnson, Nixon, Ford, Carter, Reagan, Bush, Clinton, Bush, Obama, Trump, and Biden. The same occurs frequently in leadership changes in academia, athletics, business, nonprofit, and other organizations.

While there can be significant differences in the personalities of successive leaders, if their visions for the organization also differ significantly, then the potential for disruptions within the organization is great. Just as changing the culture of an organization is a lengthy process, so is implementing a radically different vision. Gaining alignment throughout the organization with a significantly different vision will be one of, if not *the* most challenging tasks you face.

Generally, changes in the vision for an organization are incremental. While the differences might appear great at the leadership level, because of organizational inertia, the effects of the change in vision being felt within the organization will diminish as they spread. While people at the top are dancing to a different tune, those at the bottom continue to do the same old slow shuffle.

You must establish a direction by visualizing a future destination—*where* the organization should go. Your articulated vision lets people know what success looks like. Typically, vision statements have an aspirational element. They evidence hope for and within the organization.

When designing a distribution center for a client, it is one thing for the design team to prepare detailed drawings of the facility and equipment but quite another for them to visualize how the system will operate. Mentally transforming a static design into a dynamic operating system is similar to establishing a vision for an organization. However, organizational visions have less to do with the physical appearance and daily operations of the organization than with its aspirational end state.

Good hockey players skate to the puck. Wayne Gretzky, considered by many to be the greatest of all time, skated to where the puck was going to be. Visioning is taking your organization to where you believe the future is going to be. Anticipating future opportunities and challenges is a key component in visioning.

In higher education, it's relatively easy to see what the future will be regarding entering freshmen in fifteen years, because they are alive and enrolled in school. As chancellor, it was obvious from the Arkansas data that UA needed to more aggressively recruit students from out of state to meet our long-range enrollment goals. It didn't take a visionary to see where the puck was going or what the future would be if we didn't change our recruitment strategy. All that was required was an analysis of the data. As John Roberts told the students, "Data will take you where you need to go." It did for me.

During my chancellorship, UA's vision was to be "a nationally competitive, student-centered research university serving Arkansas and
the world."

MISSION

Just as purpose establishes *why* an organization exists and vision defines
what it's to become, mission answers *how* it's to accomplish its vision.
Peter Drucker emphasizes in *Managing the Nonprofit Organization*
that mission comes first. He notes that a mission statement must be
operational; it must focus on what the organization is committed to
doing. Importantly, actions must flow from the words. When their
actions support the mission statement, individuals in the organization
know they contributed to achieving the goals.

In *Discover Your True North*, Bill George calls mutual respect the basis
for empowerment and enumerates what you can do to gain the respect of
colleagues: treat others as equals, listen actively, learn from people, share
life stories, and align around the mission. Alignment of purpose, vision,
and mission are essential for effective leadership.

GOALS

We are a goal-oriented society, and far more goals are set than achieved.
Often, goals are established without being measurable. Consider New
Year's resolutions: "I'm going to lose weight" or "I'm going to be a better
person." For the first goal, how much weight? Over what time frame?
For the second goal, how will you know if you are making progress? By
what date will you suddenly "be a better person"?

You must have some way to appraise progress. As researchers, politicians, pastors, and numerous professionals know, it can be difficult,
if not impossible, to accurately measure progress toward achieving certain goals, but you and others will still make judgments about progress.

During my interview for UA chancellor, Richard Hudson, then the university's vice chancellor for government and public relations, asked me to describe my leadership style. I did so using a metaphor: kudzu, a plant that grows wild in the southern part of the US. You can't see kudzu growing, but if you turn your head and look back, it will have grown. I told him that like kudzu, on a day-to-day basis, he might not see improvements, but after five years, he'd be surprised, and, after ten years, our progress would be stunning.

Goals need to be specific. They need to be captured in writing, not stored somewhere in your memory. When goals can be measured, they need to have time frames. Also, they need to be stretch goals—achievable, not totally out of reach, but not easy to reach either. Progress needs to be tracked and feedback provided to people pursuing the goals. An important leadership responsibility is influencing people's beliefs, getting them to believe it's possible to achieve those stretch goals.

Getting people to believe is a slow process. In *12 Angry Men*, Juror #8, played by Henry Fonda in the 1957 film, gets all the other jurors to believe it's possible the defendant in the murder trial is innocent. Repeatedly, he says, "It's possible!" As arguments against the boy's guilt are dispelled, one by one, momentum builds for his innocence.

The same thing occurred at Georgia Tech as we made progress toward meeting five-year goals and at Arkansas with our 2010 goals. We never achieved unanimous agreement at either institution, but enough people believed the goals were achievable for nearly all of them to be realized, and we made far greater progress toward the goals we didn't meet than we would have without setting them.

Who establishes goals? Should they be top-down or bottom-up? As usual, it depends on the goals being established. I established the five-year goals for Georgia Tech's College of Engineering and the 2010 goals for the University of Arkansas. The Campaign Steering Committee established the goals for the Campaign for the Twenty-First Century, and the commission's members set goals for the 2010 Commission. Depending on the situation and goals, either the leader or the people engaged in achieving the goals should set them.

Confucius said, "When it is obvious that the goals cannot be reached, don't adjust the goals; adjust the action steps." Instead of abandoning a goal, find other ways to achieve it. Don't become overly locked in on a particular strategy or set of tactics. Step back and look for another way to achieve the goal. During the early stages of my chancellorship, Lewis Epley, chair of UA's trustees, encouraged me to be open to alternate ways to accomplish what I returned to my alma mater to do. He counseled me to wait on the right time, to be flexible, and to look for back doors and side doors to my goals. I listened and endeavored to be flexible.

OBJECTIVES

When Texas Instruments (TI) retained me in 1978 to develop its corporate materials management strategy, I was introduced to TI's OST (objectives, strategies, and tactics) process. As the name implies, after establishing objectives, we create strategies, then identify the tactics required to achieve the strategies. With TI's process, the objectives were general statements of what was to be achieved, the strategies were plans for achieving the objectives, and the tactics were actions to be taken in support of the strategies.

After visiting all TI sites in the United States, I prepared and submitted my recommendation for its corporate strategy for materials management. Following the strategy's adoption, SysteCon, the consulting company I cofounded, was tasked with facilitating the implementation of the strategy at TI's sites, resulting in SysteCon growing rapidly in size and reputation.

STRATEGIES

What strategies will you use to achieve the goals and objectives? More than two thousand years ago, Sun Tzu said, "Thus, what is of supreme importance in war is to attack the enemy's strategy." He also said, "All men can see the tactics whereby I conquer, but what none can see is the strategy out of which victory is evolved." It's vital to change strategies as conditions change. Strategic thinking is applicable to any leadership opportunity, not just war.

Drucker points out, "There is an old saying that good intentions don't move mountains; bulldozers do." He notes that strategies are the bulldozers that transform mission and plans from good intentions to accomplishments.

At one point in his career, Drucker was opposed to the term *strategy*. He thought it was too closely associated with the military and was often meaningless. He eventually became an advocate for strategies because they are action-focused. He reluctantly accepted the term because strategies are something you *work* for, not *hope* for.

Tyson Foods' strategy in support of its mission is to sustainably feed the world with the fastest growing protein brands. Business strategy case studies for Alibaba, Amazon, Apple, Airbnb, Baidu, DuckDuckGo, and Google (Alphabet) are provided by Gennaro Cuofano on Four WeekMBA.com. He illustrates that strategies need to change as business environments change.

TACTICS

Tactics are where the rubber meets the road, the actions you will take to meet the goals and objectives. Strategic plans should be developed around the tactics. Importantly, tactics must align with strategies, and strategies must align with goals and objectives. A challenge is knowing when to be hands-on and when to have your nose in and fingers out in the execution of tactics.

As with strategies, your tactics must change as your circumstances change. A wise leader won't be wedded to tactics or strategies and will know when it's time to make changes.

CORE VALUES

Thomas Peters and Robert Waterman write in *In Search of Excellence*, "Our experience is that most businessmen are loathe to write about, talk about, even take seriously value systems. To the extent that they do consider them at all, they regard them only as vague abstractions." That was written in 1982; what a difference forty years makes! Today, the failure to identify and publicize a company's core values is a dereliction of duty. Not only do people within the organization expect them to exist, but so do other stakeholders.

Core values relate to both organizational values and personal values. If you haven't done so, I believe you'll find it beneficial to prepare a personal purpose statement, to document a direction for your life, and to prepare personal vision and mission statements, as well as identify your personal goals, objectives, strategies, and tactics.

Drucker notes, "Organizations, like people, have values. To be effective in an organization, a person's values must be compatible with the organization's values. They do not need to be the same, but they must be close enough to coexist. Otherwise, the person will not only be frustrated but also will not produce results."

Lencioni notes in *The Advantage*, "The answer to the question *How do we behave*? is embodied in an organization's core values, which should provide the ultimate guide for employee behavior at all levels."

There are different kinds of values: aspirational, accidental, permission to play, and core values. For Lencioni, "Core values lie at the heart of the organization's identity, do not change over time, and must already exist. In other words, they cannot be contrived."

From 2018 to 2020, Andrew F. Braham, UA civil engineering associate professor; Matthew A. Waller, dean of the Sam M. Walton College of Business; John R. English, dean of the College of Engineering; and I interviewed a wide range of leaders for a podcast series, *LeadershipWWEB*. Braham, who spearheaded this idea, felt students would benefit from hearing values-based leadership interviews. The interviewees repeatedly discussed how their personal values aligned with the values of the organizations they led. Not only do effective leaders walk their talk, but they walk their values.

There is a magnetic effect when people with common core values come together. Simon Sinek points out in *Start with Why* that "For values to be truly effective, they have to be verbs. It's not 'integrity'; it's 'always do the right thing.' It's not 'innovation'; it's 'look at the problem from a different angle.' Articulating our values as verbs gives us. . . a clear idea of how to act in any situation."

STRATEGIC PLANNING

In numerous corporate seminars, I've reminded the participants, "Planning, doing, changing—you're paid for three things." None of us has the luxury of standing pat. As Mike Duke reminded the leadership students, "Change is occurring at an exponential rate," so we must adjust, accommodate, adapt, and anticipate. To respond to change individually is one thing, but to do so as an organization requires planning.

Drucker notes in *Managing the Nonprofit Organization* that strategic planning is neither a box of tricks nor a bundle of techniques. It isn't forecasting. It doesn't deal with future decisions. It deals with the futurity of present decisions, and it does not attempt to eliminate risk. So what does he contend strategic planning is? "It is the continuous process of making present entrepreneurial decisions systematically and with the greatest knowledge of their futurity, organizing systematically the *efforts* needed to carry out these decisions, and measuring the results of these decisions against the expectations through organized, systematic feedback."

He adds, "Planning starts with the objectives of the business. In each area of objectives, the question needs to be asked, '*What do we have to do now* to attain our objectives *tomorrow*?'" He notes the danger of adding new things to the plan without subtracting things from current practices. This calls for discipline.

In general, the strategic planning process uses an organization's core in aligning its mission with its purpose and vision, aligning its strategies with its goals and objectives, and aligning its tactics with its strategies. Throughout the strategic planning process, keep in mind a statement Eisenhower attributed to a soldier: Plans are worthless, but planning is everything. When asked by a reporter if he was worried about Evander Holyfield's fight plan, Mike Tyson responded, "Everybody has a plan until they get punched in the mouth."

In analyzing visionary companies, Collins and Porras write in *Built to Last*, "Visionary companies make some of their best moves by experimentation, trial and error, opportunism, and—quite literally—accident. What looks *in retrospect* like brilliant foresight and preplanning was often the result of 'Let's just try a lot of stuff and keep what works.'"

When it comes to planning, I'm an advocate of using the same approach used in setting goals: Think big. Harry Truman observed, "You can always amend a big plan, but you can never expand a little one. I don't believe in little plans. I believe in plans big enough to meet a situation which we can't possibly foresee now." Plan with a purpose, not for planning's sake. Planning has been an integral part of my career. Like John "Hannibal" Smith of *The A-Team*, "I love it when a plan comes together."

Approached properly, by involving stakeholders, documenting an organization's vision, mission, goals, objectives, strategies, tactics, and core values adds value. A synergistic benefit is alignment of processes. More importantly, it aligns people with the organization's direction. Engaging people in the process builds and connects the team. It aligns the team members with one another. Direction matters. But alignment matters more!

CHAPTER 8

Cultures

I n the leadership class, the visiting leaders repeatedly cited a lack of fit with the organization's culture as the primary reason for high turnover rates. This is a truth borne out in my own experience. Within a few months at Tennessee Eastman Company, I realized I wasn't a good fit for its culture.

Having joined the company following the completion of my bachelor's degree in 1961, I wasn't prepared for the paternalistic approach Eastman Kodak Company took toward its employees. I respected and liked the people I worked with, and I liked the location, in Kingsport, Tennessee. After all, it's where I met Mary Lib, who was a teacher in the high school. But something about the company didn't sit well with me. It was difficult to put into words, but I chafed at what I perceived to be an underlying attitude about what it took to be successful at Eastman.

Many things seemed formulaic. You could tell what a person's position was by the size of the office and its furnishings. If the person received a promotion without having to relocate, either the size of the office was changed by moving partitions or the furnishings were upgraded or both. There seemed to be an expectation about where you lived, what civic and social clubs and churches you joined. Admittedly, as with many companies, the early 1960s culture changed over time. Following Eastman Kodak spinning off its chemicals, fibers, and plastics business in the 1990s to form Eastman Chemical Company, I joined its board of directors. Its culture appeared to have changed, or perhaps I had.

I was a rash and independent young man, fresh out of college, having read Ayn Rand's *The Fountainhead* and *Atlas Shrugged*, as well as William Whyte's *The Organization Man*. Following graduation, with lofty goals of becoming the next CEO of a major corporation without becoming *an organization man*, I was determined to succeed, and I was going to do it my way.

When the annual United Way Campaign was launched in the fall of 1961, my supervisor informed me what my "fair share" was—the amount I was expected to contribute, based on my salary. It rubbed me the wrong way. If I'd not been told how much to give, I probably would've given more, but I didn't like being told what to do. Taking orders has never been my strong suit.

Over time, I mellowed or matured and learned to not let minor issues cause me to lose sight of my overall goals. Organizational culture is real, it's important, and it's powerful. Craig Hickman and Michael Silva note in *Creating Excellence*, "Individual leaders, not organizations, create excellence." They point out excellence does not occur "without laying a strong foundation of strategic thinking and culture building." Culture and strategy are foundations for excellence, but excellence occurs only through strong leadership. Peter Drucker is credited with saying, "Culture eats strategy for breakfast." Regardless of who said it first, it underscores the importance of an organization's culture and the attention it merits.

Mike Duke told the leadership students, "The success of an organization is linked inextricably to its culture and purpose." Donald Smith told the students that cultural fit was a major factor in hiring people. Chris Lofgren told the students he would rather have a company with a great culture and an okay strategy than a company with an okay culture and a great strategy. Lofgren reminded them, "Leaders are stewards of culture." John Roberts said, "My most important duty is maintaining our culture."

In *Leadership: The Inner Side of Greatness*, Peter Koestenbaum identifies two sides to leadership, personal and strategic. He notes a company's culture resides within the personal side and that culture must support strategy. Koestenbaum notes, "In an effective company, it is the culture that translates strategy into tangible results. . . . Compared to culture, strategy is easy. Strategy is mechanical and, if necessary, can be bought. Culture, by contrast, is personal and is brought into being only through unusual personalities—ultimately, only through character."

It's essential when you are considering joining an organization to assess its culture and decide if you will be a good fit within it. If you won't, then you have three choices: Don't join the organization, join the organization and adapt to its culture, or change the organization's culture. Among the three, the most difficult choice depends on the person. Some people are capable of making the necessary adaptations; likewise, some, albeit fewer, are in a position to change and are capable of changing the culture. Of the two, adapting to the culture—going along to get along—is the simpler choice, but this is where *fit* is proven or not.

Leaders and upper managers must be fully invested in the change for it to be successful. In *Change is Good . . . You Go First*, Mac Anderson and Tom Feltenstein note, "Although the culture of any company starts at the top, it is the managers who will make it or break it, especially in times of change. Their attitude, their commitment, and their understanding of the change mission will be key to your success." Supervisors might not be the decision-makers, but they can be the decision-wreckers.

The challenge in changing an organization's culture is its ingrained memory. Not unlike metal alloys possessing shape memory, an organization's culture over time can revert to what it was before a new leader changed it. Leaders come and go, but organizations remember! To avoid reverting to old habits, leadership continuity is essential.

Numerous examples exist of leaders prioritizing increasing diversity within management ranks who're followed by leaders who don't place the same value on diversity. Consequently, the gains made during the predecessor's leadership tenure are soon lost. The same occurs when priorities change regarding the importance placed on product quality, customer service, servant leadership, and a host of here today, gone tomorrow management priorities.

Don't be surprised if, after you leave an organization, several of the changes you enacted disappear. Also, don't be surprised if you hear about it from people who resisted those changes when you were the leader.

KNOWING THE CULTURE

In *Lead with a Story*, Paul Smith notes, "An organization's culture is defined by the behavior of its members and reinforced by the stories they tell." He suggests finding the stories that exemplify the culture you want to foster and sharing them broadly.

Although each company's culture is unique, in *Corporate Cultures*, Terrence Deal and Allan Kennedy identify the following types: tough-guy, macho culture; work hard/play hard culture; bet-your-company culture; and process culture. In *Corporate Culture and Performance*, John Kotter and James Heskett identify three categories of corporate cultures: strong cultures, strategically appropriate cultures, and adaptive cultures.

Doug McMillon told the leadership students, "Change must be a part of an organization's culture." He added, "Other than our purpose and values, Walmart's only constant is change."

In a set of cultural myths associated with visionary companies, Collins and Porras include "Visionary companies are great places for everyone to work." The reality, they note, is "Visionary companies are so clear about what they stand for and what they're trying to achieve that they simply don't have room for those unwilling or unable to fit their exacting standards." They categorize the cultures for several of the companies they examined as cult-like, noting these are "great places to work *only* for those who buy in to the core ideology; those who don't fit with the ideology are ejected like a virus."

Margaret Townsend, while serving as J. B. Hunt's senior vice president of engineering and technology, talked to the students about the importance of learning the history and respecting the culture of the organization you join. Previously, she worked at GE, Microsoft, Avaya, Washington Mutual, and Tempur-Pedic. When asked why executives fail when brought into a company from outside, she said she had asked a very senior executive if he thought she would be successful in a job she was being considered for, and he replied, "Yes. You are qualified, but sometimes a body just rejects the organ." She pointed out, "Changing jobs at the executive level is a risk, and it is a risk you are paid to accept. Through potentially no fault of your own, it might not work out, and you will need to be prepared to move on if that happens."

Having worked at several universities, Jeff Long, then UA's vice chancellor and director of athletics, told the students, "What works best for one organization will not necessarily work best in another organization." You must learn an organization's culture before you can make changes. How do you determine if you'd be a good fit for an organization's culture? First, you must know what its culture is. You must also know yourself and assess accurately how your strengths, weaknesses, and leadership philosophy align with the culture. Unfortunately, while some aspects of an organization's culture are visible, other aspects lie beneath the surface and aren't easily detected.

In *Organizational Culture and Leadership*, Edgar and Peter Schein identified three levels of culture: artifacts, espoused beliefs and values, and basic underlying assumptions. Artifacts are visible manifestations of the organization's culture; they can be seen, heard, and felt as you interact with people in the organization and tour its offices and facilities. How people dress and interact, how offices are designed and arranged, and how employee parking is designed can provide clues. Additionally, published corporate values, the mission statement, and organization charts can be informative. How people communicate (face-to-face, email, text messages), as well as how meetings are organized and how frequently they occur, can prove beneficial. Be wary of drawing conclusions from limited evidence, though. Your eyes can deceive you. Too often, first impressions are influenced by your background and experience. For example, if you worked in a rigid, formal organization and observed an informal, loose organization, you could easily reach an incorrect conclusion that the organization is very inefficient.

Espoused beliefs and values include ideals, goals, values, aspirations, ideologies, and rationalizations shared by people within the organization. Typically, these are established by the organization's founder. However, over time, transformations occur. What a company espouses can differ significantly from what actually occurs. So as you're told the organization's beliefs and values, you should take them with a grain of salt until you've observed them in action.

For a leader, it's critically important to recognize that multiple cultures exist: an organization's culture, an individual's culture, and the leader's culture. Basic assumptions underlying the organization can conflict with basic assumptions underlying an individual's culture. Many US companies face this internationally.

Culture does not happen by itself. It has to be nurtured and managed. Good culture is one of the soft things that makes a company a better place to work and makes it stronger in the marketplace. However, despite the adjective, soft things are usually hard. Every company has an overarching culture and often has subcultures based on geography, departments, offices, and so forth. The key is that subcultures need to understand they're subcultures; they need to celebrate the good differences and not clash with the overall culture of the organization. In a growth environment, culture must adapt to the environment in order to enable growth.

An organization's culture is interconnected with its purpose, strategies, and values. Their combination influences how people view an organization. Leaders are responsible for modeling the combination. Your behaviors will positively or negatively impact the organization and its associates.

In *Primal Leadership*, Goleman and his coauthors note, "Many cultures place tremendous value on strong personal ties, making relationship building a *sine qua non* of doing business. In most Asian cultures—as well as in Latin America and some European countries—establishing a strong relationship is a prerequisite for doing business." What is considered acceptable business practice in some countries is a violation of the Foreign Corrupt Practices Act in the US.

In *Leading with Integrity*, Alan Kolp and Peter Rea address the challenges companies face when operating in countries with different cultures, especially those in which what is considered acceptable behavior in one is judged to be illegal in another. There are vast differences in the cultures of Canada, England, and Germany on one hand and China, India, and Middle Eastern countries on the other. In some countries, job opportunities for people are based on performance and competence; in other countries, job opportunities are based on social class, birth, and personal connections.

How do you decipher the culture of an organization? It's not easy. Edgar and Peter Schein conclude in *Organizational Culture and Leadership* that "The process of deciphering cannot be standardized, because organizations differ greatly in what they allow the outsider to see." In *Corporate Cultures*, Deal and Kennedy suggest a number of ways to gain an understanding of what an organization's culture is: study the physical setting, read what the company says about its culture, test how the company greets strangers, interview company people, observe how people spend their time, understand career path progressions of employees, learn how long people stay in jobs (particularly middle management), look at the content of what is being discussed or written about the company, and pay particular attention to the anecdotes and stories that pass through the cultural network.

Word of mouth, institutional reputation, employee turnover, third-party opinions, and a host of other ways of gathering information can help, but instinct is likely to prove more accurate than anything else in deciding if you're going to be a good fit for the culture of an organization.

Over my career, I worked in numerous organizations, each with a different culture. After Tennessee Eastman Company, I worked within the cultures of Virginia Tech, Ethyl Corporation, North American Aviation, The Ohio State University, Virginia Tech (again), Georgia Tech, National Science Foundation, and University of Arkansas. Extensive consulting experiences with Texas Instruments provided me with an exposure to its culture. Although I served on boards of directors for Russell Corporation, Eastman Chemical, Motorola, Motorola Solutions, Logility, and J. B. Hunt, I'm sure I didn't gain as accurate an assessment of their cultures as I'd have if I'd been an employee.

Marvin Bower, former managing director of McKinsey & Company, is credited with defining company culture as "the way we do things around here." Kolp and Rea observe, "Corporate culture is vital to strategic success, since there are both healthy and unhealthy cultures. *Corporate culture* is a short-cut for describing the way of life in a particular business." You need to assess how things are done in an organization and be brutally honest in assessing yourself to decide if you're a good fit.

The pastor of a church we attended once told me about a visitor who'd asked if the members of his church were friendly. The pastor asked, "Were the members of your previous church friendly?" When the visitor responded affirmatively, the pastor said, "You're going to find members of this church are friendly, too." When another visitor asked the same question but responded differently to the pastor's question, the pastor said, "You're going to find the same here." In the end, frequently, the answer to questions of fit are more a function of the person than the organization—but not always. If you aren't a hit-the-ground-running kind of person, you shouldn't try to run with those who are. There's a reason birds of a feather flock together: They fit!

ADAPT TO OR CHANGE THE CULTURE?

No doubt, there will be some aspects of the culture you like and some you don't. If those you like are consistent with your core values, then adapting to the culture is likely to be successful. If the culture is antithetical to your core values, avoid it.

Leaders shouldn't assume they know the culture of their organization. What they think they know can be quickly dispelled by doing as Shakespeare's Henry V did at Agincourt. In disguise, he practiced managing by wandering around: He walked among the troops to gauge their morale and receive a performance review. Henry V's practice appears to be the basis for the American and British television program *Undercover Boss*.

It shouldn't be necessary to go in disguise, but it'll be revealing for a leader to ask people at all levels of the organization to describe the culture of the organization. Few descriptions will likely be the same. Don't be surprised if it fits the parable of the elephant and the blind men. People describe what they believe it to be, based on their experiences. Different subcultures will exist in different segments of the organization. By contacting a broad cross-section of people, you can piece together the patchwork quilt of an organization's culture.

Any change you make can have unintended consequences. Therefore, as Mike Duke advised the leadership students, "Don't identify what should be changed until you have identified what should not be changed." In *Corporate Culture and Performance*, Kotter and Heskett affirm the need for leaders to be patient when effecting cultural change. For the ten companies they studied in which major cultural change occurred, the time required ranged from four to ten years, with an average of more than six and a half years.

Changing corporate culture is more difficult and more time consuming than changing corporate strategy. To effect a change in the culture, you must have buy-in at all levels of the organization.

The 2003 *Columbia* shuttle disaster was a particularly stark example of what can come of a toxic organizational culture. A scathing report by the *Columbia* Accident Investigation Board concluded the disaster was the result of "cultural traits and practices detrimental to safety" that were allowed to develop and organizational barriers that censored dissent and "prevented effective communication of critical safety information." Kolp and Rea observe in *Leading with Integrity*, "Changing processes is difficult but possible, and it is easier than changing the collective values that define a corporate culture."

Bill George notes in *Discover Your True North* that a culture of empowerment throughout an organization begins with how its leadership behaves every day. He writes that leaders "cannot preach empowerment and then behave in a hierarchical manner to get near-term results, or they lose credibility with their colleagues. Nor can they reward or even tolerate power-driven managers who behave like jerks to get results and often play political games in their organizations. These people need to be moved out of the organization for the culture to be internally consistent with empowerment. Then they need to reward leaders at all levels who empower their colleagues and subordinates and recognize them publicly."

Once you've concluded an organization's culture must change, what kind of culture do you want to create? Chris Lofgren advised the students to "Create a culture in which ideas, not people, compete." While serving as its president and CEO, Donald Smith led a cultural change at Tyson Foods. He advised the students to "Create a culture so strong it will reject those who try to reject it." John Roberts reminded the students "We have to break the mold to change the culture." Changing culture is hard, but sustaining the change is even harder. Remember what happens when heat is applied to shape-memory metals.

In *The New Corporate Cultures*, Terrence Deal and Allan Kennedy note, "Once you have an idea about the cultural lay of the land in your company, you need to exercise some personal leadership to begin the process of building into the company the kind of culture you want. . . .What you do have to do is stand up and be counted on for what you believe in and why you consider it essential that others in your company share these beliefs."

Which do you want, a strong culture, a strategically appropriate culture, or an adaptive culture? Effective leadership coupled with an adaptive culture is the key to sustained corporate performance. Kotter and Heskett point out in *Corporate Culture and Performance*, "The single most visible factor that distinguishes major cultural changes that succeed from those that fail is competent leadership at the top."

Based on their research, they drew several conclusions and identified four requirements for successfully effecting cultural change.

Changing the Culture at UA

I can testify as to the effectiveness of the methods identified by Kotter and Heskett. My experience attempting to change the culture of the University of Arkansas aligns with their conclusions perfectly. North Central Association, the UA's accrediting body, visits campuses every ten years. They visited the UA campus the year before I became chancellor. A decade later, following a visit in 2007, the commission issued its report, stating, "the University of Arkansas has transformed itself. . . . The visiting team was impressed with and commends the university for the sense of direction and accomplishments . . . as well as the overall morale of faculty, staff and students.

"UA is on a new trajectory, one that is rapidly moving it to truly become a world-class student-centered research university. . . . The 2010 Commission approach to institutional planning and change could be used as a highly successful model by other institutions of higher education interested in deep and extensive planning and transformative change." The transformation detected by the North Central Association visiting committee reflected a change in UA's culture, but its report provided several recommendations for further improvement. Important work remained.

As a leader, leading a change of culture will be one of your most challenging assignments. To be successful, you must walk the walk and talk the talk of a servant leader. Model the culture you want for your organization. Be patient, passionate, persistent, and consistent. Communicate, communicate, communicate cultural expectations. Model the behavior you expect of others. Create and cultivate an environment in which people are comfortable and relaxed—one in which they enjoy what they do, one where work is fun. Don't take for granted the culture is as it should be. Continually validate by communicating across the organization. Set the tone at the top. People are counting on you to lead. Don't let them down. More importantly, don't let yourself down.

CHAPTER 9

Decisions and Mistakes

A rkansas banker Reynie Rutledge admitted to the students, "You always want to do the right thing, but most of the time, you don't know what the right thing is." If it were easy, others in the organization would have already done it.

When ethical, moral, and legal issues are not involved, deciding what the right thing is can be quite difficult. Often, the question boils down to *right for who*? As the leader, when what is right for one party is not right for another, you must decide—and you need the wisdom of Solomon to make both parties happy. Unless your decision is a win-win, one party will believe you made a mistake.

A friend shared that while he served as the engineering dean at a major research university, he was frustrated with the lack of faculty support for his decisions. He believed that, even if a donor were to make a sizeable gift to the college and he decided to offer equal bonuses to each member of the faculty and staff, no one would be happy. Some faculty members would argue that the size of the bonus should be based on the number of papers they'd published, the magnitude of external research support received, the number of student credit hours taught, professorial rank, and so forth. Someone would want to form a committee to develop a formula to determine how the money should be allocated. My friend said it would be simpler to use the money to purchase equipment or software.

I'd like to claim the dean's frustration wasn't justified. I can't. Likewise, I'd like to claim it'd only occur with an engineering faculty, but I can't. Likewise, I can't claim such reactions are limited to academia. I've experienced it in business, government, and nonprofit organizations.

When you make decisions involving people, some (perhaps many) will second-guess you. Leadership isn't a popularity contest; it's a decision-making activity.

DECISIONS

Great Britain's former chancellor of the exchequer, Nigel Lawson, is credited with saying, "To govern is to choose. To appear to be unable to choose is to appear to be unable to govern." In like manner, to lead is to decide. To appear to be unable to decide is to appear to be unable to lead. Decisions accompany leadership. Leaders soon learn that not making a decision *is* a decision.

Judith McKenna reminded the students, "Decisions do not occur in a vacuum. Anticipate the repercussions." She said, "Tough decisions need to be approached with genuine empathy, something learned but not taught."

Many if not most important decisions need to be made without all the information, but you can rely on life experiences. Making the no-regret decision can help guide your choice. In fact, the decision may not need to be made yet.

While teaching a course on methods improvement at Virginia Tech in 1964, I told the students to adopt an Aristotelian approach and, to improve their work methods, to use a 6W1H process: asking why, what, who, when, where, which, and how? At the time, I didn't realize I'd use the same process in making decisions.

Why?

Just as I was taught in an undergraduate methods improvement class, in teaching the same course I emphasized that the students should start with *why*. Little did I know that forty-five years later, Simon Sinek would publish *Start with Why* and would be featured in a TED Talk. Adopting a questioning attitude has served me well. It always begins with *why*, and *why* is coupled with the remaining questions.

Frequently, decision-makers want to determine, first, what the decision should be. Before doing so, they should determine why a decision needs to be made. As I noted above, not making a decision *is* a decision, but you are likely to be asked to make a decision when a decision isn't required. What will be the implications if you simply ignore the opportunity to make a decision? Will it go away? Remember the Eisenhower matrix. Neither you nor your lieutenants need to address every decision opportunity. Be selective. It's essential for decision-makers to answer the *why* question before deciding.

In the process of asking *why*, don't forget to ask *why not*. Push against boundaries. Go beyond the tried and true. To encourage "thinking outside the box," ask *why not*.

After determining a decision must be made, consider what the effects of the decision will be, including who will be impacted and what new problems will arise. Consider carefully what decision truly needs to occur.

What?

Peter F. Drucker observes in *Managing the Nonprofit Organization*, "The most important part of the effective decision is to ask *What is the decision really about?*" Make sure you identify the root cause of a problem before you solve it. Had the NCAA board of directors given more thought to the underlying issue with student-athlete transfers and compensation, perhaps they would've realized piecemeal decision-making creates more issues.

Two examples related to what decision is required come to mind based on my experiences with SysteCon.

A division of Westinghouse requested our assistance in designing a unit load automated storage and retrieval system for a new distribution center to be located in South Carolina. After James M. Apple Jr., a SysteCon partner, toured the Pittsburgh distribution center, he gathered data, analyzed throughput and storage requirements, and determined a full pallet load automated storage and retrieval system (AS/RS) wasn't the correct solution; instead, they needed a small package order-picking system. The client's understanding of what they needed had been incorrect.

A division of Federated Department Stores was another SysteCon client. The facility we designed included an AS/RS and automated guided vehicles; it served as a distribution center and cross-docking facility. After the system was installed, the division CEO called to express concerns about the system. Hugh D. Kinney Sr., cofounder of SysteCon, visited the facility in an Atlanta suburb and saw the issue was neither software nor hardware, it was humanware. For the first time, supervisors had offices in the distribution center and were spending time in their offices instead of supervising operations on the floor. The issue was quickly resolved by having managers manage. Once more, what the client thought was the problem was incorrect.

You must also decide what kind of decision you need to make and what the consequences are if you make the wrong one. As Amazon's founder Jeff Bezos put it in a 2021 article for *Inc.*, "There are decisions that are irreversible and highly consequential; we call them one-way doors, or type 2 decisions." Jason Aten, the author of the article, adds, "In type 2 cases, [Bezos] always looks for more information, since the decision is very important, and once it's made, there's no going back. Most decisions, Bezos says, are two-way doors, or type 1 decisions. These are less consequential. Make the wrong choice and you can go back. The problem, he says, is confusing the two and taking too long to make type 1 decisions." You have to determine *what* type of question you're trying to answer.

Who?

Exemplary leaders make fewer decisions than most people believe. In *The Contrarian's Guide to Leadership*, Steven B. Sample advances two general rules for decision-making. His first rule is "Never make a decision yourself that can reasonably be delegated to a lieutenant." When you try to make all the decisions yourself, you become the bottleneck for the organization, and you're left with no one to appeal to for reconsideration. To develop decision-making skills within your team, you must empower your team members to make decisions.

As UA chancellor, I relied heavily on the vice chancellors to lead their organizations. I depended on them to handle the day-to-day management of the university. Deciding who'll make the decision is important. As Sample puts it, you want to avoid having a two-front war: debating who should make the decision and debating what the decision should be.

When?

Sample's second rule is "Never make a decision today that can reasonably be put off to tomorrow." If delaying the decision is reasonable, then allowing for more time provides an opportunity for gathering additional information. Conditions change rapidly; by waiting until the decision needs to be made, the reason for making it can disappear.

The key word in both of Sample's rules is *reasonably*. For his first rule, clearly, if a bet-the-farm decision is being made, the leader must make it. Likewise, for his second rule, there are situations in which rapid decision-making is essential, such as athletic competitions, military battles, hospital emergency rooms, and the New York Stock Exchange trading floor.

When I arrived at UA in 1997, Carnall Hall was an abandoned, fenced off, and condemned former women's dormitory that had been declared an environmental hazard. Within a few months of my arrival, one trustee in particular strongly encouraged me to demolish it. Even though it was an eyesore, I resisted. I simply didn't think it was the right thing to do. But I didn't have a good alternative.

Founded in 1872, the university included women in its first graduating class, but women did not have an on-campus residence option until 1906, when Carnall Hall was built. Ella Carnall graduated from the university in 1881 and taught English and modern languages from 1891 to 1895. During this period, the university nearly closed because of financial difficulties. At a meeting of the faculty, Ms. Carnall appealed to the faculty to forego salaries to keep the university afloat. She was successful. Remembering the role she played, the residence hall for women was named for her and continued to function in that capacity until the 1960s. Thereafter, it housed a number of university organizations until it was closed in the 1990s.

At UA Board of Trustees meetings, I was asked frequently when Carnall Hall would be demolished. Complicating the situation was an activist group who mounted a campaign to save the hall. Members of the group wrote letters to the editor in the local newspaper, appeared in interviews on local television stations, and occasionally paraded outside campus with "Save Carnall Hall!" signs.

For more than a year, I put off the decision while asking the vice chancellors to provide me with alternatives. Fortunately, a private developer in Fayetteville came forward and proposed a public–private partnership to convert the building to the Inn at Carnall Hall, an upscale hotel serving the university area. The restoration was quite successful, and the inn became a coveted place for alumni and visitors to stay when they visited campus. In retrospect, I don't know how much longer I could've delayed its demolition. Fortunately, I'll never know.

When faced with a tough decision, some leaders prefer to kick the can down the road. They avoid the decision or form a committee, anticipating nothing tangible will result. These aren't actions exemplary leaders will take. Delaying a decision isn't the same as ignoring it. Instead, it's leaving the door open in anticipation of better solutions.

The downsides to putting off decisions are obvious: Your followers might conclude you're incapable of making decisions, are afraid to make them, or are a procrastinator. Clearly, you don't want to develop such a reputation. In deciding *when* to decide, keep your fingers on the pulse of the organization, and listen to your heart.

UA's former vice chancellor for student affairs, Johnetta Cross Brazzell, told the leadership class students, "Sometimes you can make a change without making a change." She shared an example in which she wanted to replace someone on her team. She didn't have to act, because the person chose to leave for a position elsewhere. Personnel matters don't always resolve themselves on their own. In her case, it did.

Photographer, leadership author, and consultant David Pincus told the students the best advice he'd received as a photographer was, "When you think you have the shot, turn around." He'd spend hours waiting for the right moment to take a photograph of a given scene, but, just before doing so, he'd turn and look at the surrounding scenes to ensure there wasn't a better shot to be had. So it should be with leaders: Just before making a decision, pause, consider the alternatives again, and then take the shot. Decide!

Where?

Generally, it's best to make a decision as close to the point of impact as possible so you can better understand its ramifications. However, clarity is essential through the organizational hierarchy. The following

example illustrates a failure to achieve clarity (and effective communication) through the organizational hierarchy. During the spring semester of
1999, UA's chief financial officer met with me to discuss an issue related
to the UA Apprentice Program. He said that, in previous years, individuals who completed the apprentice program were given jobs by the
university. However, given the financial conditions within the Facilities
Management Division, where technical staff were employed, they were
currently unable to hire. I asked if promises had been made regarding employment following completion of the program. He said none
had been. I asked how many people would be impacted; he said seven
or eight. I told him to meet with legal counsel and university relations
to make sure he touched all the bases. In retrospect, I should've asked
more questions.

Nothing happened for several weeks. One morning when I arrived
at the office, I received a phone call from President Sugg, asking what
was going on. That morning, a front page article in the statewide newspaper announced thirty-one people were being laid off at the university.
I told Alan I had no idea but would find out.

UA's CFO came to my office to tell me what had happened following our previous talk. After analyzing the finances of the division, he'd
learned the budget problem was greater than could be solved by not
hiring graduates of the apprentice program, so he met with the division's leadership, and they developed a solution: lay off all apprentices
and others based on job seniority, including several husband and
wife teams.

He hadn't kept me in the loop because he was trying to give me
deniability, but I was ultimately responsible. He apologized and offered
his resignation, which I refused. He'd made a mistake, but he had good
intentions. I told him I would handle it but let him know this couldn't
happen again. It never did.

I met with employees and their supervisors and apologized for our
mistakes. I assured them no one was being laid off and found other
ways to handle the budget. Letting decisions be made at the points of

impact is a good thing, but you dare not be kept out of the loop. In the end, deniability will not carry the day. The buck stops with you!

Which?

Among the decisions to be made, which should be reserved for you, the leader? Bet-the-farm decisions definitely are yours to make. Hiring, compensating, evaluating, developing, promoting, and replacing members of your leadership team are on your list of decisions. Decisions likely leading to controversy or negative press are also best made yourself. Anyone can deliver good news, but the leader should deliver bad news.

Recalling the Eisenhower matrix, the leader makes the important, urgent decisions. Which decisions a leader makes depends on the decisions, their impact, and the consequences.

How?

Will you make your decision based on a combination of advice, analysis, intuition, judgment, and destiny? Will you make it based on ballots? There will be occasions when voting is an appropriate approach. In general, however, it's best to not take a vote if you aren't going to be governed by the outcome.

My industrial engineering education caused me to rely heavily on an analytic approach to decision-making. It influenced my approach to consulting and to leadership. As a consultant, I relied on a six-step process for designing integrated systems: define the problem, analyze the problem, generate alternative designs, evaluate the alternatives, choose the preferred design, and implement the design.

The most important step in the design process is the first. If you define the wrong problem, you won't obtain the best design for the integrated system.

The best decisions generally involve a combination of facts and intuition. I also relied on my own experiences, the experiences of others, and the advice of trusted people. After discussing a situation with the leadership team, we tended to reach consensus. I prefer team-based decisions. I listened and asked questions but didn't share my feelings on the matter until others had spoken. Sometimes I didn't indicate where I came down on the matter, because I wanted to let the issue ripen. But in the end, the decision was mine. If the outcome was positive, I credited the team; if it was negative, I was to blame.

Martin Luther King Jr. said, "A genuine leader is not a searcher for consensus, but a molder of consensus." Exemplary leaders don't put everything to a vote. But they also don't unilaterally declare what will be done. Instead, they guide the discussion until general agreement is achieved.

It's important to have a very diverse team involved in making big decisions. You need the benefit of optimists, pessimists, and realists, right-brain thinkers, left-brain thinkers, and whole-brain thinkers, short-term focused and long-term focused individuals, risk-averse and risk-seeking people, and a team with different personalities and a wide array of strengths and weaknesses.

When making decisions, consider the probabilities of different future outcomes. The Roman philosopher Seneca is credited with saying, "Luck is when preparation meets opportunity." If you've done your homework and are prepared, you'll be surprised how lucky you are.

A major factor in decision-making is the use of judgment. Not everything can be quantified and that which can be quantified can't always be done with 100 percent accuracy. Judgment doesn't mean flipping a coin. After considering all facts, estimates, and advice available, use your best judgment, then be prepared for things to not go the way you anticipated. Sometimes worse, sometimes better, but never exactly as predicted.

Beware of the sunk cost fallacy—sticking to a path just because we've already invested time and effort into it. From experience, I know how difficult it is to walk away from past decisions and investments.

Leaders make mistakes when they get married to a particular decision and refuse to file for divorce when things don't go as planned. I witnessed it multiple times on corporate governing boards.

After interviewing leaders of a wide variety of organizations, David M. Rubenstein notes in *How to Lead*, "All leaders take risks, but the risks that combat leaders take are somewhat different. . . . No one wants an indecisive or uncertain military commander leading the troops." Followers don't want an indecisive or uncertain leader. They want a leader who can decide when a decision is needed.

MISTAKES

In 1960, after the New York Yankees lost to the Pittsburgh Pirates in the seventh game of the World Series, Yogi Berra said, "We made too many wrong mistakes." Some mistakes are more costly than others.

Mistakes can be contagious; they can lead to other mistakes. Failure to recognize when a mistake occurs is generally more serious than the original mistake. Even worse is recognizing a mistake occurred but ignoring or failing to remedy it. Most egregious, though, is attempting to cover up a mistake. Cover-ups, denials, passing the buck, and playing the blame game are surefire ways to destroy your reputation and the morale of your team. Legendary college football coach Paul "Bear" Bryant reportedly said, "When you make a mistake, there are only three things you should ever do about it: admit it, learn from it, and don't repeat it."

Greg Brown told the students, "The only thing worse than making a bad decision is not correcting it." On another occasion, he told the class, "Worse than making a mistake is not doing something about it when you realize it is a mistake."

After mishandling a cable television issue when he was at Ameritech, Brown said he learned the following lessons: obtain input from others before making a decision, inform your boss before announcing a big decision, and focus on the customer, not the competition. This is good advice for all leaders, best followed prior to—not after—making decisions.

Why?

When a mistake occurs, determine why it occurred. Was it because of a misunderstanding? Was it the result of innocence, inexperience, or poor communication? How you deal with the mistake is highly dependent on why it occurred.

Why did the debacle involving the Facilities Management Division occur? I failed to follow up with the vice chancellor and learn what steps were being taken, he failed to keep me informed, and his lieutenants failed to recognize the consequences of their decisions regarding who would be laid off.

If we didn't answer the question of why the mistake occurred, nothing would be learned from it. Failing to answer the question will likely result in similar mistakes in the future.

What?

Importantly, what kind of mistake was made? Was it a minor mistake or a major mistake? Were any laws broken? Was there an ethics violation? What will be the short-term and long-term implications of the mistake?

Pam McGinnis told the students that the biggest mistakes leaders make relate to people. She said, "The most difficult mistake is overestimating or underestimating the ability of one of your employees." She also said, "Bad business decisions are not mistakes. They are opportunities to make the next decision."

Who?

John Steinbeck said, "I guess a man is the only kind of varmint sets his own trap, baits it, and then steps in it." I disagree with the gender limitation, but it's true that too many mistakes leaders make are due entirely to themselves. After making a mistake, the leader asks, "Why didn't I anticipate the trouble my action caused?"

Who made the mistake? Was it you or was it a member of your leadership team? If it was you, then it can't be overlooked; remedy it quickly. Don't make another mistake by trying to cover it up. If, on the other hand, a member of your leadership team made the mistake, it can present a learning opportunity for them and an opportunity for you to demonstrate empathy.

When?

Timing and frequency are important aspects of any mistake. Often, the mistake is entirely due to poor timing. President George W. Bush notes in *Decision Points* that his mistake regarding Katrina was one of timing: "The problem was not that I made the wrong decisions. It was that I took too long to decide." So has it been with me.

On Saturday, February 23, 2002, basketball coaches Tubby Smith and Nolan Richardson chatted briefly following UA's loss to the University of Kentucky. At the press conference following the game, Richardson was asked what he and Smith discussed. Reportedly, Richardson said, "If they go ahead and pay me my money, they can take the job tomorrow."[1] The game was played at Kentucky, and I wasn't aware of the comment until Sunday, when I attended an indoor track meet on UA's campus.

Soon after I arrived at the track meet, I was asked by a reporter for my reaction to Richardson's statement. Because I was unaware of it, I asked what he'd said. When he told me, I said I thought it must've been a response "in the heat of the moment."

Later that afternoon, I left the track meet to attend a portion of the UA women's basketball game against the University of Georgia. While seated courtside during the game, I was approached by Fred Vorsanger, who managed Bud Walton Arena, where basketball games were played and where offices for the men's basketball coaches were located. Vorsanger said he regretted hearing what Richardson had said at the press conference. I told him the same thing I said to the reporter: that it must've been a heat of the moment response. Vorsanger said Richardson told him the same thing on Friday as the team was leaving the arena for the airport. I was shocked, because I'd reached an agreement with Richardson that he wouldn't make public comments indicating unhappiness with his employment.

Upon returning to the track meet, I saw Frank Broyles, UA men's athetics director. He was very upset about what Richardson had said. After talking with him, I decided it was time for Richardson to be replaced. (Because of an awkward relationship between Broyles and Richardson, Richardson's contract placed on me the responsibility of firing him.) While meeting with Broyles, I called Alan Sugg, UA president, and told him of my decision. He concurred and said he would inform several UA trustees. I told Broyles we needed to meet with Richardson on Monday and inform him of my decision.

Broyles asked if we could delay doing so because he was committed to fly to Georgia that evening to play golf at Augusta National Golf Course and would not return until Wednesday. The men's basketball team was playing at Mississippi State University on Wednesday, so we would have to wait until Thursday, February 28, to meet with Richardson. It was important for us to meet with Richardson as soon as possible. I should've told Broyles to cancel his trip, but I didn't. Big mistake!

Monday morning, I met with Scott Varady, UA's legal counsel, and informed him of my decision and asked him to advise me on how to handle Richardson's dismissal. I also met with Roger Williams, associate vice chancellor and director of university relations, and asked him to facilitate press releases regarding the coaching change. Later that day, Richardson held his normal Monday afternoon press conference during basketball season.

The Associate Press reported, "At a news conference Monday, Richardson complained about news coverage and noted that only white reporters were at the news conference. 'When I look at all of you people in this room, I see no one who looks like me, talks like me, or acts like me," he said."[2]

When Broyles and I met with Richardson on Thursday, he concluded he was being fired for what he said on Monday, not what he said following the game on Saturday. Subsequently, Sugg, Broyles, and I were sued for racial discrimination and violating Richardson's constitutional right to speak out on subjects of race. Multiple witnesses testified my decision was made on Sunday. We prevailed in the suit and its appeal in federal courts.

If Broyles and I'd met with Richardson on Monday, before his press conference, I believe things would've played out quite differently. But I continued to make similar mistakes.

Richardson's successor, Stan Heath, was unable to meet expectations for the men's basketball program. He was fired by Broyles on March 25, 2007. His successor, Creighton University's coach, Dana Altman, was introduced to the media and fans on Monday, April 2, 2007. That evening Altman and his wife, Reva, joined Broyles and his wife, Gen, at the UA chancellor's residence for dinner. During dinner, it was obvious to Mary Lib and me that Altman and Reva were uncomfortable. She was tense. He hardly said a word during dinner and ate very little.

Following dinner, Broyles departed for Augusta National Golf Club to attend the Masters tournament. Given my sense of discomfort regarding the Altmans, I should've told Broyles he needed to be available during Altman's first day on the job. But I didn't. Another big mistake!

Apparently, Altman didn't consult Reva before accepting the job offer on Sunday. Their high school daughter, Audra, with them on the trip to Fayetteville, was distraught over the move and remained in the hotel with a friend who had accompanied her.

The next morning, I received a telephone call from a member of the athletics staff informing me Altman was having second thoughts about being our coach. With Broyles in Georgia, I met with Altman to learn his concerns and assure him of our support. I was unable to dissuade him about leaving. That afternoon, we held a press conference announcing Altman's decision to return to Creighton. If I'd trusted my instinct and asked Broyles to remain, would it have changed Altman's decision? I doubt it. He had many other things on his mind.

Where?

At an important banquet in April of 1999, UA's vice chancellor for university advancement, David Gearhart, introduced major donors and members of UA's leadership in attendance. He introduced a particular attendee as "the dean's wife" rather than as a state senator, to which she and the dean took offense. As the evening unfolded, the dean accosted Gearhart and made a scene, using crude language and behaving unprofessionally. Numerous people in attendance witnessed this, as did a media representative.

After I learned what occurred and discussed the matter with my executive team, I met with the dean and indicated his behavior was inconsistent with my expectations of members of UA's leadership team. I encouraged him to think about what actions he or I should take regarding his mistake. A few days later, he resigned as dean and returned to a faculty position. Had he made this mistake behind closed doors and, perhaps, in the office of the vice chancellor, I would have handled it differently. However, where it occurred elevated it and led to his resignation.

Similarly, had Nolan Richardson made his "If they go ahead and pay me my money, they can take the job tomorrow" statement privately, the consequences of the mistake could have been quite different. Where mistakes are made matters!

Which?

Two types of errors tend to occur in decision-making: A type I error is rejecting someone or something that should be accepted; a type II error is accepting someone or something that should be rejected. Type II errors tend to be more visible then type I errors. When someone is hired and soon thereafter is fired, a type II error obviously occurred.

While I was chancellor, we hired two men's basketball coaches and one women's basketball coach; I participated in the selection of each and all three failed to deliver satisfactory results. Numerous corporate acquisitions don't prove to be successful, resulting in type II errors. As a board member, I voted for many acquisitions that failed.

Fortunately, type I errors are less visible. Among coaching candidates we didn't select, two took teams to the NCAA Tournament Final Four.

While I was serving on the Russell Corporation board of directors, a small start-up athletics clothing firm approached members of management seeking to be acquired by Russell. Governing board members agreed unanimously with management that it wouldn't be a good investment. We rejected the overture from Under Armour—an obvious type I error.

The challenge, of course, is that anything you do to minimize the probability of making one type of error increases the probability of making the other type of error. To guarantee you won't make a type II mistake in hiring, you don't hire anyone—ensuring you make numerous type I errors. Similarly, to guarantee you won't miss out on acquiring a future Under Armour, you acquire every start-up athletics company and make numerous type II errors.

Recognize both types of errors, and don't let risks have undue influence on your decisions. Mistakes are going to be made. You want to encourage people to take appropriate risks. You should celebrate rather than punish mistakes that result from these types of risks.

How?

How you respond to mistakes depends on the answers to the six W questions. If you made the mistake, admit it, apologize, fix it, learn from it, and move on. If others made the mistake, take appropriate actions, make necessary changes of policy and training, step back, assess, and explore alternatives. Regardless of who made the mistake, be resilient, be positive, be empathetic, and be encouraging.

Describing the downing of Korean Airlines flight 007 on September 1, 1983, by a Russian pilot, an incident that was denied by the Soviet Union, Colin Powell noted in *My American Journey*, "I drew some useful lessons from the incident. Don't be stampeded by first reports. Don't let your judgments run ahead of your facts. And, even with supposed facts in hand, question them if they do not add up. Something deeper and wiser than bits of data inform our instincts."

John White III shared with the leadership students three ways to deal with mistakes:

1. Admit to yourself it is a mistake and own it.

2. Acknowledge the mistake to those who are affected by it.

3. Correct the mistake.

General Jim Mattis notes in *Call Sign Chaos*, "There's a huge difference between making a mistake and letting that mistake define you, carrying a bad attitude through life." Don't let mistakes define the person who makes them. If a mistake occurs, you want to know about it. "Good news needs to travel fast, but bad news needs to travel faster."

General Marty Steele shared with the students advice he gave troops he led in combat: "Seize the day. Bloom where you are planted. Subordinate yourself to the task at hand. And seize off of each other's strengths, rather than attack each other's weaknesses." Steele ensured that mistakes were remedied. Under his command, the people making mistakes were not castigated by their fellow marines. Everyone learned from each other's mistakes. They realized that no one is perfect. But, in their work, lives were on the line; they had to make sure they had each other's back.

John Roberts said, "Mistakes are good educators if you welcome them." Jeff Long advised, "Use mistakes people make as teachable moments."

Throughout my career, the most significant thing I've learned about mistakes is to not let them define you. As Greg Brown told the leadership class, "Leaders are remembered for their greatest mistakes." Then, he advised, "Don't be a victim!" Following a tough loss, coaches remind their teams to not let one loss become two losses. Learn from your mistakes, but don't dwell on them.

CHAPTER 10

Leadership Teams

Leadership is all about the team. Leaders are responsible for assembling, refereeing, assessing, advancing, compensating, and changing the team.

ASSEMBLING

When Yogi Berra, long-time manager of the New York Yankees, was asked what makes a good manager, he replied, "Good players!" Likewise, good leaders are made by good team members. In the end, your success as a leader will be based on the success of your team. Assembling the team is the most important task.

Greg Brown said he looks for people with high IQ, self-awareness, good judgment, and integrity; he also said he looks for competence and values, as well as quality and fit. Donald Smith said he placed greater weight on trust than ability. John Roberts said he looks for people who are reliable, creative, self-starting, communicative, articulate, and not overreaching.

UA chancellor Joseph Steinmetz identified the following attributes of people he hires: They are passionate and a self-starter who can work independently. They think inclusively and act decisively. They handle people with sensitivity, have charisma, and are observant of the needs of others. He looks for those who can lead and rally people around a cause.

Johnetta Cross Brazzell said, "I only want to hire people with aspirations, who are creative and ambitious. My job is to help them achieve." She also said, "Hire people who are active participants." She added, "I couldn't afford slackers," and advised the students to "Be clear about where you want to go and what you want to do. Decide the difference you want to make in the lives of others. Engage and support others along the way in your leadership journey."

Rubenstein reported that Virginia Rometty said curiosity—a desire to learn—was the most important trait she looked for in people she hired.

When choosing someone for your team, the best indicator of future performance is past performance. Add strength where you're weak and value performance over promise. Shelley Simpson is very intentional in forming teams based on strengths of team members. She uses StrengthsFinder to ensure members of the teams possess the variety of strengths needed for the problem. General Marty Steele uses Myers–Briggs personality assessments to achieve a diversity of personalities on teams.

When queried by David Rubenstein about the success of the hedge fund Citadel and the securities trading firm Citadel Services, its founder and CEO Ken Griffin said in *How to Lead*, "When you can put together the right team with the right mission, you can accomplish great things." When Nike's Phil Knight was asked about his skill set, he said, "I've been pretty good at evaluating people."

Your effectiveness as a leader comes down to how well you select people for your team. Unlike baseball players who can have a batting average of less than 35 percent and be inducted into the Hall of Fame, you must make good choices more than 50 percent of the time. Just one mistake in selecting a key member of the team can result in removal from your leadership position.

In assembling a team, it's critically important for the team to bond, for individuals to trust and respect one another. For bonding to occur, the team must trust one another.

If you inherited your team, let team members demonstrate their capabilities. Political elections aside, when a new leader makes wholesale changes in the team, it sends more ripples through the organization than I suspect the leader realizes.

During my interview for the UA chancellor position, a staff member asked who I'd bring with me from Georgia Tech. I said I'd only be bringing my wife, and she'd be fully engaged in supporting me but wouldn't be compensated by the university. A few years later, two Georgia Tech colleagues joined me, filling positions as deans. However, they weren't players to be named later. When openings occurred, I thought of them, as well as others in my network. Although I encouraged them to apply for the positions, search committees recommended they be chosen to fill the openings.

General Mattis notes, "Throughout my career, I've preferred to work with whoever was in place. When a new boss brings in a large team of favorites, it invites discord and the concentration of authority at higher levels."

When an organization needs to move in a different direction, a new leader is usually required. So, if you've been brought in as the new leader, it's very likely you'll need to make several changes in the makeup of your executive team. A hard fact you must face is the people who brought the organization to this point are unlikely to be the people who can take it to where it needs to be.

J. B. Hunt's John Roberts told the leadership class, "The things that got you here might not get you there." His observation applies equally to an organization and an individual's career.

Interestingly, Schneider National's Chris Lofgren (a J. B. Hunt competitor), in the same semester, told the students, "The things that get you to where you are today are often the things that stop you from getting where you need to be tomorrow." Not only must the leader continue growing, evolving, and adapting, but so must members of the leadership team. Standing pat is not a winning strategy in today's competitive world.

Changing people might not be your only challenge. It might be necessary for you to change the makeup of your team to acquire the right skill sets. Using Jim Collins's bus metaphor, not only do you need to change the people in the seats, you need to change the seats. As chancellor, I asked the provost to change seats and become the CFO, and this was one of the most effective personnel moves I made.

John White III shared with the leadership class three steps he used to gain followership: spread the vision relentlessly (like a broken record), let people know you care about them, and highlight people's strengths.

Availability is not a skill set. This is true in all settings, but it's particularly true in consulting. At SysteCon, if an engineer wasn't currently assigned to a project, it was tempting to add the person to a new engagement with a client. However, if the person's skill set wasn't what was needed, we knew it'd be a mistake for the client and for SysteCon to add them to the team. Forcing a person with the wrong skill set on a team is like pouring new wine into old wine skins. Distasteful!

If you're given the opportunity to assemble a team from scratch, start with character, and end with fit. In between, include diversity, competence, passion, and humility.

Diversity

When they hear the word *diversity*, most people think of gender, race/ethnicity, or sexual orientation. In addition to these, strive to incorporate as many Myers–Briggs personality types and as many StrengthsFinder types as you can. Also, achieve a breadth of experiences and ages. Make sure your team consists of people who think differently than you. Depending on your organization's mission, include a diverse mix of geographical backgrounds and languages. A team's strength is linked inextricably to its diversity.

If your organization doesn't have a history of full inclusion, you'll receive pushback when you begin changing the culture to incorporate it. It's hard work, but the results will make the effort worthwhile. I speak from experience.

What's the point in assembling a team of Tweedledees and Tweedledums, people who look, think, and believe alike—or, even worse, who all mimic you? How can you expand your capabilities if everyone is just like you? A common mistake leaders make is assembling a team of yes men or yes women, although I've never met the latter. If you don't have people on your team who'll disagree with you, you're bound for trouble. If you're never wrong, why do you need a team? If you're the smartest person in the room, then you didn't assemble a bright team.

Another mistake leaders make is excluding mavericks from the team. General Mattis emphasizes in *Call Sign Chaos* the importance of nurturing maverick thinkers. They can provide the edge needed to win. Although it's taken far too long for some to accept the strength a diverse team offers, it's taken even longer for many to accept inclusion of maverick thinkers on the team. Because of their importance to the organization's success, Mattis advised people be assigned to guide and protect maverick thinkers "much as one would do for any endangered species."

Importantly, a leader must take on additional responsibilities by protecting a maverick and explaining to others the strengths the maverick brings to the organization. When a maverick won't follow the rules, perhaps the rules need to change or you need to have different rules for different people. You don't lead everyone the same way, do you? So why should everyone play by the same rules? It's important (and challenging) to educate team members on the value a maverick brings to the team. In the end, if the value a maverick brings to the team is worth it, make exceptions for exceptional people.

An inclusive organization should be able to include mavericks and provide a climate for them to be successful. Of course, if the maverick totally disrupts the organization, then you must decide if the gain is worth the pain.

When the National Football League is preparing for its annual draft, questions arise regarding which player each team will select. Will a team choose the best player available or the best player available filling the greatest need? The same questions arise in assembling your leadership team, but it's much more complicated than drafting a football player, where there is a known set of candidates. Such a draft pool doesn't exist for leadership teams. After going through the search and selection process, you must decide if any candidates available at the moment are acceptable. If you're expecting perfection, you're going to be disappointed.

Don't be wedded to a job description when hiring. If you spot someone whose strengths are not an exact match to the job description but the person would be a valuable member of the team, hire the person as quickly as you can. It's far better to fit the job to the person than force a person to fit the job.

Competence

You'll be judged by the weakest link in your chain of command, so make sure all team members are strong in their areas of responsibility. You can work around personality clashes, but you can't overcome incompetency. In the first offering of the leadership course, a student asked Mike Duke what he looked for in people he hired. Without hesitating, Duke said, "Character, competence, and people skills."

Assemble a team with high intelligence and emotional quotients; of the two, the latter is far more important. In fact, not unlike universities overemphasizing ACT or SAT scores in making admission decisions, an overemphasis on IQ can lead to hiring mistakes.

Angela Duckworth makes a compelling case in *Grit* for choosing team members based on that trait, a combination of passion and perseverance, not ACT or SAT scores. She notes, "Students in [an experiment] who had higher SAT scores were, on average, just slightly less gritty than their peers. . . . Our potential is one thing. What we do with it is quite another."

Passion

Passion is critically important in a leadership team. In Rubenstein's *How to Lead*, Ken Griffin said he looks for passion and accomplishment in people he hires. Do they love—not like—what they do, and do they "have a demonstrated track record of having made good decisions and having accomplished things in their lives"?

Passion is attitude. Not everyone can hire based on a person's accomplishments, but you can hire based on an assessment of the candidate's passion. You want people on your team who are eager, who run toward opportunities, who love what they do, who get up in the morning looking forward to going to work, and who don't consider what they do a job but a calling.

No doubt because many of the students in the leadership class were seniors and looking forward to gainful employment, many asked the guest leaders what they looked for in people they hired. Doug McMillon said he "seeks people who build trust, are honest, smart, and hardworking." Another guest leader said, "passion and hard work, intelligence, curiosity, and emotional intelligence." She also highlighted competence and integrity.

Margaret Townsend said she looks for people who are energetic, passionate, discerning, and able to embrace reality when adding people to her team. She told the students that, early in her career, she was told, "You are not paid to be right. You are paid to make right prevail." She emphasized the importance of having emotional intelligence and passion in the workplace. She said, "You find out who you are and what you love in the risks you take." Townsend reminded the students, "You are better at your job if you have perspective and additional interests."

Humility

An exemplary leader will be humble. Throughout the book are numerous examples of humble exemplary leaders. They didn't say, "I did it!" Instead, they said, "We did it" or "You did it." Abraham Lincoln was revered for his humble approach to leadership. He set his ego aside when he assembled his cabinet by choosing people with divergent opinions and people who were his political rivals. According to John Dickerson's *The Hardest Job in the World*, he wrote that Lincoln said about his cabinet choices, "These were the very strongest men. I had no right to deprive the country of their services."

REFEREEING

Because you lead a team consisting of high-ability, smart, competitive, and passionate people, be prepared to serve as a referee. No doubt, it will require all your skills as a mediator. Not to worry! An abundance of material on conflict resolution is available, but in the end, it will come down to relationships—among the disputing parties and between them and you, the leader. As Salacuse notes in *Leading Leaders*, "My own experience and observations have led me to conclude that the essence of leadership—of leadership in action—is not a quality at all. It is a relationship—a relationship between a leader and the persons led."

How you handle disputes will depend on the issues involved. Occasionally, the answer will be obvious to you but not to the parties in dispute. For example, it might require you to clarify your guidance. Don't be surprised when mountains are made of mole hills. Sometimes, the smallest things can create the most intense conflicts. Pay attention to the little stuff.

As Salacuse notes, "A certain amount of competition and conflict among professionals in high-talent organizations is productive and can lead to improved performance because it causes individuals to exert increased efforts. Too much conflict, however, can cause a decline in productivity and even lead to organizational paralysis."

The disputing parties will want you to be a judge and declare the winners and losers. Instead, strive to be a mediator. Listen carefully to all sides of the dispute. Let everyone be heard. Avoid making quick judgments. Search for middle ground. Ask questions. Make sure people are talking. Avoid taking a position on the issue, unless it involves an ethical, legal, or policy matter.

Abraham Lincoln was confronted with a situation involving two of his cabinet members, Secretary of the Treasury Salmon P. Chase and Secretary of State William H. Seward. Chase was jealous of Seward's influence and friendship with Lincoln. Working behind the scenes, in 1864, Chase complained to Republican senators about Seward's performance and said Lincoln did not consult all members of the cabinet about important decisions. A delegation of senators met with Lincoln and urged him to remove Seward and reorganize his cabinet. When Seward learned of the meeting, he submitted a letter of resignation, which Lincoln put in a coat pocket. This was the last in a string of resignation letters from Seward; Lincoln had declined his earlier submissions.

As Donald T. Phillips describes in *Lincoln on Leadership*, after thinking about the situation, Lincoln brought the delegation of senators into a meeting with his cabinet, excluding Seward. With everyone in the room, he asked all parties to resolve their disputes before anyone left. The senators were not aware the cabinet members would be in the meeting and the cabinet members were unaware of Lincoln's plans. Chase was placed in an awkward position; he could not side with the senators, because his cabinet colleagues would know he was the cause for the senators' concerns. So Chase admitted that Lincoln did consult the cabinet on important matters and Seward performed his duties admirably. The senators were embarrassed and Chase was exposed as a fraud. Chase's hopes of replacing Lincoln as the Republican Party's nominee for president were dashed. He resigned the next day. If all else fails, Donald Phillips noted in *Lincoln on Leadership*, try getting all parties to the dispute together, "lock them in a conference room—sometimes on a Saturday—and compel them to stay together until peace is made."

As UA's chancellor, I had to deal with a situation involving two individuals who reported to the provost. After giving the provost several months to resolve it, I intervened. I had good relations with both parties and fully expected we could resolve the matter. We met on a Friday afternoon. I let them talk. They both laid out the issues as they saw them. After there were no more words to be said, I said they needed to resolve it; I wouldn't take sides, and we would remain there until it was resolved. We sat silently for what seemed like hours, but it was probably less than thirty minutes. Then, one agreed to the other's position. I asked if this settled the matter. Both said it did, and they left.

I'd like to say there were no further disputes between the two individuals, but I can't. I believe the root cause was much deeper than either was willing to confront or admit. Perhaps jealousy or resentment was the underlying issue. However, they continued to work together and to lead their organizations effectively.

Following Lincoln's acceptance of Chase's resignation, he was visited by Congressman Samuel Hooper of Massachusetts and Treasury Registrar Lucius Chittenden; they both expressed regrets at Chase's resignation. Lincoln handled the situation masterfully. After listening to them and explaining why he made the change, he acknowledged Chase's value to the nation. As Doris Kearns Goodwin notes in *Team of Rivals*, when Lincoln said, "And there is not a man in the Union who would make as good a chief justice as Chase," Chittenden concluded, "Lincoln 'must move upon a higher plane and be influenced by loftier motives than any man' he had known."

Several important leadership lessons are provided in Lincoln's handling of Salmon B. Chase. Chase was one of Lincoln's rivals for the presidency, but Lincoln appointed him to his cabinet. Chase continued to undermine Lincoln and make life miserable for him, but Lincoln overlooked those things because of his competency in managing the treasury. Finally, when Chase was causing discord within the cabinet, Lincoln acted. However, he did so without malice. Instead, he thought of another way Chase could benefit the nation and appointed him chief justice of the Supreme Court.

As a leader, you might need to play the role of referee. Indeed, there will probably be times when you think all you do is referee egos. Consider purchasing a referee's shirt and a whistle to let team members know you won't ignore disputes arising within the team. Far worse than having disputes among team members is a leader who ignores them.

Take a deep breath, and remember how Lincoln handled disputes in the middle of war. Maybe it'll instill within you the resolve to continue pressing forward. Everyone on the team might not like one another, but they need to respect one another. A key to them doing so resides with the leader. As you demonstrate respect for each member of the team, that respect will be contagious; your team members will respect one another. Praise in public, discipline in private, and be sensitive to the sensitivities of your team members.

ASSESSING

Annual performance assessments won't cut it. Continuous assessments won't, either. The former occur too infrequently, and the latter lose their relevance. People need time to process feedback, make adjustments, and demonstrate the feedback was effective.

It's important to periodically have face-to-face discussions with each team member regarding their performance and opportunities for growth and improvement. However, there should be few, if any, surprises. Your team members should know you'll give positive and negative feedback when needed. They should also know you have their backs.

Feedback has been called by many the breakfast of champions. I value feedback. However, obtaining objective, candid, and accurate feedback is one of the toughest challenges a leader faces. As Shelley Simpson told the students, "It is difficult to get candid feedback because friends will let you off the hook." Judith McKenna reminded the students, "Feedback is not the most important thing. What you do with it is."

Coleman Peterson shared an example in which he received candid feedback from his supervisor. He said the supervisor taught him "how to hold people accountable by punishing them and moving forward without holding their mistakes over them in the future." He said his supervisor never again mentioned the incident causing the candid feedback. Jeff Long advised, "After levying criticism regarding a person's performance, don't let the criticism carry over; let it go, and move on."

Also, giving feedback can be challenging. Early in my leadership, I made an unforgiveable mistake in performing performance appraisals. I wasn't as sensitive to the sensitivities of people on my team as I should've been. I used 360-degree feedback without editing the comments. I was naive. Because the students completed faculty evaluations by providing anonymous comments online and I was accustomed to reading raw comments, I shared raw comments with individual team members. One person was devastated. From my mistake, I learned that the assessment process needs to be tailored to the individual. It is not a cookie-cutter process. Therefore, know the strengths, weaknesses, and sensitivities of each person on your leadership team. Not everyone is ready for or wants feedback, but they're the ones who need it most. In *Beware Those Who Ask for Feedback*, Richard Moran contends that those who ask for feedback "are really asking for validation."

From being on the other side of assessments, people need a more detailed assessment than "You're doing a great job. Keep it up!" They need specific suggestions: areas to be improved, things to change, new things to do. Generalities don't cut it. Be specific. No one is perfect, so there must be things each person can improve.

Donald Smith shared with the students a hypothetical example of a person with a mannerism that irritated some people. The person's supervisor didn't want to make a big deal about it because the person's work performance was outstanding, so the supervisor said nothing. Multiple supervisors took the same approach as the person advanced within the organization. When being considered for a vice presidency, the mannerism was cited as a reason for the person not being selected. By overlooking something that could prove detrimental to the person's career advancement, Smith said, those supervisors weren't doing their jobs. Being a leader is not a popularity contest, so share good news and bad news with team members when assessing their performances.

Recently, I recalled Smith's example when a friend was removed from a leadership position. The supervisor cited a particular mannerism as justification for my friend's removal. No one had ever mentioned it in numerous performance appraisals. I'd never noticed the mannerism. My friend paid the price for ineffective feedback sessions with current and previous supervisors. What was the problem? "You talk too much!" Why hadn't anyone said to my friend, "Talk less! Smile more!"?

In assessment sessions, don't just focus on past performance and opportunities for improvement. Also focus on the future by addressing the career goals and aspirations of all members of your team. Ask for ways you can help them achieve their goals. Don't limit consideration of their goals to your team or organization; if the goals are best achieved elsewhere, then offer to support their achievement.

Focus on performance goals. You get what you measure, so establish quantifiable goals for each team member. Request goals from each team member. When you meet, compare your goals for them with their goals for themselves. Reach agreement and ensure the goals are a stretch.

One of the greatest challenges in performing assessments is getting people to see themselves as others see them—to recognize improvement opportunities, not so much in job performance, but in enhancing their respect and influence. During my first year as chancellor, I met with all the direct reports to my direct reports. I asked what the strengths and weaknesses of their leaders were and what I could do to help them accomplish their goals. After approximately nine months, I met with each direct report, provided my written appraisal, and discussed what I could do to help them achieve their goals. Sessions with members of my leadership team were valuable; one was quite memorable—my meeting with legendary football coach and men's athletics director J. Frank Broyles.

To put things in perspective, I grew up in Arkansas and knew what the athletics program was like BB (before Broyles) and AB (after Broyles). Prior to accepting the offer to be chancellor, I met with Homer Rice, Georgia Tech's athletics director, whom I had a strong relationship with; I chaired the search committee for the football coach and for the men's basketball coach.

Rice and Broyles were very close. Rice presold me on Broyles. When I arrived, Broyles knew I wasn't only a fan of his but also someone who wanted to help him. During my first year as UA's chancellor, we met numerous times to discuss various aspects of his program. In November, Broyles called and said we needed to talk. He concluded he needed to replace the football coach. I said I'd come to his office and discuss it.

When I arrived, Broyles asked how I wanted to handle the selection of a new coach. I said it was up to him, and after he had talked with Rice, we formed a committee chaired by a dean. It included former players and members of the faculty athletics committee. Houston Dale Nutt Jr. was hired. (His ten-year record was seventy-five wins and forty-eight losses, resulting in eight post-season appearances in bowl games.)

In my first performance assessment meeting with Broyles, I made observations and asked questions about the performance of his coaches and the performance of student athletes in academics and sports for each of his sports. Toward the end of the session, I said, "Frank, when people come to a basketball game, they see only white students in the pep band, cheerleading squad, and pom squad. Also, when people look at your staff, they see several former football players, but they're all white. As a result, some people conclude you are a racist. I know you aren't, so what can I do to help you overcome this incorrect perception?" Without saying or doing anything else, everything was different in the fall. Broyles addressed every issue I raised. I couldn't have asked for a better response, and this came from an icon, a living legend.

When Coleman Peterson met with the leadership class, the students asked him about the challenges he faced as an African American leader in increasing racial and gender diversity within Walmart. Peterson said he doesn't think the vast majority of Caucasians are racist; instead, they are blind. They don't see the need for change, because they're unable to see things through the eyes of non-Caucasians. He said the same is true regarding hiring and promoting women; many male leaders are unable to see things through the eyes of women.

The assessment process provides a vehicle to help people see themselves as others see them. However, for it to work, a leader must have high EQ, or emotional intelligence. To achieve high EQ, leaders must first know themselves. The toughest person you will ever have to lead is yourself. Once you've become brutally honest regarding who and what you are, then you'll be able to develop self-awareness or empathy and become effective in relationship management.

In Rubenstein's *How to Lead*, Indra Nooyi took giving feedback to members of her executive team to a new level while serving as chairman and CEO for PepsiCo. She wrote letters to their parents. She thanked them for the gift of their child to PepsiCo, adding, "it opened the floodgate of emotions. Parents just started to communicate directly with me. It's been an amazing experience, because now I write to about four hundred executives' parents."

ADVANCING

Helping your team members achieve their career goals should be one of your top priorities. Exemplary leaders measure their success by the successes of their team members. Provide opportunities for growth, development, and exposure for your team members. As you develop a reputation for launching superstars you will find an abundance of budding superstars wanting to join your team. Mary Pat McCarthy told the students her measure of success was the number of people she led who became partners at KPMG. If you care for your people, you want them to succeed and to help them do so.

When my son, John, left Andersen Consulting, a colleague he mentored joined him at Manugistics and followed him to Capgemini. When he moved from Capgemini to Adjoined Consulting, his colleague anticipated he would be moving, too. However, White told him it was in his best interests to remain and be a leader at Capgemini because he was ready to step into a senior leadership role. While having his colleague with him in a new venture would contribute to White's success, he was more committed to his colleague's success. As it turned out, White assessed the situation correctly and his former colleague proved to be an exceptional leader. Sometimes advancing the team requires sacrifices.

As you identify the strengths within your team members, you can also help them advance their careers by facilitating lateral moves in the organization. Perhaps your head of internal audit would be ideally suited to lead your human resources efforts. Perhaps your provost would be ideally suited to become your chief financial officer. The former occurred at Fortna when my son was CEO; the latter occurred when I was UA's chancellor.

COMPENSATING

Reportedly, on President Reagan's desk was a reminder of there being no limit to what a person can do or where the person can go if the person doesn't mind who gets the credit. Effective leaders ensure the credit goes to the team. They publicly compliment team members.

While compliments are appreciated, my father told me, "The proof of the compliment is in the paycheck." No doubt, the importance of his paycheck was a direct result of him going through the Great Depression and the small salary he received as a public school administrator.

After seeing in the newspaper what my salary was when I was hired to be the UA chancellor, my father said my annual salary was more than he received in salary over his entire career. I was humbled. I am also embarrassed society doesn't pay teachers more. However, I also realized rewarding members of my leadership team included more than their paychecks.

Although it was hard to do, given the attention I received statewide, I tried to let the spotlight shine on them, not me. I tried to follow Lincoln's example and let the team receive the credit while I shouldered the blame. At the same time, I endeavored to model what I expected others to do, rewarding performance, not position. Just because people are located in lower positions in the organization does not mean their pay must be less than for those in higher positions.

For example, I had no difficulty paying coaches more than I was paid as chancellor for the same reason it was not difficult for me to approve paying a law professor more than a sociology professor, paying an economics professor more than a music professor, or paying a biomedical engineering professor more than a history professor. Salaries are driven by market forces. To attract and retain top talent, you must pay what the market demands.

One of the many mistakes I made as chancellor was not learning how much my predecessor was paid. As engineering dean at Georgia Tech, I was paid quite well. When I was offered the position of chancellor, President Sugg asked what I wanted my salary to be. I said I thought it would send a bad signal regarding the University of Arkansas if its chancellor was paid less than the engineering dean at Georgia Tech. Also, I said I didn't want an increase in salary. My salary was $230,000. I didn't realize $230,000 was 60 percent more than my predecessor was paid.

When my salary was announced, it created quite a controversy. Not only did Sugg and the trustees have to defend it, but so did Governor Mike Huckabee. When asked about it in a television call-in show, he said he was sure they could hire someone for far less, but he doubted such a person would be as effective as I would be. He also said he was confident my fundraising abilities would prove my salary was a bargain. I was unaware of the furor until I arrived months later.

The combination of selling SysteCon, retiring from Georgia Tech, and serving on multiple corporate governing boards resulted in my university salary not being a major concern to me. However, it was a great concern to many within the university and state. For several years, when Sugg offered me a raise, I declined. One year, he said I had to take an increase in my salary; otherwise, I'd be creating an issue for my successor. So he set my compensation at the average of what peers in the Southeastern Conference were paid.

CHANGING

As was illustrated in the episode involving two of Abraham Lincoln's cabinet members, changes will occur in the makeup of the team. Such changes might arise as a result of members voluntarily leaving, but in assembling the team, changes also occur because someone needs to be removed.

The weak link in a team will be obvious, if not to the leader then to other team members. When it becomes obvious a change is needed, don't delay. When asked what they would have done differently, several leaders told the students they would have acted sooner to remove someone from the team.

The 80-20 rule applies to teams. Eighty percent of a leader's time is spent dealing with issues created by 20 percent of the team members, or 80 percent of a team's contribution is the result of 20 percent of the team members. I've never known a team to consist of members who made equal contributions or required equal attention.

If members aren't pulling their weight, changes are needed. As Machiavelli would advise, do it sooner rather than later. When making the change, do it with sensitivity and empathy. Provide an opportunity for people being removed from the team to make graceful exits. If it can be "their idea" to leave, all the better. As Johnetta Cross Brazzell said, "Sometimes you can make a change without making a change."

The key to your success as a leader will be the people you lead. Give careful attention to who you select to be on the team and how you lead them. Assemble a diverse team with complementary strengths. Advance and compensate them well. Don't assume each team member should be led the way you want to be led. Instead, learn the most effective way to lead each individual on the team. When a change is needed, make it. Personnel issues are not like fine wines; they don't improve over time.

Drawing on their experiences, guest leaders provided students in the leadership class with an extensive set of reflections on practical leadership. A compilation is available at https://JohnAWhiteJr.com/WhyItMatters.

CHAPTER 11

Leadership Nitty-Gritty

As a leader, how do you define success? How will you measure success? Mike Beebe, the governor of Arkansas at the time he spoke to the leadership class, said he defined success as enjoying what he does. John Roberts said, "Life is short and very sweet. Keep your eye on what is important and makes you happy." Roberts also said he used his faith and his family to measure personal success and included his effectiveness in sustaining corporate culture in measuring his professional success. Greg Brown said success is a frame of mind; it is having the freedom to do what you want to do. He also said there are no shortcuts to success. Shelley Simpson told the students that, as they go through the seasons of life, success will look different.

Adriana Lopez Graham said she measures success by the development of people; she emphasized the importance of knowing your weaknesses and strengths and being very intentional in addressing your weaknesses. UA's Joe Steinmetz said, "The joy of leading is seeing others succeed and being able to facilitate their success."

Mike Duke and UA's engineering dean, John English, independently said success is leaving the campsite better than you found it. John White III said something quite similar: "Leave things better than I found them." Duke also defined success as winning. Roberts said, "There is no substitute for winning. When a team wins, it gels."

Johnetta Cross Brazzell said making a difference in the lives of people she mentored gave her the greatest satisfaction and her definition of success shifted over her career from focusing on herself to focusing on her team. Mary Pat McCarthy measured success by the number of people she mentored who were named partners in the firm.

Judith McKenna told the students her "definition of success is being able to do something I enjoy and knowing my family is just fine. Family comes first." Admiral Mike Johnson defined success as small victories. Chris Lofgren said you must define success for yourself, and you should realize your definition will change. Jeff Long reminded the students success is a journey. Admiral Jack Buffington defined it as doing a good job and having people appreciate you. Donald Smith said, "Your success is defined by whether or not you have understood your purpose and you have patterned your life to fulfill it." Then, he shared his leadership purpose: "To do God's will." Smith added, "Successful people are the ones who make difficult things look easy."

Coleman Peterson said he had shifted from focusing on being successful to being significant. Peterson's statement resonated with me, because it turned success from being inwardly focused to being outwardly focused. One can only be significant by having an external impact. Servant leadership is all about significance.

When a student asked General Marty Steele how he defined success for himself, he replied, "I don't think of life that way. Life is a journey. If I must choose, success is something yet to occur." Steele recognized the ultimate judgment of success is at the end of the race, not during it. So it is with leadership.

Ultimately, the measure of success should be team based, not leader based. If a report card is to be completed for the leader, who should complete it? Their team members? What about those the leader reports to, such as a governing board? What about those the governing board reports to—the shareholders?

Shareholders vote on annual proxy statements but also by buying and selling stock. Governing boards also vote, as they assess the performance of the CEO. In the end, the success of the leader depends on the performance of the team. Therefore, a measure of the team's success is a measure of the leader's success.

LEADING LEADERS

Leading Leaders by Jeswald Salacuse resonates with me because almost all of my leadership experiences have involved leading other leaders. The subtitle of his book, *How to Manage Smart, Talented, Rich, and Powerful People,* is an apt description of people I led at Georgia Tech, the National Science Foundation, SysteCon, and the University of Arkansas, as well as in professional societies and organizations and on corporate boards. It certainly applied in my work with friends, donors, and volunteers at Georgia Tech and the University of Arkansas.

Salacuse notes that a particular challenge of leading leaders is when the team members are specialists or otherwise prestigious, such as accountants, engineers, entrepreneurs, investment bankers, lawyers, management consultants, physicians, portfolio managers, research analysts, and scientists. In the case of universities, tenured professors,

Nobel laureates, and other eminent members of the faculty are not easily led. Hospital administrators face similar challenges.

Salacuse goes on to point out that the challenge of leading leaders is found in both for-profit businesses and nonprofit organizations
alike. CEOs are faced with similar challenges when leading or interact-
ing with governing boards. The challenges result from a leader having
limited authority over the people being led.

While reading his description of the challenges of leading leaders, I
couldn't help but think, "Amen!" multiple times. No doubt you've heard
the expression, "Managing professors is like herding cats." The expression is quite unfair to cats. Mary Lib and I have owned cats, and they
were less independent and less challenging than many professors I've
known. In fact, I recall a particular tenured, full professor who refused
to take on assignments; when no salary increase was forthcoming, he
remarked, "That's okay. I'll just do more consulting."

My leadership of volunteers in professional societies and at church
prepared me for leading academics. To persuade people to do things,
when logic didn't work, I appealed to their pride, ego, collegiality, peer
pressure, and sense of purpose. Success resulted in greater team unity.

Many of those Salacuse identifies as leaders who must be led are
what Peter Drucker calls knowledge workers. For a significant fraction
of his career, Drucker addressed the challenges of leading knowledge
workers. In his landmark study of management, *Management: Tasks,
Responsibilities, Practices*, published in 1973, he calls special attention to
the need for effective leaders to be imaginative and courageous. Drucker
notes the things that motivate manual workers are generally ineffective in
motivating knowledge workers. He argues that fear, as a motivator, must
be replaced with opportunities for self-motivation and self-direction.

In "They're Not Employees, They're People," published in *Harvard
Business Review* in 2002, Drucker notes, "Executives will have to learn
what the effective department head in the university or the successful conductor of the symphony orchestra [has] long known: The key to
greatness is to look for people's potential and spend time developing it.

"Similarly, leaders in knowledge-based businesses must spend time with promising professionals: Get to know them and be known by them; mentor them and listen to them; challenge them and encourage them."

Leadership is highly situational and contingent. Situation dictates the leadership approach. The approach depends on the people being led and how they are best led. When leading leaders, it's likely you'll be leading people who know at least as much as you, who have at least as much influence as you, who are more experienced than you, who can turn a blind eye and deaf ear to what you do and say, and who can find other employment paying at least as much as you pay. The best way to lead leaders is the best way to lead anyone—by inspiration, persuasion, perspiration, persistence, and patience.

MENTORING

When I was in college, I don't believe the word *mentoring* was in my vocabulary. If it was, I rarely used it. But over my career, I had many mentors, people who provided wise advice and counsel or served as role models. My Virginia Tech leader and friend Paul Torgersen was a mentor, but we never used the word. Until shortly before his death, I don't think Paul knew how much influence he had on my life and career. There're many others who don't know how much I depended on them as I wandered along life's pathways. Not only did many not realize their impact on me, but neither did I at the time. Only through reflection later in my leadership journey did I appreciate what I learned from so many.

Mentoring is a subject of great interest to students. Within UA's Department of Industrial Engineering, a number of mentoring circles are available; alumni meet regularly with students to answer questions and provide advice as they prepare to enter the workforce. In addition, each untenured faculty member is assigned a mentor who is a tenured professor.

Many of the leadership students asked the visiting leaders about mentoring. John Roberts said, "Mentors taught me things I didn't know and things I didn't know I didn't know."

Coleman Peterson identified three qualities of a good mentor: They manage well and set clear objectives, they provide good and constant feedback, and they are candid. He said, "For mentoring to be effective, there must be trust and respect between the individuals." In another offering of the course, he said, "Mentor relationships can be too structured and mechanical. Mentoring works best when there is a relationship between the individuals."

Shelley Simpson said, "In selecting a mentor, find someone with an attribute you desire and learn from the person." Mike Duke told the students, "There isn't a beginning and an ending with a true mentor." He also identified characteristics required of a good mentor: mutual trust, integrity, and the courage to be candid.

Johnetta Cross Brazzell reminded the students, "You are setting an example for someone." She was extraordinarily effective mentoring her team, and many of them went on to hold vice president and president positions at other universities.

John White III said, "Be purposeful in choosing a mentor." Reminding students mentorship is not a one-way street, he said, "You need to have mentors. Invest in them if you want them to invest in you." He said the impact mentoring had on his career was massive.

Being very process oriented, White developed a mentoring process. Specifically, he recognizes that every engagement with someone is a learning opportunity. He said the students could learn from others what they should do or learn what they shouldn't do; both are valuable. He cautioned them to be selective in choosing mentors and to define the attributes, skills, experiences, or traits they value and want to emulate or adapt.

There is no cookie-cutter approach to mentoring. One size doesn't fit all. The mentorship must be tailored to the needs of both the mentor and the mentee. Once you've defined what you're looking for from a potential mentor, White recommended you approach the person with specific requests. Often, those you want as mentors are very busy, so you need to be specific about why you want them, what you hope to learn from them, and ways you want to improve. Doing so will make it almost impossible for them to say no.

Once someone agrees to be your mentor, the work begins. Find time to meet, be prepared for the meeting, and specify what you want to focus on. Come prepared with great questions to gain insights, demonstrate commitment, define ways in which you can help your mentor or make the mentor's life easier, ways in which you can put what you've learned into practice, and demonstrate your appreciation in words and deeds. In short, demonstrate that the time spent investing in you is valuable and that you take the investment seriously. Mentors need to know you're invested in them, too. If it's the right kind of relationship, mentors will go out of their way to help make you successful.

NETWORKING

A leader's network contributes significantly to their success, both personally and as a leader. Internal networks facilitate two-way information flow quickly and accurately. Having people who will provide a heads-up is priceless. Likewise, external networks can provide objective assessments of your effectiveness as a leader. Receiving objective, candid feedback is one of the greatest challenges a leader faces. The leader's network might be the only way such feedback occurs.

Margaret Townsend told the students, "Be nice to the people you network with in your career. You never know what doors might open as a result."

Networking is how I was able to serve on corporate boards. It's also how I became a candidate for the UA chancellor position, how I was appointed to the National Science Board, how I was selected to lead the Engineering Directorate at the National Science Foundation, and a host of other career-boosting things. Leadership matters, but so does networking.

I thought I was very good at networking, but my son makes me look like a novice. White advised the students, "Use a touch strategy to build your network." He said, "Don't let relationships die, cultivate them."

White is intentional in his networking. Again, he has a process that has proven very effective. He advised the students to maintain contact with people in their network, not to make contact only when they want something. Instead, they should look for opportunities to share something that would benefit or be of interest to them. If they read a book, article, or something on the Internet they think they would be interested in, send them a copy, or suggest they read it. If they see a movie or something on TV that reminds you of them, give them a call or send an email or text message and let them know. Stay in touch.

Networking requires an investment of time. You need to stay top-of-mind by keeping your network top-of-mind. Little things mean a lot! White has worked at five companies, been on numerous boards of directors and advisory boards, and served in leadership roles for a number of professional societies. He has interviewed *only once* for a job or role during his career—his first job out of college. All other roles and opportunities came through his network. Networking matters!

SAY IT IN THE ROOM

Donald Smith shared with the leadership class how he dealt with a phenomenon I experienced many times during my career: informal meetings occurring after formal meetings. A meeting occurs in which the leader summarizes the conclusions and agreements from the meeting; then, when people leave the room, they revisit what was said in the meeting and express disagreements with the conclusion. Typically, those who disagree say little, if anything, during the formal meeting. In expressing negative viewpoints, they undermine the leader and spread discontent among people who attended the formal meeting.

Smith had a saying: "Say it in the room." He was very emphatic about the need, once agreement is reached in the room, for the agreement to continue outside the room. Members of the leadership team must speak with one voice.

DON'T FENCE ME IN

You're likely too young to remember Cole Porter's cowboy song, "Don't Fence Me In," sung by cowboy radio and movie stars Roy Rogers and Gene Autry (among others), but the words to the song came to mind frequently when I served in leadership positions. Leaders can be fenced in by people who blame the leader for unfavorable decisions. What they don't realize is they're also fencing themselves in by doing so. If you're a member of the leadership team and you say to one of your followers, "The leader decided to do this, but I didn't support it," what've you done? You just scored a twofer: You not only diminished your follower's regard for the leader but also the follower's regard for you. You demonstrated that you don't have enough influence to change the leader's decision. Whether you agree with the leader's decision or not, give every indication of being totally supportive.

There is another way members of the leadership team fence themselves in: when a request is made by a follower and the leadership team member says, "Let me consult the leader, and I'll let you know." What just happened? If the leader agrees, the member of the leadership team demonstrated a lack of authority to make the decision or an inability to make it; if the leader doesn't agree, the member of the leadership team demonstrated an inability to sell the request to the leader. Instead of mentioning the leader when responding to the follower, the leadership team member should have said, "Let me think about your request. I

want to consider all aspects of it, then I'll let you know my decision."
Words matter. Choose them carefully.

You're passing the buck when you, as a member of the leadership
team, say to a follower, "I agree with you, but let me check with the
leader." Look at what you did. You, again, scored a twofer. You set up
the leader and yourself. First, if the leader doesn't agree, you made the
leader look bad and demonstrated a willingness to do so; second, you
showed you aren't necessarily aligned with the leader's decision and
you aren't aligned with the leadership team.

Don't back yourself into a corner, and don't back your leader into a
corner. Doing so serves neither the leader nor you. The leadership team
must speak with one voice. It must be aligned. Check your ego at the
door and function as a team member.

MOMENTS THAT MATTER

Leaders must be cognizant of moments that matter to their stakeholders. Just because a particular moment doesn't matter to you doesn't
mean it doesn't matter to others. Because of the demands on a leader,
moments that matter to others can fall through the cracks. Having a
diverse team, including someone with great institutional memory and
someone with strong human resources (HR) skills, can minimize that.

HR professionals understand the significance of moments that matter to employees. Aaron McEwan, vice president and advisory leader at
Gartner, said, "Many experiences that affect employees at work are outside the control of the organization, such as the birth of a child or the
relocation of a spouse for work. What matters is how HR handles these
memorable moments when they occur. . . .

"Today, 16 percent of HR functions are experimenting with a
'moments that matter' approach, and 56 percent of HR leaders are
interested in identifying 'moments that matter' for their organization.

"Moments that matter allow us to learn more about what's really important to our people, rather than the moments that HR and leaders think matter. . . . More importantly, they enable action. When we identify the moments that matter to employees, we have clear next steps for HR to take action on to improve the employee experience."[1]

DEFINING MOMENTS AND TIPPING POINTS

Defining moments and tipping points are opposite sides of the same coin. The same set of events can be labeled either, depending on the context. A defining moment for someone can be a tipping point for an organization and vice versa.

Greg Brown shared with the leadership students two very difficult periods during his leadership of Motorola. Prior to the company separating its cell phone business, economic conditions within the firm were dire, to say the least. Over a short time frame, Brown lost more than thirty pounds, wasn't eating or sleeping, and was worrying about what he should do as CEO. Late one night—or, more accurately, early one morning—his wife, Anna, interrupted his pacing back and forth and asked what he was doing. After Brown shared his doubts and uncertainties with her, she delivered tough love and told him there were sixty thousand Motorolans waiting on him to lead. She also said, "If you don't believe in you, why would others believe in you?"

Years after the separation of Motorola into Motorola Solutions and Motorola Mobility, as Brown was leading Motorola Solutions, an activist investor pressured him to take an action he didn't support. As the activist investor gained support from other directors, Brown told Anna he was considering resigning as chairman and CEO. Again, Anna caused Brown to shift his thinking. She asked what he thought would happen if he agreed to do what the activist investor wanted. When Brown said he didn't think anything would come of it, she asked what he had to lose by going along with the investor's recommendation. When it failed, everyone would know Brown's original opposition was correct; if it didn't fail, he wouldn't be any worse off than if he resigned, but no one could say he walked away from the company he led successfully for many years. As usual, Anna was right. Brown continues to lead Motorola Solutions.

Paraphrasing Maya Angelou, Brown advised the students, "When things are not going well and you are in a situation you don't like, change it, or change the way you think about it." He also told them, "Look for two or three people who will love you, care for you, and tell you the truth."

In the course of your life and leadership journey, specific events will impact you. The impact can be significant or insignificant. For the former, its significance might not be obvious immediately. In retrospect, you will realize it was a defining moment, that it changed you in fundamental ways. The same can occur for the organization you lead.

When the impact is insignificant, you might give the event a momentary thought, but life goes on as usual. While such events might *define* moments, they are not *defining* moments. Upon returning to the office following attendance at an out-of-town conference, a colleague asks how the conference was and you respond, "Lousy!" Actually, the conference itself was terrific, but there were flight delays and the room at the hotel was next to the elevator, causing you to be awakened numerous times during the night. The flight delays and elevator noises defined the moment for you, not the conference.

Hundreds of defining moments occurred over my career, some more significant than others. These include choosing to transfer from the Missouri School of Mining and Metallurgy to the University of Arkansas, committing to excel academically in graduate school, leaving Virginia Tech for Georgia Tech, going to the National Science Foundation, and leaving Georgia Tech for the University of Arkansas. Numerous choices I made and opportunities I had were influenced by events quite independent of anything I had done.

The following pivotal events from my UA chancellorship illustrate the challenge in deciding if events are defining moments or tipping points.

Increase in Chancellor's Scholars

As mentioned previously, the 1998 UA fall semester freshman class at the University of Arkansas included 492 Chancellor's Scholars. It was a 1,100 percent increase, compared to the 1997 freshman class, and sent a message across campus and across the state: The University of Arkansas is on the move. My invitation to high-ability students to join us in a journey to excellence was accepted by a record number. Many faculty members doubted our ability to shed a "party school" reputation so quickly. The 1998 freshman class caused the faculty members to change their minds; they began to believe achieving our goals of academic excellence were possible. A shift in attitudes began emerging on campus.

Murder on Campus

On August 28, 2000, a murder and suicide occurred on the UA campus. I was meeting with my executive committee when an assistant joined us and reported shots were fired in Kimpel Hall. We adjourned the meeting. Bob Smith, UA's provost; David Gearhart, vice chancellor for university advancement; and I went immediately to the UA Police Department, where we were joined by Roger Williams, associate vice chancellor and director of university relations. To ensure media representatives were apprised of developments, I conducted three news conferences that day. The next morning, I was interviewed by *Good Morning, America*. Also, on Tuesday, we held an all-university forum on the tragedy, at which I addressed the university community.

I don't know why, but a shift occurred in how I was perceived by statewide media after the tragedy. Perhaps they saw me, for the first time, as a person, not an administrator. Regardless of why it occurred, there was a definite shift in the tone of my media coverage. This wasn't my perception alone; members of the executive team, President Sugg, and several UA trustees drew the same conclusions.

An editorial in *The Morning News* on Friday, September 1, 2000, included the following: "We offer high praise to the University of Arkansas Chancellor John White and everyone else at the university who handled Monday's tragedy on campus with skill, sensitivity and forthrightness." In addition, "Chancellor White and others in the administration really stepped up to deal with the impact, realizing first how quickly and how widely news of the shootings would spread and trying to assure those in the university community and all their distant friends and relatives that the campus was secure and that there was no continuing threat to anyone's safety. The shootings occurred near the noon hour on Monday and by 2 p.m. officials had set up the first of five different press conferences that would be held in the span of three days. Each time, White himself and all the key officials and police officers were there to answer questions and impart information to the campus community and to the public as quickly as it was available to them." The editorial closed with, "We give Chancellor White himself considerable credit for the UA's response to this crisis.

"These have been, without doubt, his finest hours at the helm of the Fayetteville campus.

"We also applaud all of the people around him who facilitated the flow of information to us all and who will be there in the days and weeks and semesters to come as the university heals."

Basketball Fan Wins $10,000

On January 8, 2002, a fan won $10,000 at a men's basketball game. Mary Lib and I were at the Arkansas versus Mississippi State game when Michael Collyar was selected for a Fuji-sponsored half-time competition. If Collyar made a layup, he'd receive a prize and be given a chance to make a free throw for an additional prize. If the free throw was successful, he'd be given a chance to make a three-point shot for another prize. And if the three-point shot was successful, he'd be given a chance to make a half-court shot for $10,000. He had to make all four shots within 24 seconds.

We watched as Collyar made the layup, free throw, and three-point shot. Then, with people in Bud Walton Arena holding their breath, the half-court shot hit the backboard and went through the hoop. The crowd erupted; Collyar was ecstatic.

Then, Matt Shanklin, UA's assistant athletic director for marketing and licensing, said something to the public address announcer, who then announced Collyar stepped over the half-court line and wouldn't receive $10,000. As it was reported by Kristin Netterstrom in the student-run newspaper, *The Arkansas Traveler*, "The once cheerful crowd immediately booed loudly as Collyar received his parting consolation pack of a T-shirt and a camera with film. The student section began yelling, 'Fuji sucks. Fuji sucks.' Shanklin didn't fare any better. As he began to walk around Bud Walton Arena, boos bellowed from everywhere, including from UA Athletic Director Frank Broyles, who was waving his hands and booing Shanklin along with the rest of the crowd.

Netterstrom wrote, "'It was the loudest booing I have ever heard,' Collyar said. 'Some people have said it was louder than any referee has gotten booed.'

"As Broyles was booing and telling Shanklin to give Collyar the money, UA Chancellor John A. White, who was sitting at half court with his wife, Mary Lib, and US Sen. Tim Hutchinson, R-Ark., made his way down to the announcer's table."

When I saw Broyles leaving the arena and walking toward the media break room, I excused myself, walked down to the floor, and told Shanklin to have the PA announcer say the fan would be paid. Shanklin said the insurer wouldn't pay, because a video recording of the shot showed Collyar stepped over the line.

My response was, "Tell the announcer the student will be paid $10,000. Also, tell Frank he'll pay $5,000, and I'll pay $5,000."

Broyles's payment would come from the Razorback Foundation, and mine would come from the UA Foundation. I returned to my seat. The announcement was made, fans were happy, and we won the game against Mississippi State. Soon, I'd learn, I won, too.

Little did I realize while I was watching to see what Broyles would do, apparently eighteen thousand fans were watching to see what I would do. My actions were instinctive. It was the right thing to do, so I did it.

The next issue of the *The Arkansas Traveler* included an editorial titled, "White's small gesture giant step for him." The editorial began, "During the Arkansas-Mississippi State men's basketball game Tuesday night at Bud Walton Arena, Chancellor John A. White performed his best feat yet during his tenure at the UA.

"Though the spin later that night told a different story, White is the one who said December graduate Michael Collyar's half-court bank shot should count."

The editorial included the following: "During his rocky tenure, White made many a blunder and has been criticized for being too stern and not personal enough, especially with students. That all changed Tuesday night. With a small gesture, he ensured that a recent graduate will long remember his days at the UA as a Razorback fan and helped dispel his image as a cold, stand-offish person. About the only praise White received Tuesday was from Collyar, who gave him a long hug at the announcer's table.

"By the end of the night, though, Shanklin and the sports information department had done enough spinning to make Rumpelstiltskin seem slow. In everyone's eyes, Broyles and White together made the decision to give Collyar the money. But what few people know is that White immediately took action not only to give Collyar a big graduation present but ensure that he will be a lifelong fan of the Razorbacks and of the university. For the first time in his tenure, White really showed what few have known: He is a kind-hearted person who truly cares about the UA and its image. Long chastised for not showing care for students, in a single action White demonstrated much of that care with a simple gesture."

The editorial ended with, "Because he didn't do so Tuesday, White should take a bow today for his actions. He deserves it. And after a rocky start, White showed everyone that he finally has arrived in Fayetteville."

Accompanying the editorial was a cartoon of me by Dusty Higgins, the illustrator of this book, with a huge heart and holding a basketball. The story of the $10,000 half-court shot and how it was handled was alive and well in Arkansas. The editorial writer was correct: It impacted how students perceived me. It was also another example of a little thing that meant a lot.

Permission granted by *The Arkansas Traveler*, January 14, 2002. All rights reserved.

Walton Family Gift

On April 11, 2002, UA announced a $300 million gift from the Walton Family Charitable Support Foundation. At the time, it was the largest gift made to a public university. I believe it still is.

The Walton family made a huge difference in my chancellorship. Also, the families of George and Boyce Billingsley, Lee Bodenhamer, Bob and Marilyn Bogle, J. B. and Johnelle Hunt, Julian and Nana Stewart, Don Tyson, and Willard and Pat Walker, among others, and numerous companies stepped up and impacted the success of my tenure as chancellor. However, the Walton family stepped forward first and set the example.

I remember so well my first meeting with Mrs. Helen Walton. We had lunch at Fred's Hickory Inn in Bentonville in July of 1997, a few weeks after I arrived to be the UA chancellor. I told Mrs. Walton about my parents, who had combined service of over seventy years in the Arkansas public school system.

I told Mrs. Walton about my mother, Ella Mae McDermott White, raised in Dermot, Arkansas, named for her great-grandfather, Charles McDermott. In the middle of the Great Depression, she had no money but wanted to go to college. She heard that a school bus ran every day between Dermot and Monticello, where Arkansas A&M College (now the University of Arkansas at Monticello) was located, and was told she should go see the college president and apply for a job to earn money for college.

When my mother arrived, a line of people stretched out of the building, all waiting to see the college president. It was late in the afternoon before she was able to see him. The president told her there were no more jobs available. He asked how much money she had. "Not any," she replied. He asked what her father did for a living, and she told him he was a plumber.

"Doesn't he have any money?" the president asked.

"No, sir," she said. "People give him what they can from their gardens when he works for them." The president asked what else he did, and she said, "Nothing. He's a plumber."

"He doesn't do anything else?"

"Well, he raises bees."

"Bees!" exclaimed the president, as he slapped his desk. "You bring me some honey, and you can go to college."

My mother rode the bus each day carrying two one-gallon jars of honey for the dining halls. That's how she was able to go to college, where she met my father.

I told Mrs. Walton I needed someone to throw a big rock into the lake and make a splash big enough for people across the country to know the University of Arkansas was here to play. I wanted it to create ripples that would go on forever and let them know we were here to stay. Mrs. Walton reached over, patted me on my arm, and said, "We'll help."

Mrs. Walton was present, with Governor Mike Huckabee, for my announcement on October 6, 1998, of the Walton's $50 million gift for the business school. When I said I didn't realize her rock was going to be the size of a mountain, she laughed.

Permission granted by *Arkansas Democrat-Gazette*. All rights reserved.

My requests of financial support from the Walton family began with my request in 1998 for $1.5 million to bail me out when so many students responded to our Chancellor's Scholarship offer. The Walton's $300 million gift in 2002 followed their $50 million gift in 1998 for the business school, named for Sam M. Walton. His name made a huge difference, but the $300 million gift was a catapult for the University of Arkansas.

When we announced the Campaign for the Twenty-First Century on October 26, 2001, our goal was to raise $500 million. By the time we received the Walton's $300 million gift, we'd raised almost $300 million. Their gift was a matching gift for new money raised following its receipt. Therefore, we raised the goal to $900 million. On April 15, 2005, we raised the goal to $1 billion. By the time the campaign ended on June 30, 2005, we'd raised a total of $1.046 billion.

The Campaign for the Twenty-First Century provided funds for 132 endowed faculty chairs and professorships and 1,738 scholarships and fellowships. More than 41,600 new donors participated in the campaign, and the total number of individuals who contributed reached 72,641. In sum, benefactors made 304,328 gifts and pledges to the campaign.

When I was informed we would receive the $50 million gift, there were two strings attached. Dean of the business school Doyle Williams and I had to commit to remain at the university for five years. When Rob Walton called to say the family agreed to fund our proposal for $300 million and they needed a letter from me and David Gearhart, UA's vice chancellor for development, I asked, "If it was a five-year commitment for $50 million, how many years is it for $300 million?" Rob Walton laughed and said, "Another five years." We received the first gift in 1998. By my math, two five-year commitments meant I honored my commitment in 2018, when I stepped down from the UA chancellor position and returned to my first love, the most rewarding leadership position I've held, teaching.

Which of these four events would you categorize as a defining moment versus a tipping point? My decision to be front-and-center with the media following the murder/suicide and my *decision* to award $10,000 to Michael Collyar changed how I was perceived. Recalling the definition of a tipping point, the key word is decision. Both changes resulted from decisions, responses to events. I consider them tipping points; others might consider them defining moments because they changed how they defined me.

The arrival of 492 Chancellor's Scholars in the freshman class of 1998 and the $1.5, $50, and $300 million gifts from the Walton Family Charitable Support Foundation significantly impacted the momentum for change within the University of Arkansas. I consider them defining moments for the University of Arkansas; some might consider them tipping points. Regardless, they were important milestones.

Things beyond your control—unexpected things—can have significant impacts on your leadership journey. When they occur, trust your heart. Do the right thing. You never know whose perceptions of you will be impacted by your actions. When great things happen, don't take too much credit. When bad things happen, don't take too much blame. Stay the course. When tipping points occur, use them as opportunities to lead. Recognize defining moments for what they are, tectonic shifts caused by forces you might not see but can feel.

KEEPING SCORE

In 1908, Vanderbilt University invited alumnus Grantland Rice to address a gathering of its alumni. Few expected his work "Alumnus Football" to become his most famous, ending with the oft-quoted lines "For when the One Great Scorer comes to mark against your name, He writes—not that you won or lost—but how you played the Game." These lines were drilled into me and my fellow high school students in order to plant seeds of sportsmanship and integrity and build strong character. Obviously, I didn't fully embrace Rice's message. Not only did I want to play the game right, but also I wanted to win! I didn't treat it as *either/or* but as *and*.

Keeping score doesn't matter, unless you want to accomplish something. Then, it really matters. British mathematician Lord Kelvin noted, "When you can measure what you are speaking about, and express it in numbers, you know something about it. When you cannot express it in numbers, your knowledge is of a meager and unsatisfactory kind." I don't agree with everything Lord Kelvin said, such as "Heavier-than-air flying machines are impossible," but I believe you get what you measure.

However, not everything important in life can be measured. In *Leadership on the Line*, Heifetz and Linsky wrote "Meaning cannot be measured," and pointed out we can become so obsessed with counting things that we lose sight of our mission, our goal, our purpose in life. However, they observe, "Of course, measurement is a profoundly useful device, but it cannot tell us what makes life worth living. The challenge is to use measurement every day, knowing all the while that we cannot measure that which is of essential value."

When trying to effect significant change in the culture of an organization, it's essential to demonstrate progress. Making progress toward achieving goals increases momentum. As people begin to see the battleship—or, in our case, the flagship—changing course, beliefs change. Instead of believing it is *possible* change *can* occur, they believe it is *probable* change *will* occur. Finally, they accept that change *is* occurring.

To provide evidence of progress, I like to keep score and let others see the results. Some people must see change occurring before they become supportive. Through my interactions with Bob Kaplan and Bob Camp, I became a fan of the balanced scorecard and benchmarking; they became important tools in my leadership toolkit.

Given my industrial engineering education, I used data to support my arguments for change. I was influenced by W. Edwards Deming, who said, "In God we trust, all others must bring data." However, I prioritize information over data. I didn't support collecting data for data's sake, but used data to inform people of the opportunities for improvement and to show what was possible because others had achieved it.

DILBERT © 2022 Scott Adams, Inc. Used by permission of Andrews McMeel Syndication. All rights reserved.

At Georgia Tech, at the National Science Foundation, and at the University of Arkansas, we relied heavily on benchmarking to communicate the necessity of change and to demonstrate progress. Leaders of the various schools within the College of Engineering at Georgia Tech believed their programs were great. We wanted them to realize they were good, not great, and what was required for them to become great. We asked leaders to benchmark against top-ranked programs. Once they saw where their programs fell in a set of benchmark measures, they and members of their faculty understood the need for change. Soon, every program was advancing in the rankings. As they advanced, surveys indicated faculty morale also increased.

SLICING PIES

Not long after I returned to be UA's chancellor, John Lewis, a native of Fayetteville, former classmate, and successful banker, told me the major differences between attitudes in Arkansas and Texas, where he had worked for several years. Lewis said Texans have an abundance mentality and Arkansans have a scarcity mentality. In Texas, entrepreneurs and wildcatters are celebrated. In Arkansas, people who succeed are not encouraged in the same way.

An unpleasant mental picture reared its head when I heard Lewis's remarks. It contained a pot of boiling water into which live lobsters were tossed. If a lobster tried to crawl out of the pot, other lobsters grabbed it and pulled it back into the boiling water. Misery loves company. If they aren't succeeding, some people don't want others to succeed.

There is a feeling among many that if someone else is successful, their chances of also becoming successful are reduced. If someone else gets a large slice of the pie, they'll get a smaller slice. I was raised to believe we should focus on doing all we can to make the pie bigger so everyone gets a larger slice. When you see a fellow lobster trying to crawl out of the pot, help it. Who knows? It might get to the top, reach back, and pull you out of the pot.

Mike Duke knew Walmart needed to increase the number of women in executive positions. He also knew more minorities were needed in executive positions. The vast majority of Walmart's customers were women, and an increasing number of its customers were minorities. It made sense, morally, socially, legally, and economically for Walmart to provide more opportunities for women and minorities to advance within the company.

Was Duke's position unanimously supported by his leadership team? Is the world flat? Some seemed to think so, because they didn't see how his efforts would lead to corporate success. When a senior lieutenant questioned the wisdom of Duke's goal, Duke said, "It is not a zero-sum game!" Then, he explained how the pie was going to become bigger and opportunities for white males would also increase. Increasing opportunities for women and minorities doesn't represent a decrease in opportunities for white men; it isn't an *either/or* but an *and* opportunity.

PRUNING

Despite everything we learned in mathematics, effective leaders add by subtracting. Instead of doing many things acceptably, they do fewer things exceptionally. The danger of doing a great job is you'll be a magnet for more jobs that you can be great at. You must learn to decline what would otherwise be wonderful opportunities. Leaders must be selective about the things they do in order to excel in doing them.

Successful people are likely to become unsuccessful when they try to do too much. Being busy is not necessarily being productive. It's easy to become caught in the vise of efficiency versus effectiveness, trying to do things right instead of doing the right things.

Effective leaders prioritize and make choices. They also embrace change. Andy Jassy, Jeff Bezos's CEO successor at Amazon, said one of the most important lessons he learned at Amazon is the importance of embracing change, not resisting it. "You can't fight gravity," he said, and you are much better off "being ahead of whatever direction the world is headed than you are howling at the wind or wishing it away or trying to put up blockers."[2]

Resistance to change is in our DNA. It manifests itself when we're successful. When Hall of Fame University of Texas football coach Darrell Royal was asked by a reporter what changes he would make before a big game, Royal said he'd "Dance with who brung ya." Everyone accepts the need to change when they're losing, but few are willing to do so when they're winning. But when you're winning can be the best time to make changes. Repair the roof when it isn't raining. In highly competitive conditions, if you're standing still you're losing ground.

Avoiding letting sunk costs affect decisions is one of the toughest things for leaders to do. Making changes when things are going great is a sibling to ignoring sunk costs. When making changes, give careful consideration to what you're willing to change and the changes you'll resist. Shakespeare understood the need to prune. In *Richard II*, the gardener said, "Superfluous branches we lop away, that bearing boughs may live." Prioritization is key.

In the first two verses of the fifteenth chapter in the Gospel according to John, Jesus said, "I am the true vine, and my Father is the gardener. He cuts off every branch in me that bears no fruit, while every branch that does bear fruit he prunes so that it will be even more fruitful." Notice that not only branches bearing no fruit must be pruned, so must branches that bear fruit. Doing so produces even better fruit. Expert gardeners know this. So do expert leaders.

Review your calendar, review your to-do list. Prepare your don't-do list. Subtract, delete, eliminate, exclude, prune, prioritize. Do less to do more. Just as in designing material handling systems where handling less is best, doing less is best in leading.

BULLY PULPIT

Leaders have responsibilities beyond their job descriptions, including social responsibilities to the communities in which they live and work. They can fulfill these responsibilities in multiple ways, including but not limited to serving on community advisory boards, sponsoring youth groups, providing financial support to nonprofit organizations, and so forth. Yet another way to fulfill social responsibilities is to use the leadership position as a bully pulpit and speak out on issues.

Two of my hot button issues have been and continue to be providing opportunities for women and minorities. One of the most discouraging things I've observed is roadblocks for women in the workplace. The glass ceiling is not a figment of women's imaginations. Justice Ruth Bader Ginsburg faced and overcame discrimination when she graduated from law school; in her case it was based on her being Jewish, a woman, and a mother.

Christine Lagarde, president of the European Central Bank, was told she would never become a partner in the firms she worked for because of her gender. Even today, when she walks into a room full of men, she can sense the disdain they have for her. In Rubenstein's *How to Lead*, she said, "It's less now, for sure, but when you are in a minority, that's what you experience."

One guest leader shared with the students what happened when she attended an important business meeting. She said it took her breath away when she entered the room and realized she was the only woman in the room and the only representative of her company.

More than one woman meeting with the leadership class identified a challenge many women leaders face: a false and sometimes crippling belief that one's successes are the product of luck or fraud rather than skill. One guest leader said she fights with an internal struggle of thinking, "I'm not good enough. I'm not smart enough."

Many girls are told they're not good enough in science, technology, engineering, and math (STEM). In her American Association for the Advancement of Science presidential lecture, Sheila Widnall addressed the cumulative disadvantage women face in STEM fields. It should not be surprising women leaders feel they must out-perform men to receive comparable recognition. As one guest leader said to the leadership students, "If I were a man, I truly believe I would have far exceeded the position I have today." Many women feel this way, and for valid reasons. At the same time, the guest leader told the women in the class, "The worst thing you can do is have a chip on your shoulder."

Another guest leader told the students she was mistaken for a waitress at an important business meeting and was asked if she would get someone a glass of champagne. She responded, "No, actually, you can get one for me." Good for her!

Leadership barriers for women have by and large been created by men, and men must remove them. Old boys' networks need to face reality: Women are often more qualified than men to take on leadership positions.

However, men aren't the only culprits in creating barriers for women. One guest leader shared with the leadership students an incident involving a woman supervisor who took her work, replaced the guest leader's name with hers, and took credit for the work. The guest leader quoted Madeleine Albright, former US ambassador to the United Nations and the first female US secretary of state: "There is a special place in hell for women who don't help other women."

A women who is a barrier to women advancing within an organization is known as a queen bee—one who succeeded in a male-dominated world without encouragement and support of other women. The queen bee's attitude is *I made it the hard way, so must you.* Once she made it over the bar, the queen bee raised the bar for others following her. With few exceptions, women who met with the leadership class shared experiences of dealing with a queen bee at some point in their careers. Unfortunately, queen bee syndrome is alive and well in academia, business, government, health care, the military, and other male-dominated fields.

A different but equally disturbing phenomenon occurred among African American leaders in Arkansas. While I was serving as Georgia

Tech's dean of engineering, we successfully increased the number of African American students and faculty, with support we received from the Atlanta chapter of 100 Black Men of America, Inc. Because we were so successful in recruiting outstanding African American engineering students to attend graduate school at Georgia Tech, an administrator from MIT visited with me to learn why so many African American undergraduates from MIT were choosing to attend graduate school at Georgia Tech instead of remaining at MIT. I said it had nothing to do with Georgia Tech and MIT but everything to do with Atlanta and Boston. I said the 100 Black Men worked with us to send a message to top African American students and faculty that they were needed in Atlanta. Former Atlanta mayor and United Nations ambassador Andrew Young was helpful in our recruiting efforts. A member of my staff was treasurer for the Atlanta chapter of the 100 Black Men. Being located in Atlanta was a strategic advantage in recruiting outstanding African Americans, and we capitalized on it.

Things were different in Arkansas. Several African American leaders within the state had a more parochial view than those in Atlanta. Many times, my efforts to fill administrative positions with African Americans were resisted, because the people we hired were not from Arkansas. We were able to make progress, but not as much as I wanted or the university and state needed. I missed having 100 Black Men of America as a partner.

A week or so after I became chancellor on July 1, 1997, I met with communications specialists from each college, the alumni association, and media relations. They wanted to interview me for articles they were writing. I remember vividly the first question I was asked, "What do you miss most about Georgia Tech, Chancellor White?"

I also remember my reply, "It's not Georgia Tech I miss. It's Atlanta. What I miss is its diversity. This place is too white for me."

Everyone in the room was white and stunned.

I followed up with, "Do you know how many African Americans there are in this building? Five! Do you know how many Asian

Americans there are? Two! Do you know how many staff members are Hispanic or Latino? The same as the number of Native Americans: none! We need to change things. The University of Arkansas needs to look like the state we serve." I used my bully pulpit to send a message of increased opportunities for underrepresented minorities.

I didn't just say this on campus. When I spoke to the Rotary Club in Rogers, about twenty-five miles from the university, I said the same thing. Needless to say, several Rotarians were as stunned as the communications specialists.

Warwick Sabin, president of the student government association on campus, and I met many times during my first year as chancellor. In one meeting, I asked what the university did to celebrate the birthday of Dr. Martin Luther King Jr., and the answer was nothing. While dean of engineering at Georgia Tech, I made a big deal out of King's birthday, and I thought we were missing an opportunity to make a statement for diversity on behalf of UA. I asked Sabin if he thought he could obtain the student government association's recommendation for the university to honor Dr. King by celebrating his birthday with a holiday. Enthusiastically, Sabin did so. Upon receipt of the group's recommendation, I called President Sugg and told him. He agreed. Thereafter, King's birthday was celebrated by our campus. People noticed, especially underrepresented minorities in northwest Arkansas.

Using the bully pulpit is quite different from being a bully in the pulpit. There's no reason for a leader to resort to intimidation or other bullying tactics. If you must be a bully to get things done, you're not a leader; you're a boss and not a very good one!

FAILING

Mistakes can produce failure, but not all failures are the result of mistakes. Events out of your control can lead to failure, when nothing you could have done would have resulted in success. Everyone fails. Despite the best laid plans, despite having an incredible team around you, you too will fail. The question is how you'll deal with it when you do.

One of the most successful responses to failure was Ernest Shackleton's leadership following his failure to reach the South Pole in his expedition to the Antarctic from 1914 to 1916. After having to abandon their ship, *Endurance*, which had been trapped in and crushed by polar ice in the Weddell Sea, Shackleton was able to lead his men home safely.

What made Shackleton's success all the more remarkable was it occurred following two previous failures to reach the South Pole. He failed in 1902 as a member of Robert F. Scott's three-man team, when they were within 460 miles of the pole, and in 1908, while leading an expedition, he turned back within 97 miles of the pole. Despite both failures, he was knighted by King Edward VII for his valiant efforts. Then came the two-year trek to get his team home safely from the Weddell Sea.

Perhaps not surprisingly given his determination, in 1922 Shackleton led a third Antarctic expedition, during which he died of a heart attack, at the age of forty-seven, while his ship was moored at a whaling station in South Georgia.

Although I'd heard of Shackleton's journeys, I didn't appreciate the enormity of the challenges he faced until I visited Shackleton's Hut at Cape Royds in the Antarctic in 2001. The hut was constructed in 1908 by members of the expedition Shackleton led from 1907 to 1909. It was restored in 1960 to a condition nearly identical to when Shackleton's team occupied it. Because of the low humidity and freezing temperature at Cape Royds, the conditions inside the hut were as though he and his team members had just left it. It was literally frozen in place. Walking into the hut was like stepping into the early 1900s. It was surreal.

One of the great success stories at Walmart, its supercenters, is the result of a failure. After touring large-scale retail stores in France, Walmart's founder, Sam Walton, was convinced they would be successful in the US. Calling them hypermarts, in the 1980s and 1990s, he opened four stores in Garland, Texas; Topeka, Kansas; Arlington, Texas; and Kansas City, Missouri. Compared to Walmart's stores at the time, hypermarts were quite large, greater than two hundred thousand square feet. They included a mini-mall, a food court, an arcade, a bank, and other kiosk operations, much like a shopping mall of the time.

Although the experiment was unsuccessful, based on what was learned from the experience, Walmart began opening supercenters, roughly half the size of hypermarts, and without many of the unique features of hypermarts, such as arcades and banks. Over time, supercenters have expanded in size and incorporated many features of hypermarts. It appears hypermarts were about a decade ahead of their time.

Numerous examples of product failures exist, such as Ford's Edsel, Coca-Cola's New Coke, and so on. Also, numerous examples exist of product failures turned into successes, such as Super Glue and 3M's Post-it Notes.

For a number of years, entrepreneurially focused companies advocated failing fast. Then, it evolved to fail fast, learn faster. Companies were striving to create a culture where people were not afraid to take risks and to fail. Failures were celebrated as long as failures were the result of genuine attempts to succeed and people were taking calculated risks and being innovative.

Donald Smith advised, "Give people permission to fail." As a leader, you don't want to instill within your followers a fear of failure, resulting in them being unwilling to step out of their comfort zones and try new things.

IF THE HAT FITS, WEAR IT

Elected leaders frequently say they "wear many hats" in an apparent attempt to separate their actions and decisions outside the office from those inside the office. I'm sorry, but that doesn't wash. Exemplary leaders live integrated lives. They wear the hat of leader regardless of where they are. You cannot simply leave the hat in the office when you engage in social, recreational, family, or other activities.

While serving as Walmart's president and CEO, Mike Duke was still Walmart's president and CEO wherever he went. When he went shopping, played golf, attended a church service or football game, dined in a restaurant, or attended a concert, he was still Walmart's president and CEO. Anything he said in any of those settings was being said by Walmart's president and CEO.

What you do, where you go, what you say, and who you associate with will be examined with a magnifying glass. Leaders live in fish bowls. People watch everything they do. If you're going to be a leader, you have to act like a leader all the time, not just some of the time.

Bill George states in *True North: Discover Your Authentic Leadership*, "To [live] an integrated life, you need to bring together the major elements of your personal life and professional life, including work, family, community, and friends, so that you can be the same person in each environment." He also notes, "Integrating their lives is one of the greatest challenges leaders face."

If the leader's hat fits, wear it everywhere—all the time!

CHAPTER 12

Moving On, Getting Fired, Retiring

MOVING ON

Successful leaders often reach a point when they realize little opportunity exists to positively impact the organization or the people they're leading. In such situations, it's time to move on to the next chapter in their leadership journeys.

Peter Drucker notes, "Sometimes a change—a big change or a small change—is essential in order to stimulate yourself again. . . . When you stop learning in a job, you begin to shrink." He adds, "When you begin to fall into a pleasant routine, it is time to force yourself to do something different. . . . Nothing creates more fatigue than having to force yourself to go to work in the morning when you don't give a damn." I moved on multiple times. After being at Tennessee Eastman Company less than two years, I moved on to Virginia Tech. After teaching there for three years and receiving my master's degree, I moved on to Ohio State. After teaching and completing work on my doctoral degree, in three and a half years, I moved on and returned to Virginia Tech. After serving on the faculty for five years, I moved on to Georgia Tech. My twenty-two and a half years at Georgia Tech included multiple times when I moved on: I founded the Material Handling Research Center and served as its director for five years. While serving as a professor, I cofounded SysteCon and sold it to Coopers & Lybrand after seven years. On loan to the federal government, I served for three years in leadership positions at the National Science Foundation. For six years, I served as Georgia Tech's engineering dean, after which I moved on to the University of Arkansas. After serving as chancellor for eleven years, I moved on to a full-time appointment as a professor. After serving as a professor for eleven years, I moved on to retirement.

Most of my decisions to move on weren't a result of burnout or boredom but of interesting opportunities. However, I was getting bored while serving as research center director, and I moved on from being chancellor when I felt I'd accomplished what I intended and had fulfilled my commitments to the Walton family. The decision to sell SysteCon was influenced heavily by my desire to stop juggling the responsibilities of being a member of the Georgia Tech faculty and being the rainmaker for SysteCon. Had I not moved on to Arkansas, I suspect I wouldn't have remained at Georgia Tech many more years before retiring.

In making a decision to move on, keep in mind, like Goldilocks and the Three Bears, you have three choices: move on too soon, move on too late, or move on at the right time. Because identifying precisely the right time seems to never be obvious, I prefer moving on too soon. My risk-averse nature leads me to move on when people still want me to stay longer, to not overstay my welcome.

When you move on, don't burn bridges. Nothing good will come of it, for you or for the organization you leave. The only person you'll hurt by burning bridges is yourself. Your future prospects won't improve by damaging relationships you've established, and you'll damage your reputation.

When I moved on from Tennessee Eastman Company to teach and attend graduate school at Virginia Tech, I maintained good relationships with my colleagues at Eastman. In fact, when I moved on from Eastman, I might've been the only person not labeled a traitor by my former colleagues. Many took decisions to move on personally, as though the person leaving was saying, "I don't want to work with you." No doubt, my decision was viewed differently because I was going to graduate school and would return to work at Eastman in the summer. Also, while teaching at Virginia Tech, I recommended many students to pursue employment at Eastman. Regardless, little did I know that more than thirty years later I'd be on its board of directors. Likewise, when I moved on from Virginia Tech to Ohio State, I hadn't planned on returning and being on Virginia Tech's faculty.

Moving on can be viewed by others as a promotion, demotion, or lateral move. What others think isn't important. What's important is what you think. Many people revitalized their careers by moving on to very different work opportunities. When faced with choices, follow your heart, not your head. You can overanalyze things. It's always better to run toward something than run away from something. If you choose to move on because you're running away from current responsibilities, be careful. Move on because something or someone is pulling you, not pushing you. You don't want to find yourself going from the frying pan into the fire. Despite what others may claim, the grass is seldom greener on the other side of the fence.

When you've made a bad choice, don't follow up with another bad choice. If you've dug yourself into a hole, stop digging. Find another place to dig.

GETTING FIRED

Sometimes you have little choice in whether you will move on. It is not unheard of for a leader to be removed—fired. If your firing comes as a surprise, either you haven't been paying attention or those who fired you haven't been doing their job effectively. Conditions can change to the point that a different person is needed in your position. When this happens, try to handle it like the Wizard of Oz.

Prior to the Wizard dealing with Cowardly Lion's desire for courage, when the entourage of Dorothy, Scarecrow, Cowardly Lion, Tinman, and Dorothy's dog, Toto, arrived for its audience with him, Toto pulled back a curtain, exposing him as an ordinary man. Seeing this, they realized he couldn't deliver on his promises. They were crushed.

Immediately, Scarecrow said to the Wizard, "You humbug!"

Chagrined, the Wizard responded, "Yes, yes, exactly so. I'm a humbug."

Then, Dorothy exclaimed, "Oh! Oh! You're a very bad man."

The Wizard responded, "Oh, no, my dear. I'm a very good man. I'm just a very bad wizard."

When you are fired recognize the decision was about the job, not about you. The coaches of athletics teams seem to have a better understanding of the realities of job separations. As one coach said, "You've either been fired or you're going to be fired."

Your resilience is put to the test when you're fired. After falling off a horse, you have to get back on. If possible, bounce back quickly. Otherwise, take time to identify your options. Don't rush into another bad situation. You can blame others the first time, but if repeated firings occur, few will believe the fault lies elsewhere.

Numerous business leaders, coaches, and politicians have bounced back after being fired. Michael Bloomberg, Steve Jobs, Robert Redford, Lee Iacocca, Bill Belichick, Mark Cuban, Jon Gruden, Jimmy Johnson, Bernie Marcus, Arthur Blank, Truman Capote, Walt Disney, Jamie Dimon, Jimmy Carter, George H. W. Bush, and Donald Trump were fired at some point in their careers.

Jeff Long, athletics director at three universities (Pittsburgh, Arkansas, and Kansas), told the students that taking a step back or sideways during your career can position you for better positions in the future. He encouraged them to not treat losing a job as failure but as an opportunity to recalibrate what they want to do next. Then, you can aggressively create a better future for yourself. While you can't change the future, you can participate in defining it for yourself.

LEADERSHIP TRANSITION

How leaders hand batons to their successors is quite important. Exemplary leaders want their organizations to continue thriving under new leadership. However, this isn't always the case, especially if the transition wasn't well received by the previous leader. How a former leader is viewed by those who remain in the organization will be affected by how effectively the transition occurs.

Here, as with many other leadership matters, a variation of the Golden Rule comes to mind: Prepare the way for your successor in the same way you wish your predecessor had prepared the way for you. Do all you can to effect a smooth transition—if not for your sake, then for the sake of those you leave behind.

President Reagan initiated a tradition of leaving a note in the Oval Office for the next POTUS. Reagan left a note for George H. W. Bush on stationery showing a cartoon elephant covered in turkeys, captioned, "Don't let the turkeys get you down." He encouraged his successor to rely on the stationery and conveyed his best wishes for success.

Bush's note for Bill Clinton conveyed encouragement and support.

Following Bush's death, Clinton stated, "No words of mine or others can better reveal the heart of who he was than those he wrote himself. He was an honorable, gracious, and decent man."

Clinton left George W. Bush a note in which he, too, conveyed encouragement and support, as well as noting the joys and burdens of the position. In turn, Bush left Barack Obama a similar note. Obama's note to Donald J. Trump was lengthier and more formal than his predecessors' notes to their successors.

Although Trump didn't concede the 2020 election to Joseph Biden with a congratulatory phone call, didn't welcome Biden and the incoming First Lady to the White House, and didn't attend Biden's inauguration, he left "a very generous letter" for Biden, according to *The Washington Post*. Saying it was private, Biden declined to share its specific contents.

Exemplary leaders do all they can to effect smooth leadership transitions. They don't burn bridges after crossing them. Instead, they strive to ensure strong and supportive bridges for those who follow.

RETIRING

I'm a double retiree. I retired from Georgia Tech in 1997, when I moved on to Arkansas, and I retired from Arkansas in 2019. Several months after my second retirement, my son called and asked what I was doing.

When I said I was preparing to teach an online course, he responded, "Dad, you're supposed to be retired. You worked all those years so you could enjoy life and do what you want to do."

I replied, "I'm doing what I enjoy and want to do. I was fortunate, I got to do it for fifty-six years and be paid for doing what I love, teaching." Then, I said, "John, retirement means you continue to work, but you don't get paid."

Many retirees tell me they're working more than they did before retiring. The difference, they say, is they're enjoying more what they're doing now. When I hear it, I'm reminded of how fortunate I was to find a vocation in which my square peg fit perfectly a square hole. For so many others, what I took for granted is a dream or hope.

Retirement provides opportunities and challenges. For too many, the challenge is turning the last page of a chapter without constantly wanting to go back and relive the chapter. Those whose identity is captured in the title on a business card are most vulnerable to the challenge of retirement. What can they do next? How can they contribute? How can they make a difference?

Retirement for leaders provides abundant opportunities, especially opportunities to lead. But there are also opportunities to become effective followers. Having led, I recognize that retired leaders understand the challenges other leaders face and are in a position to help.

After stepping down from UA's chancellor position and returning to a full-time faculty position, my goal was to model what an effective faculty member should be. My department heads and deans were generous in their praise for my efforts to serve colleagues, students, and them. After being a leader, then a follower, I believe the best training for followership is leadership. Find an organization you'll bring your passion, abilities, knowledge, and leadership experience to. Become a follower by volunteering to serve.

Your leadership journey doesn't end. It transitions. It's likely you'll be fired at some point during your leadership journey. It's guaranteed you'll move on multiple times, and you might even flunk retirement a few times before you finally retire. Even then, your journey continues. Transition from leadership to followership. Lead by following.

PART 3

Reflections

CHAPTER 13

Keys to As

How might I summarize my leadership journey? What advice might I have that has not been captured in previous chapters? Although numerous students receive straight As in their classes, relatively few leaders receive As from everyone they lead. Over time, the number of As a leader receives generally decreases. Friends come and go, but enemies accumulate. Movement between *liked* and *disliked* lists tends to be on a one-way street; as a leader makes more decisions, more people place the leader on their *disliked* list.

At a midpoint in my career, I began identifying things I associated with exemplary leaders and labeled them "Keys to As." No doubt, as you review the set of keys on my leadership key chain and reflect on your leadership experiences, you will add and subtract keys.

ATTITUDE

Exemplary leadership begins and ends with attitude. Churchill said, "Attitude is a little thing that makes a big difference." Attitude matters! It matters a lot. It matters the most!

Many years ago, during an after-dinner speech, for the first time, I was heckled. After my speech, an Air Force officer approached me and said I should just ignore the heckler, who had seemingly overindulged during the cocktail hour. He said he asked the individual before dinner, "Which do you think is worse, ignorance or indifference?" The response was "I don't know, and I don't care."

I'm certain the Air Force officer made up the story, trying to ease my frustration. However, as I thought about his words, I concluded that indifference is much worse than ignorance. It is very difficult to deal with people who have a bad attitude. If they are ignorant, you can attempt to educate them. But if they are indifferent, what can you do?

In speaking to the leadership class, Greg Brown said, "Be an energy giver, not an energy taker." Attitudes are contagious. A person with a bad attitude is an energy taker. A person with a good attitude can light up the room.

I recall my father sharing the pleasure he had in teaching students who were eager to learn. I also recall him saying, "Working with a student who has a bad attitude and doesn't want to learn is no fun at all. It's like going bird hunting and having to carry the dog." Anytime I encounter someone with a bad attitude, I recall his words.

We can't control a lot of things in life, but we can control our attitude. Also, we can control our effort. Attitude and effort can be a powerful combination. Judith McKenna reminded the students, "You choose your attitude." Shelley Simpson said she was not a gifted athlete in high school, but she worked hard, won the hustle award, and became a starter on the team. She told the students, "One thing you can control is how hard you work."

While serving as assistant director of NSF, responsible for leading the Engineering Directorate, my attitude shifted from focusing on me to focusing on the nation. In our highly competitive and technologically savvy world, I realized the US couldn't compete with other countries if we depended solely on universities producing predominately white male engineering graduates. The need for increased participation of underrepresented minorities and women in engineering was critical and obvious.

In a lunch meeting with Erich Bloch, NSF's director and former IBM executive, we discussed the need to expand the nation's human resources in what has become known as STEM fields. When I requested an increase in the Engineering Directorate's budget, Erich reminded me that, if it's a priority, I shouldn't need new funds to pursue it. So, with a new attitude, I reduced the budgets of all but one of the engineering divisions in order to provide a 50 percent increase for the division having major responsibility for engineering education and human resources. The results exceeded my expectations.

The number of women and underrepresented minorities supported by the Engineering Directorate increased dramatically. Many became leaders in their universities.

ALIGNMENT

If a leader is unable to align people within an organization with its purpose, vision, mission, goals, objectives, strategies, tactics, core values, and other essential attributes, then the likelihood of achieving success is nil.

If tires on your vehicle are not aligned, you're in for a rough ride. The same holds if members of your leadership team are not aligned. Not only must individuals be aligned, but an organization's purpose must align with its vision, which must align with its mission. Likewise, an organization's tactics must align with its strategies, and they must align with its goals and objectives.

How do you achieve alignment? With John Wooden, as revealed in *Wooden on Leadership*, it included teaching his players how to put on their socks and how to tie their shoes. It began with the basics, and every practice focused on fundamentals. As best he could, Wooden left nothing to chance.

John White III used the book *Extreme Ownership* by Jocko Willink and Leif Babin as a vehicle to achieve alignment by striving to have everyone at Fortna take ownership, to step up and take responsibility for achieving organizational success. Basically, he challenged each team member to commit to doing everything as perfectly as possible

Striving to achieve alignment will test your ability as a leader. Communication and repetition are essential. Letting people know what is expected of them comes first. In the end, if some individuals are incapable or unwilling to align, replacing them with people who are capable or will align becomes necessary. Jim Collins's metaphorical bus only has seats for people who are aligned with where the bus is going, aligned with the bus driver, and aligned with fellow passengers.

ACUMEN

A key to being an effective leader is being smart—not brilliant, but smart. Acumen means having the discernment to know when to make decisions and judgments. Correct timing is required for decisions and judgments to be good. Making quick decisions and judgments isn't a necessary condition for acumen; having the ability to make qood, quick decisions and judgments is. Leaders often make decisions and judgments too quickly or too slowly; knowing when to decide is evidence of acumen.

ASPIRATION

For as long as I can remember, I've aspired to be what Frank Broyles called "a difference maker." In my high school commencement address, I used the following quotation from Henry David Thoreau's *Walden*:

"If you have built castles in the air, your work need not be lost; that is where they should be. Now put the foundations under them." Years later, in reading *Good to Great*, I understood immediately what Jim Collins meant when he described BHAGs (big, hairy, audacious goals). They were Thoreau's castles in the air.

When she met with the leadership class, Mary Pat McCarthy challenged the students to excel, to run toward opportunities, not away from them, reminding them, "We did not raise the bar for you to run under it." Effective leaders raise the bar; they don't lower it.

I set stretch goals for organizations I led and for myself. We didn't achieve all of them, but I believe greater progress resulted from striving to achieve them than would have resulted from mediocre goals. In an *Arkansas Democrat-Gazette* profile about me, Cyd King included a quote from one of my Georgia Tech colleagues: "'John White is very demanding. He sets very high goals and he expects everybody including himself to achieve those goals.'" King wrote, "White has been described as a change agent obsessed with turning the state's flagship campus into a nationally ranked research institution. His oft-stated goal has been the cornerstone of his administration and has, at times, drawn ire from others across the state."

During my years at Georgia Tech, I became a fan of Lewis Grizzard, a writer for the *Atlanta Journal-Constitution*, who wrote numerous books filled with humor and wisdom. His books always had eye-catching titles, my favorite of which is *Shoot Low, Boys—They're Ridin' Shetland Ponies*. Too many leaders aim too low. I aimed high. I raised the bar. I set BHAGs. I built castles in the air.

My greatest challenge as a leader was changing attitudes and expectations. I was usually in a position of leadership for a very good organization. Indeed, many in the organization and several members of the governing board believed the organization was "good enough," so changes weren't needed. I knew we could do better.

Although several of my associates thought I was a perfectionist, I explained: "I'm often pleased, but never satisfied." It's the curse of being an industrial engineer; I know there is always a better way. I believe when you expect more from people, you get more. To continuously improve, I needed to raise the level of my expectations and the level of expectations of people I led.

One of my BHAGs for the University of Arkansas was to raise a billion dollars in a campaign for private support. Based on my years at Georgia Tech, Ohio State, and Virginia Tech, I knew Arkansas needed to raise the bar significantly in securing private support. Excluding athletics, the university typically raised between $10 million and $15 million each year. Based on the challenges we faced, we needed to raise $100 million annually. The UA's endowment was $119 million when I arrived in 1997; it needed to be $1 billion. We needed to shift the decimal point one place to the right in annual giving and the endowment.

Other than Mary Lib, only David Gearhart, vice chancellor for university advancement, knew I believed we needed to mount a billion-dollar development campaign. In recruiting Gearhart, we met for dinner in Crystal City, Virginia. Attempting to persuade him to join me, I shared my BHAG. Many years later, Gearhart shared that, following our meeting, he told Jane, his wife, that he loved my optimism, passion, and vision for the university, but that I was crazy: I believed we could raise a billion dollars at Arkansas. Gearhart shared this story with the UA campaign steering committee when we achieved my BHAG.

Just before going into a meeting on the UA campus for the board of trustees to vote on my appointment to be chancellor, a reporter from *The Arkansas Traveler*, the student-run newspaper, asked if she could interview me. I agreed but said I had limited time because the trustees were waiting.

She asked, "What's the first thing you're going to change as chancellor?"

I quickly responded, "I'm not going to change anything, but *we're* going to change a lot, and we're going to start with attitudes and expectations."

I knew this would be my greatest challenge because UA was viewed widely as the best university in the state. However, my aspiration for the university was much greater than just being the best in the state.

In my first meeting as dean with Georgia Tech's engineering faculty, after discussing my goals and aspirations for the college, I shared several things that bugged me. For example, it really bugged me when alumni, faculty, and students proudly proclaimed Georgia Tech was the best engineering program in the South. After reminding them Georgia Tech's bookstore sold T-shirts stating, "Georgia Tech, MIT of the South," I said I wouldn't be satisfied until I saw T-shirts in MIT's bookstore stating, "MIT, Georgia Tech of the North."

At Georgia Tech and Arkansas, I worked to elevate aspirations within the faculty by differentiating and associating. Specifically, at Georgia Tech, we benchmarked against the best US engineering programs, instead of regional engineering programs; at Arkansas, we benchmarked against the best public universities in the nation, not the state. Too many people were shooting low because they thought competitors were ridin' Shetland ponies. Furthermore, in Arkansas, the aspiration adjustment needed to go well beyond the UA faculty. It needed to include alumni, trustees, governmental leaders, public and private high school administrators, guidance counselors and teachers, as well as members of the media and the general public. We had to overcome an "It was good enough for me, so it's good enough for mine" attitude that existed with too many people within the state.

Finally, as important as it is for a leader to have aspirations, it is far more important for the leader's aspirations to be for the team, not the leader. My goal was to be the leader of the best team, not the best leader of a team. The focus must be on the team, not the leader. Judgments of leadership quality must be based on team performance, not a leader's performance.

AMBITION

You may well ask, "Isn't ambition the same as aspiration?" They're close cousins, perhaps even opposite sides of the same coin, but they're not identical twins. Consider the following differentiation:

"Aspiration is what you hope to do in life, but it is the ambition that drives you to work hard to achieve that goal."[1] If aspiration is included in a leader's list of strengths, most people consider it a good thing. However, if a leader claims to be ambitious, some people often react negatively to the claim.

Despite what Brutus tries to convey about Caesar in *Julius Caesar*, being ambitious is a good thing. Wouldn't you prefer to be led by someone with ambition than someone without it? If overdone, ambition can turn into greed, arrogance, pomposity, and selfishness. But what if the person's ambition is for the people being led to be immensely successful? Wouldn't you want such an ambitious person to lead you? What if the leader's ambition is for the team to be the best it can be? I believe ambition is a good thing so long as *best* is measured by the team's success. As with aspiration, what matters with ambition is the target of the leader's ambition and how it's manifested.

Strive to be the best leader you can be. Remove *I*, *me*, and *my* from your vocabulary and replace them with *we*, *us*, and *our*. Be a servant leader, not a leader to be served. Be a *selfless* leader, not a *selfish* leader.

AVAILABILITY

Journalist, biographer, and historian Richard Brookhiser said in *George Washington on Leadership*, "One hundred percent of leadership is showing up—at the necessary moments." Being there at critical moments matters. Soon after my arrival as chancellor, Frank Broyles, in his heavy Georgia accent said, "Chancellor, weddings are optional, but funerals are mandatory." He told me one of his major donors died and the funeral service was on Saturday afternoon. Broyles was unable to attend the funeral, because he was contracted to be the color analyst with play-by-play announcer Keith Jackson for an ABC network televised broadcast of a football game on the West Coast. "The family never forgave me," Broyles said. Following his advice, I attended many funerals while serving as UA chancellor. When a prior commitment prevented me doing so, Mary Lib attended and expressed my condolences to the family members.

ACCOUNTABILITY

Leaders must be accountable. Although a leader can delegate authority to others, accountability cannot be delegated. President Truman is remembered for having a sign on his desk stating, "The buck stops here." He also said, "If you can't stand the heat, you'd better get out of the kitchen." Churchill rightly noted, "The price of greatness is responsibility." Accountability accompanies responsibility.

Nothing demoralizes a team more than having a leader refuse to be accountable.

The adage "When the going gets tough, the tough get going" was demonstrated over and over during the COVID-19 pandemic. Too many leaders ducked, danced, blamed, and pointed fingers. Too few took responsibility. A separation of the wheat from the chaff occurred when the going got tough.

As a leader, it's important to remember what Chris Lofgren told the students in the leadership class, "Managers hold people accountable. Leaders create an environment in which people hold themselves accountable."

One of the most powerful things a leader can do is apologize. In *What Got You Here Won't Get You There*, Marshall Goldsmith identifies twenty habits standing in the way of a leader achieving greatness; the seventeenth habit is refusing to express regret. Goldsmith devotes a chapter to the subject of apologizing and calls it his "magic move."

Apologizing is the ultimate demonstration of accountability. Controversy followed soon after the earliest shipments of Pfizer's coronavirus vaccine went out. The controversy had nothing to do with the virus but with its availability. States weren't getting the amounts they expected. After two days of piling on by media and state officials, four-star Army General Gustave Perna, who oversaw distribution efforts, took full responsibility for the miscommunication that resulted in states not receiving their full allocation of doses. Perna said, "I want to assure everybody, and I want to take personal responsibility for the miscommunication. I know that's not done much these days, but I am responsible." Perna took responsibility for mistakes made by others. Why? He was the leader of the effort. He was accountable. He apologized.

ALLOCATION

Time management is a major challenge for leaders. Too few realize time is both a leader's most valuable resource and the leader's scarcest resource. In reading this sentence, time passed; it can never be regained. My goal is to ensure the time you invest in reading this book yields an awesome return on your investment.

Many people spend their time; too few invest it. Leaders must invest it, and they must invest it wisely. However, before they can do so, they need to know how they spend it as well. If detailed records were kept, leaders would be astonished at how little time is spent leading versus on ceremonial, urgent but unimportant, and trivial matters.

If you're not careful, you'll find yourself playing Whac-A-Mole. As soon as you complete one task, three more will appear on your to-do list. The number of people adding to your list will grow exponentially over time. As a result, many times, you'll feel like screaming, "Time-out!" However, time is flying by. There is no stopping it. There are no time-outs in leadership. It is 24/7/365.25.

So, how do you maximize the return on your investment of time? First, you must be disciplined and learn when and how to decline invitations and requests. Warren Buffett said in an article for *Yahoo! Finance*, "The difference between successful people and really successful people is that really successful people say 'no' to almost everything." The adage "No good deed goes unpunished" applies to how you allocate your time. If, at the outset, you are available to meet with everyone, then when you learn to say no, you'll come across as inconsistent, insensitive, and insincere.

In addition to declining invitations and requests, limit the length of meetings; otherwise, they will last longer than you can afford. The Pareto principle applies: 80 percent of what is accomplished occurs in the first 20 percent of the meeting. Schedule meetings for 15 minutes, and, where possible, don't sit down. (This is an instance of "Do what I write, not what I did." In retrospect, I could've accomplished far more if I'd managed better the length of meetings.) Also, having a gatekeeper is crucial; have someone interrupt you and let you and your visitors know you have another appointment.

Another way to maximize the return on your investment of time is to change your attitude. If anything on your to-do list is also on your have-to-do list, follow Greg Brown's advice to the leadership class and change the way you think about it. Think of your have-to-do list as a get-to-do list. Appreciate the opportunity you have to lead; step back, and recognize what you get to do as a leader.

In addition to being disciplined, be mindful of the breadth and depth of your responsibilities. According to Sample's formula for leadership in *The Contrarian's Guide to Leadership,* 30 percent of a leader's effort is devoted to important matters, and 70 percent is spent "reacting to or presiding over trivial, routine, or ephemeral matters." Showing up is important. However, be careful, or you'll have no time for showing up and doing the really important 30 percent, which includes independent thinking, inspiring followers, reading, writing, and reflecting.

Importantly, within Sample's 30 percent is time spent with individual members of your executive team. Lincoln was adept at doing so, according to Doris Kearns Goodwin's *Leadership in Turbulent Times.* To avoid the specter of favoritism, he spent time with each individual member of his administration.

Remember, when you prepare a to-do list, don't forget to prepare a don't-do list. You'll be asked, pressured, or expected to do numerous things you shouldn't do. You cannot continue adding things to your to-do list; be disciplined, and remove things from the list. The shorter your list, the more effective you'll be. Major in the majors, not the minors.

Recall the Eisenhower matrix from Dickerson's *The Hardest Job in the World*. Eisenhower believed "the urgent should not crowd out the important. The matrix helps everyone sort priorities, the most important process in any organization."

Finally, to maximize your productivity, you must control the agendas. Don't let agendas control you, and don't let others set the agendas. I refer to two kinds of agendas: open and hidden. An example of an open agenda is a published agenda for a meeting; a hidden agenda is what people bring when they attend the meeting. One reason leadership can be lonely is a leader never knows with certainty what each person's hidden agenda is. Very few people's agenda is making the team successful; instead, their agendas tend to be self-serving. Never go into a meeting without providing a copy of the agenda to every attendee.

Know your priorities, and stick to them until conditions change, then revise the priorities. This requires discipline—tough-minded, stubborn, persistent discipline.

AFFIRMATION

Teddy Roosevelt is credited with saying, "Nobody cares how much you know until they know how much you care." Caring for the people you lead and affirming their importance and value to you, the team, and the organization are keys to being an exemplary leader.

Leaders not only can but must affirm followers. As Lou Tice notes in *Smart Talk for*

Achieving Your Potential, "Every good leader is a genius at positively affirming other people."

When Walmart's former senior vice chairman Don Soderquist met with the leadership class, he said that a defining moment for him professionally was when Walmart's chairman and CEO, Sam Walton, told him he was extraordinary. Chris Lofgren reinforced Soderquist's comment by telling the students, "Nothing is more powerful than someone believing in you."

Jeff Long said his high school football coach saw something in him he didn't know he had, reminding him of the importance of having someone see in you an ability you don't see in yourself. Pam McGinnis delivered a similar message; she told the students a high school guidance counselor encouraged her to go to college, something McGinnis had given no thought to doing.

General Marty Steele emphasized the need for leaders to be affirming. He said it's important to convey to your followers that they "really do make a difference." He instilled this attitude in his troops. His number-one rule was that his people were not allowed to publicly say anything untoward about a fellow soldier, sailor, airman, or marine, even in jest, because of the need for intrinsic trust and confidence required of his men and women. He wanted his team members to have each other's back all the time and everywhere, not just in combat situations.

While serving as NSF's assistant director, I wanted people in the Engineering Directorate to know I cared for them. Each week, I stopped at a nearby Hallmark shop and purchased birthday cards for each person having a birthday in the coming week. I wrote a small note in each card, thanking the person for everything he or she was doing for me, NSF, and the nation. It was a little thing, but I wanted people to know I knew what they did and I cared.

At the end of my three-year appointment, NSF held a reception for me. Everyone in the Engineering Directorate was invited to stop by for refreshments and to wish me farewell. I'm sure there were some speeches, and I probably spoke about how much my time working with them meant to me, because those three years were the most impactful years of my professional career. However, what I remember about the occasion is not what I said or what people said about me. Instead, it was what happened as people drifted out of the room.

Three women were huddled together; two were consoling a colleague who was crying. When I went over to speak to them, the woman who had been crying looked up at me and said, "Oh, Dr. White, I'm going to miss you so much." I quickly assured her that I knew my successor was going to do a terrific job. She said, "Dr. White, you don't understand. You are the only person who ever gave me a birthday card. I have all three of them pinned on the wall in my cubicle."

Little things mean a lot! *Sic parvis magna* (great things from little things come)! My son must have picked up on this, because he told the students in the leadership class, "Focus on the little things." Judith McKenna told the students, "What really matters to people are the tiny noticeable things that happen every day." She said TNTs—tiny noticeable things—can be powerful!

When Mary Lib was in Washington Regional Hospital for a pacemaker and defibrillator implant, a young man walked into her hospital room and introduced himself to us. He said, "Chancellor White, you won't remember me, but when I was a UA student, you stopped one day when it was raining and gave me a ride to my class."

"Oh, yes," I interrupted. "I remember picking you up near Razorback Stadium. I tried to get you to put your backpack in the back seat, but you insisted on placing it on the floor at your feet. I took you to Bell Engineering Center."

He told us that, after graduating in electrical engineering, he'd accepted a position with Medtronic, in Tulsa, but was recently transferred to the VA Hospital in Fayetteville. When he saw my wife's name on the list of people scheduled for a Medtronic implant, he asked if he could do it, because of what I did for him that rainy morning. A few years later, Mary Lib had to have the device replaced, and there he was again. He said, "As long as I am working here, you can count on me to take care of Mrs. White."

These examples weren't big deals to me, but they were for the people on the receiving end. Little things mean a lot. Affirmation matters!

It's important for leaders to affirm their followers, but it's also important for leaders to engage in self-affirmation. In *Personal Coaching for Results: How to Mentor and Inspire Others to Amazing Growth,* Lou Tice notes, "To affirm something means to literally make it firm, solid, more real. Through repetition, what you think becomes a belief, beliefs become behaviors," and as Tice notes, "Behaviors create experiences and results."

ANTICIPATION

During a leader's 30 percent, time must be spent anticipating coming challenges and opportunities. Chris Lofgren told the leadership class that a leader needs to see around corners. A significant fraction of my 30 percent was spent thinking about the future and what changes and opportunities might be available. In general, leaders don't like surprises. They must anticipate.

An important aspect of anticipation for a leader is visioning, looking ahead. Then, what the leader anticipates is converted into a mental picture of what the future will look like for the organization. Judith McKenna reminded the students they need to look farther than one step ahead; they should anticipate the second bounce of the ball, the result of the result. Every action causes a reaction. What'll be the reaction to a leader's action? Anticipate!

Anticipating the second bounce of the ball can limit unintended consequences accompanying decisions. Indeed, because unintended consequences occur so frequently, the phenomenon led to the law of unintended consequences. A highly visible example was provided by an NCAA decision. Guidelines regarding athletic eligibility of athletes who transfer to another university were changed dramatically. The motivation for the rule change was very logical: A freshman football player arrives at a university and realizes it's not a good fit. The old rule required the player to sit out a year after transferring. So the rule was changed to allow a football player who hadn't played in more than four games to be eligible to play for another school the following year.

The unintended consequence? The guideline didn't limit transfers to freshmen. Following the fourth game of the season, because Clemson's starting quarterback from the previous season was no longer the starting quarterback, he announced he was transferring. He was neither a freshman nor a sophomore; after transferring to the University of Missouri, he had only one year of eligibility remaining. If loopholes exist, people (athletes and coaches) will find them.

It didn't take long after the student-transfer genie left the bottle for the guideline to be expanded to allow any student athlete to transfer one time without penalty. The transfer portal produced fundamental changes in recruiting and retention. Several Hall of Fame coaches opted to retire rather than deal with the turbulence created by the transfer portal.

Conspiracy theorists believed the consequence of the initial change in the student-athlete transfer guideline was intentional, an initial step to provide greater flexibility for student athletes in order to circumvent efforts by some to pay them salaries. Just as the transfer portal had significant unintended consequences, the compensation of student athletes for use of their name, identity, and likeness (NIL) is having significant unintended consequences on intercollegiate athletics.

But there is more to anticipation than looking for opportunities presented by changes and having feelings of foreboding while preparing for future problems. A. A. Milne's Pooh Bear nailed it: "'Well,' said Pooh, 'what I like best,' and then he had to stop and think. Because although eating honey was a very good thing to do, there was a moment just before you began to eat it which was better than when you were, but he didn't know what it was called." Although Pooh didn't know what to call it, we do: anticipation.

AWARENESS

When I taught engineering economic analysis, I made index cards available for the students to provide feedback on the lectures. I asked them to write the most important thing they learned during the class session on one side of the card and to use the other side of the card for any questions they wanted me to answer. I said the first 10 minutes of the class were theirs, and I would respond to their questions.

Typically, after two or three class meetings, none of the questions related to course content. Instead, they related to life. The students asked whether I was married, how I met my wife, whether I have children, what kind of car did I drive, whether I was a Democrat or Republican, how much money I made, where I purchased my suits, how many ties I owned, what they should wear when they go for a job interview, and so forth. Because the students were so interested in hearing answers to their questions, few were late in arriving to class. The questions also gave me an opportunity to provide fatherly—or grandfatherly—advice. Importantly, they made me aware of what was on the students' minds.

In addition to being aware of the needs and challenges facing their followers, leaders need to be self-aware. They need to know their strengths and weaknesses, as well as their values. Jeff Long reminded the students, "It's really important to take time to know who you are as a person, what you stand for, and what you don't stand for."

Greg Brown told them, "Check your ego at the door. Life is not linear. You must adapt to changes in life. You have to believe in yourself. If you don't, why should anyone else believe in you? It's the tough days that define you, not the good days. It's not what happens to you that matters; it's how you respond to it."

Pam McGinnis said, "You have to be self-aware. You're only going to be great if you know yourself." She advised the students to "Be conscious of how you come across" to other people. She said, "Be who you are."

While on Virginia Tech's faculty, after attending a conference in New Orleans, I was on a Delta flight to Atlanta, connecting with a flight to Roanoke. I was seated in the center seat; occupying the aisle seat was the current world's number-one-ranked handball player. During our conversation, he asked if I played handball. I told him I didn't because of a reoccurring dislocation of my left shoulder, but I played racquetball. Then, he gave me three pieces of advice. First, play with people better than I am, because it'd improve my game. Second, play to my strength, which is probably my forehand; don't try to make my backhand as strong as my forehand, because it'll weaken my forehand. Third, hit every serve and shot to my opponent's weakness, which is usually their backhand.

After returning to campus, I played with one of my graduate students, who was a very good racquetball player. I had never won a game with him, but he was smart enough to let me think it was possible. So I decided to hit every serve and every return to his backhand. I won the first game. I couldn't believe it. I was ecstatic. During the second game, I was ahead 10 to 0 and did a baby lob serve to his backhand. He lost the point, smashed his racquet against the wall of the court, walked off, and never played with me again.

Little did I realize how much the handball player's advice would influence my leadership. In considering attitude, I mentioned how I used differentiation and association to elevate aspirations of faculty members at Georgia Tech and Arkansas. I was following the handball player's first piece of advice: Play with people better than you. He said it would make me better as a racquetball player; I believed using differentiation and association would make both universities better— and it did.

His second piece of advice served as a cornerstone for my leadership approach. Knowing my strengths and weaknesses, I assembled a team with people who were strong in areas where I was weak. To be successful, I had to be brutally honest about my strengths and weaknesses.

Knowing your strengths is not easily done. Peter F. Drucker notes in *The Effective Executive*, "Most people think they know what they are good at. They are usually wrong. More often, people know what they are not good at—and even then more people are wrong than right. But a person can perform only from strength. One cannot build performance on weaknesses, let alone on something one cannot do at all."

Judith McKenna reminded the students, "Every strength, overplayed, is a weakness." Persistence, if overplayed, becomes stubbornness. Being overly focused becomes being oblivious to what is going on around you. So play to your strengths, but don't overdo it.

I've used StrengthsFinder and the Myers–Briggs personality assessment tools to help me identify my strengths and weaknesses. Also, I've relied on feedback from individuals I've worked with, as well as friends and family members. Despite these attempts, I realize it's unlikely people will provide a totally accurate assessment, because it's impossible for anyone to be totally objective. Psychologists have learned that what we see is colored by our experiences.

Daniel Goleman's pioneering work identified five skills a person needs in order to have high emotional intelligence: self-awareness, self-regulation, empathy, social skills, and motivation.[2] To truly understand others, first you must understand yourself. Self-awareness is key to being an effective leader. Emotional intelligence (measured by your emotional quotient, EQ) must be coupled with intellectual or academic intelligence (intelligence quotient, IQ). However, if you have to sacrifice one, don't sacrifice EQ. Prioritize EQ over IQ, but don't opt for stupid. You don't have to be the smartest person in the room. In fact, it's better if you aren't. Surround yourself with people who are smarter than you.

Greg Brown reminded the students, "When you think you're the smartest person in the room, that's the beginning of the end." Pam McGinnis said something very similar, "The second you think you know everything, you're obsolete."

Shelley Simpson told the students to play to their strengths. She uses StrengthsFinder extensively. When she assembles a team to attack a problem, she attempts to ensure all varieties of strengths are represented on the team. She also makes sure people understand the strengths of the team members so they maximize the potential of playing to their strengths.

What about the handball player's third piece of advice? After the graduate student walked off the court, awareness caused me to conclude that winning a racquetball game was not as important as maintaining my relationship with the student. Only in unusual situations will I attack an opponent's weaknesses. Instead of attempting to make a sale by putting down the competition, I emphasized the strengths of our organization. However, at times, I couldn't resist pointing out improvement opportunities facing the competition.

ATTENTIVENESS

While I was awaiting my time to give an address in Munich, Germany, to a large group of IBM employees, the organizers showed a film. I didn't understand the German dialogue, and there were no subtitles; however, I quickly got the message. It began by showing a man's arm; the camera backed up and showed the man and a woman lying on a blanket; the camera moved back again and showed they were in a lakeside park in Chicago; the camera moved back and showed the United States; the camera moved back and showed the planet; the camera continued to move back ten thousand light years until Earth was an invisible spot in the universe. Then, the camera zoomed in quickly, showing pictures inside the man's arm, down to a distance of 0.1 fermi or 10^{-16} meters, to the smallest microscopic elements within a cell. The film, titled *Powers of Ten*, was developed by the Eames Office of Charles and Ray Eames.

Leaders must be attentive to details without losing sight of the big picture. Mike Duke likened his approach while serving as president and

CEO of Walmart to that of a pelican. A pelican flies along at a high altitude, then dives into the water to catch a fish. Mike said he usually flew at an altitude of forty thousand feet but occasionally dived into details about the business. Doing so lets people know you are paying attention and that you care about the details.

John Wooden emphasized to his players at UCLA the importance of paying attention to details and doing small things right. He notes, "talent alone won't get the job done. Talent must be nourished in an environment that demands the correct execution of relevant details." Wooden acknowledges in *Wooden: A Lifetime of Observations and Reflections on and off the Court* that his teams never achieved perfection, but they never stopped striving to achieve it. Even though they had perfect seasons, never losing a game, he claimed they never played a game perfectly. Still, his team tried to make each pass and each shot perfectly, to perform each play perfectly, and to play each game perfectly.

Being attentive means not only seeing things as they are, but also seeing how they can be. Leaders must listen using their eyes and their ears. Listening to the words and the words behind and between the words is essential. Listening for the unspoken words is also important. Reading body language while listening can communicate a very different message than simply listening.

Sample notes in *The Contrarian's Guide to Leadership*, "The average person suffers from three delusions: (1) that he is a good driver, (2) that he has a good sense of humor, and (3) that he is a good listener." Coleman Peterson told the students in the leadership class about a meeting he had with his first supervisor following his graduation from college. The supervisor attempted to tell Peterson he was not a good listener. Peterson interrupted the supervisor multiple times, arguing he was a very good listener. From this experience, Peterson learned the importance of being an active listener. Subsequently, he listened carefully, then repeated what he heard. He said it made a big difference in his ability to communicate. Being attentive matters.

ALERTNESS

Alertness is a not-so-distant cousin of awareness and attentiveness. Awareness requires a leader to have a high-altitude view of the organization; attentiveness requires a low-altitude view; alertness, on the other hand, requires a leader to think quickly. John Wooden noted, "What all our teams had in common was not height, but quickness—physical quickness, of course, but also something of equal value: mental quickness—that is, alertness." Alertness, the ability to be constantly observing, absorbing, and learning from what's going on around you, is a critical component for the individual in charge, the leader who strives for continuous improvement.

To be alert, leaders must evaluate themselves and their competitors. They must assess accurately their strengths and weaknesses, as well as those of the competitors. They must be alert to changes in the arena within which they operate and look for opportunities to adapt and apply innovations occurring in other arenas.

Leaders must pay attention to what is happening inside as well as outside their organizations. Of the two, perhaps the latter is more important. Based on the number of businesses declaring bankruptcy, many leaders failed to either see an impending change or refused to believe the change would impact them.

Wooden believed leaders who possess the value of alertness "constantly monitor the competitive landscape and are quick to identify trends, changes, opportunities, and potential threats." He noted that they see what competitors miss because they're constantly alert, on guard, looking for signals of a need to adjust, to make changes in real time. He writes, "They are quick to see weaknesses in their organization and correct them and quick to see a weakness in the competition and take advantage of it."

ASSERTIVENESS

Because leadership is highly situational and contingent, there will be situations when assertiveness is required.

The Mayo Clinic shared the following regarding assertiveness on its website: "Being assertive is a core communication skill. Being assertive means that you express yourself effectively and stand up for your point of view, while also respecting the rights and beliefs of others.

"Being assertive can also help boost your self-esteem and earn others' respect. This can help with stress management, especially if you tend to take on too many responsibilities because you have a hard time saying no."

To be sure, there are good and bad kinds of assertiveness, just as there are good and bad BHAGs. Mathematicians use different approaches in proving mathematical theorems, including direct proofs, proofs by induction, and proofs by contradiction. Similarly, leaders employ proof techniques to support positions they take, including using data and independent experts. However, some leaders use proof by assertion ("It's true because I say it is!") and proof by intimidation ("Agree with me, or else!"). I place the latter approaches in the category of bad kinds of assertiveness.

There is a difference between being assertive and being aggressive. However, there are times when a leader will need to be aggressive, to keep the pressure on. Carville and Begala note in *Buck Up, Suck Up . . . and Come Back When You Foul Up*, "Ronald Reagan was the master of being aggressive without being unpleasant."

They also note that Newton's first law of motion applies to people as well as objects. "Our goal was to overcome the inertia of analysis, put bodies in motion and make it incumbent upon those who wanted to stop that motion to offer a powerful rationale to do so."

Noting people are less inclined to be aggressive because they don't want be offensive, Carville and Begala argue for people risking being considered offensive in order to get things done, to be successful. If you do so and don't succeed, you'll know you did your best. They observe, "The time for thinking, for planning, for strategizing, is before the first punch is thrown. After that, whoever is more agile, mobile and (especially) hostile is the one who's going to walk away a winner." Better to be aggressive and fail than to be a wimp and never try.

AMBIGUITY

Ambiguity presents a paradox because it seems in some ways to be on the opposite end of the spectrum from assertiveness. Donald Smith told the leadership students that ambiguity breeds mediocrity and that clarity breeds excellence. My purpose in including ambiguity among the Keys to As is to call attention to the need for a leader to be able to deal with it. Few things in leadership are binary: right or wrong, black or white, or good or bad. If they were, others in the organization would have dealt with them. Decisions coming to you, in your leadership position, will often fall between the obvious extremes. As a result, qualitative rather than quantitative judgments will be required. Many of your decisions will be based on intuition and instinct, not data.

I come at this topic with considerable experience, having prided myself on being a data-driven decision-maker, but I'm not alone. Accountants, engineers, mathematicians, and scientists are among those who often have difficulty dealing with ambiguity. Their data-driven and fact-based academic training leaves little room for ambiguity. As a result, when in leadership positions, they soon learn they have to use different parts of their brains.

Bennis addresses left-brain and right-brain contrasts in *On Becoming a Leader:* Left brain implies logical, analytical, technical, controlled, conservative, and administrative; right brain implies intuitive, conceptual, synthesizing, and artistic. He notes that effective leaders need to be whole-brained, because leaders need to be both intuitive and logical.

ACCURACY

Giving accurate information to your team members is critically important for a leader. It's not necessary for all information to be shared, but it'd be a huge mistake to give inaccurate information.

So is it better to be ambiguous or accurate? The answer, of course, depends on the situation. The issue is how much information to share, because once shared there is no controlling its distribution. Thomas Modly, acting Navy secretary, learned this lesson the hard way after firing Captain Brett Crozier from command of the USS *Theodore Roosevelt*. As reported in the *Wall Street Journal*, while addressing the aircraft carrier's crew over the ship's loudspeakers, Modly said Crozier was either naive or stupid for writing a letter regarding the spread of COVID-19 on the ship. Modly resigned after recordings of his remarks to the crew became public.

Admittedly, mistakes will occur regarding dissemination of information. However, if and when it occurs, corrections should be communicated immediately. Remember, your most precious asset is your reputation. Don't let your life's work in building your reputation be destroyed in the blink of a lie! Be accurate.

Churchill noted that a lie gets halfway around the world before truth gets its pants on. General Mattis adds in *Call Sign Chaos*, "In our age, a lie can get a thousand times around the world before the truth gets its pants on."

ADAPTABILITY

Not only must leaders lead in conditions of ambiguity, but they must also adapt to a rapidly changing world and they must do so quickly. Leaders must be adaptable and resilient. Wooden notes, "Adaptability is being able to adjust to any situation at any given time." Leaders cannot be rigid and inflexible. They must hold strong to their values. They must stand up and lead, especially when opposing, gale force winds are blowing in their faces. To paraphrase Thomas Paine, these are the times that try leaders' souls.

Doris Kearns Goodwin writes that Franklin Roosevelt's ability to "adapt to changing cir- cumstances, to alter his behavior and attitudes to suit new conditions, proved vital to his leadership success." She noted that during the banking crisis, Roosevelt's adaptability proved critical in fulfilling his promise to reform the banking industry and stock market. Roosevelt  was very adaptable. With him, everything could be changed. He believed changes and improvements could always occur, if necessary.

I recall an instance when Alan Sugg told me I needed to go along to get along. I replied, "I'm not a go along to get along person." I'm sure I didn't say it in the calm voice with which you read my response. However, as I reflected on what Sugg said, I realized he was right. I was being inflexible. And, in the grand scheme of things, it was on a very minor issue. I was majoring in the minors, instead of staying focused on my larger goal. I needed to pick my battles. I couldn't go to the mat on every area of difference if I was going to succeed in what I returned to my alma mater to accomplish. I had to decide if this was a hill worth dying on. Deciding it was not, I adapted, changed my posi- tion on the issue, and moved on to the next challenge.

Another dimension to being adaptable is being able to change from a "my way or the highway" leader to a leader who is willing to compromise. Learning half a loaf is better than nothing can lead to new opportunities for you as a leader and for your organization. Learning to adapt and to meet someone more than halfway can be effective in getting things done, as well as in elevating the level of respect followers have for you as their leader. It took me far longer to learn this than it should have. If I could turn back the clock, I would've been less intransigent. Too often, I failed to focus on the critical few and ignore the insignificant many.

ACCOMMODATION

Just as aspiration and ambition are close cousins, so are adaptation and accommodation. The accommodation key is intended to remind you to be inclusive, to welcome ideas, viewpoints, and personalities of all types. It's a reminder of the strength in diversity. Be accommodating; be inclusive; don't be divisive, dismissive, or patronizing.

The value of diversity has received considerable attention in recent decades. But many leaders have failed to recognize it. I find it puzzling that many view the world through such a narrow prism when it comes to forming teams; they prefer to have teams made up of individuals who look the same, think the same, believe the same, and act the same.

I'm not sure when I recognized the need to increase the participation of women and underrepresented minorities in engineering and science, but it occurred more than fifty years ago. I recall, in introducing me before I gave a presentation, Jane C. Ammons, a Georgia Tech professor, said, "John White was advocating having more women in engineering before it was cool to do so."

After being at the National Science Foundation and seeing demographic data for the US and other nations, I became known as an advocate for diversity, encouraging leaders to become more accommodating of differences in people as they assembled teams. My targeted audience was white males. I believed we had created the problem, so we needed to participate in solving it.

However, the need for accommodation extends beyond gender, race, and ethnicity. It includes accommodating different political views, geographies, personalities, strengths, and a host of other factors.

When Mike Duke set out to increase the number of women and minorities in executive positions in Walmart, a member of his executive team said he thought it would impact the company negatively. Duke responded by saying increasing diversity isn't a zero-sum game. By doing so, more opportunities will be available for everyone because it's not only the right thing to do but it's also the profitable thing to do.

He reminded the leadership team who Walmart's customers are, who makes the buying decisions for families, and how the face of Walmart needs to look like the face of the customer.

ASSOCIATION

How often have you heard, "Don't judge a book by its cover"? But don't you do so, over and over? We are quick to judge. In *Blink*, Malcolm Gladwell addressed the subject of quick judgments, documenting instances where experts do so very accurately, as well as instances where they don't. A more extensive treatment of the subject is found in Daniel Kahneman's *Thinking, Fast and Slow*.

Two aspects of association critically important for you as a leader are to be selective about people you choose to associate with and to be careful about making judgments too quickly. Not only are books judged by their covers, but people are judged by those around them. As Lee Iacocca observes in *Where Have All the Leaders Gone?*, "You can tell a lot about a person by looking at who his friends are." In *It's Easier to Succeed than to Fail*, S. Truett Cathy advises, "Associate yourselves only with those people you can be proud of whether they work for you or you work for them." Who you hang out with sends messages; be aware of the messages you send.

An important element of association is networking. Making and maintaining connections proved to be instrumental in my professional career. While I thought I was good at networking, as noted earlier, my son puts me to shame. He is organized and intentional in building and sustaining his network. He stays in touch with people better than anyone I know. There is a reason people claim, "What you know and how much you know are not nearly as important as who you know."

ARBITRARINESS

Albeit infrequently, there are times when a leader must be arbitrary. Logic, reason, and wise counsel are ignored and the leader acts arbitrarily. It's not a "my way or the highway" approach; neither is it a "speak softly and carry a big stick" approach. Instead, it's an "I hear you and I understand where you are coming from, but this time we are going to do such and so" approach.

Coleman Peterson shared with the students an instance in which David Glass, Walmart's CEO, acted arbitrarily. All division heads were told to reduce their budgets by 5 percent. Peterson tried as hard as he could to get Glass to not force him to make the 5 percent budget cut. After listening to Peterson for what Glass surely thought was far too long, he told Peterson, "Sometimes you just have to be arbitrary. Make the reductions." As Oren Harari writes in *The Leadership Secrets of Colin Powell*, Powell said, "I only have to do so much compromising. There comes a time when I can just say, 'Do it!'"

AUTHENTICITY

In recent years, authenticity has become a necessary trait for exemplary leaders. Its synonyms include accuracy, correctness, credibility, legitimacy, purity, reliability, trustworthiness, truthfulness, and validity—but not transparency. But many who ask a leader to be transparent intend for the leader to be open about all matters. Asking for transparency is quite different from asking for authenticity. A plethora of situations exist where a leader cannot be transparent, but few, if any, where a leader cannot be authentic.

Chris Lofgren told the leadership students to be authentic. John White III said, "Be authentic, because people can see right through you." Pam McGinnis advised the students, "Remain true to yourself and be authentic."

Role models are important. Studying successful leaders and identifying best practices and traits is useful for emerging leaders. However, they should not attempt to copy someone else's leadership style or traits. After completing his doctorate and joining Motorola, Chris Lofgren met with Motorola's CEO, George M. C. Fisher. Lofgren asked Fisher what he needed to do to be successful as a leader. Fisher advised him to be himself. He said, "You can only be the second best someone else." Terrific advice. Be authentic. Be you!

ACTING

Tom Peters and Nancy Austin note in *A Passion for Excellence*, "All business is show business. All leadership is show business. All management is show business. That doesn't mean tap dancing; it means shaping values, symbolizing attention—and it is the opposite of 'administration' and, especially, 'professional management.'"

As Shakespeare wrote in *As You Like It*, "All the world's a stage, and all the men and women merely players." This applies especially to leaders. As a leader, you're playing a role, you're on stage. You must sound like, look like, and act like a leader.

Wait! Isn't being authentic and being a thespian a paradox? Yes, it is. Leaders must walk the tightrope. There will be times when you must be authentic and times when you must be a thespian and act as though everything is under control.

Bennis observes in *On Becoming a Leader*, "Leadership is not just a performing art, it may be the greatest performing art of all—the only one that creates institutions of lasting value, institutions that can endure long after the stars that envisioned them have left the theater."

There's another side to the acting coin—taking actions when needed. As Bennis notes, "For leaders, the test and the proof are always in the doing." Appropriate actions might include changing roles and responsibilities, personnel changes, and changing directions for the organization. Don't be stubborn and resist making changes when they are called for. The words of Will Rogers come to mind, "If you find yourself in a hole, stop digging." Change is an essential element of a leader acting like a leader. Leadership is not just role playing.

It's great to have wonderful ideas, but if they aren't converted into action, they are merely thoughts.

ACHIEVEMENT

In the end, you can possess all attributes of a grade-A leader, but you must achieve results; if you don't, your tenure as a leader will be limited. Vince Lombardi is credited with saying, "Some of us will do our jobs well and some will not, but we will be judged by only one thing—the result."

As children, we were taught that seeing is believing. However, over time, I realized the reverse is true: believing is seeing. As Alice said in *Alice through the Looking Glass*, "The only way to achieve the impossible is to believe it is possible."

Beliefs establish the ceiling for achievements. If you don't believe you can, you can't! What we think shapes our beliefs. Emphasizing the importance of self-talk, Tice observes in *Personal Coaching for Results*, "We think and act not in accordance with the real truth, but the truth as we believe it," and "Thoughts accumulate to build beliefs."

General Tony Zinni said in *Leading the Charge* that it isn't enough "for a true leader to be a strategic thinker. He must also be a strategic *doer*."

If you possess all attributes of a grade-A leader, results will follow. However, don't take them for granted. Keep your eye on the scoreboard to ensure results are occurring. If not, you need to act. Even more, you need to achieve. Actions without results are meaningless. As Chris Lofgren reminded the leadership students, "Effort is appreciated. Results are required."

In the end, a leader is measured on the achievements of the organization. The proof is in the pudding.

ADVERSITY

I suspect you didn't expect to find adversity included in Keys to As. To be sure, I don't believe you have to experience adversity to be an exemplary leader, but it is helpful if you have. If nothing else, it helps develop empathy. Interestingly, an amazing number of highly effective leaders dealt with adversity either prior to or during their periods of leadership.

It's not the particular adversity you face, but how you respond that matters. Some people let adversity be their excuse for failing to achieve their goals; others use adversity as motivation to achieve them. Generally, it's a choice people can make. As Greg Brown put it when meeting with the students, "When bad things happen, you have a choice. How you respond to adversity is up to you." He added, "It's not about the cards you're dealt, but how you play the hand. Sometimes you're dealt the five of clubs. Play the five of clubs to the best of your ability."

Lou Tice notes, "Every problem, every adversity contains, along with the prospect of pain and loss, the seeds of opportunity and the possibility of growth and gain. Some good can come from every bad situation."

Judith McKenna told the leadership students, "When disappointments come, you need to pick yourself up and dust yourself off." She reminded the students, "The only person who can lose your credibility is you."

As described by Bennis in *On Becoming a Leader*, Abigail Adams wrote to son John Quincy Adams in 1780, "It is not in the still calm of life or the repose of a pacific station that great characters are formed.... The habits of a vigorous mind are formed in contending with difficulty.

Great necessities call out great virtues." No doubt, the crucible of COVID-19 will also produce a generation of new leaders.

While serving as UA's athletics director in 2015, Jeff Long told the students in the leadership class that the best career strategy can be taking a step backward or what some consider a demotion in order to position yourself for a job you want to obtain. He also said fear of failure can provide motivation to succeed. I hired Long in 2008 to be UA's athletics director; in 2017, he was fired by my successor's successor and hired by Kansas in 2018 to be its athletics director. In 2021, following questions about a coach he hired, Long resigned. As have many involved in intercollegiate athletics, Long made several job changes in his career and was well qualified to advise the students on how to deal with adversity.

Greg Brown told the leadership students, "Adversity does not build character, but it reveals it." April 13, 1987, has special significance to Brown. It's the day his new boss at Ameritech said he didn't want him but was forced to hire him. Also, he learned his father had colon cancer, and he learned his wife, Anna, was pregnant. His delight in learning he would become a father was overshadowed by the double whammy of learning about his father's cancer and his situation at Ameritech. After talking with Anna and one of his brothers, Brown decided to stay the course, emerged from the adversity, and was very successful at Ameritech. In fact, his success led to major career moves, resulting in him landing at Motorola.

Not long after he did, Brown was promoted to president and CEO. The timing of his promotion could not have been worse insofar as the company's financial situation was concerned. Over a period of a month, Brown hardly slept, his weight plummeted, and he was on the verge of a mental breakdown. As mentioned previously, as he walked the floor wondering what he could do, Anna reminded him that sixty thousand Motorolans were waiting for him to lead. Climbing out of the adversity pit, Brown summoned the strength and resolve to turn around the company and position it for tremendous success. (As a member of the board of directors, I observed firsthand what Brown accomplished.)

Although the adversities (and adversaries) I've faced pale in comparison with what many have faced, one instance comes to mind: Why I was rejected by every graduate school I applied to while employed by Tennessee Eastman Company.

Because of a fateful fishing trip on February 23, 1963, I was employed as an instructor by the Department of Industrial Engineering at Virginia Tech. When I accessed student files to retrieve the file of a student in my course, I accidentally retrieved my file. In it was a letter from the acting department head at the University of Arkansas; he responded to all queries from universities to which I applied for admission to their graduate program. His letter stated, in no uncertain terms, I should not be admitted because I "would be a cancer" and "would destroy student and faculty morale," among other things.

Of course, the letter didn't share the rest of the story! When the professor taught engineering statistics, he said the first test would be closed book, open tables, and nothing could be written in the tables. During the test, he examined each student's book. When the tests were returned, my paper had a grade of 80, which was marked through and replaced with a 60. After class, I asked why he deducted 20 points. He said I had cheated because I had something in my tables. I objected and told him I looked at the tables before the test, and I had not entered any notes. When he refused to believe me, I left his office, retrieved my book, and came back to show him the only thing in my tables was a cartoon character I had doodled weeks before the first test. He refused to look at the book and said it didn't matter what it was, because he said nothing could be written in the tables. When I said, "That's not fair," he responded, "Get out of my office!" I met with the department head and complained about what I considered unfair treatment. I received a grade of C in the course.

The next semester, the same professor taught statistical quality control. I met with him before classes started and said I'd demonstrate I learned material covered in engineering statistics by making an A in his course. I had the second highest grade in the class and received a grade of B+. Pluses and minuses carried no weight in computing grade point averages.

Unfortunately, the same professor taught production planning and control the next semester. Like a dummy, I repeated my earlier claim that I would make an A in his course. It was a relatively small class, so I knew at the end of the semester my class average was 20 points above everyone's in the class. I received a grade of C for "poor professional attitude." I had no recourse because the department head was on sabbatical leave and the professor was acting department head. When I read his letter regarding my admission to graduate school, I decided to show him what I was capable of.

Following completion of my master's and doctoral degrees with an unblemished record and a rapid advancement within my profession, in 1983, as president-elect of the American Institute of Industrial Engineers, I was seated at the head table for the annual awards banquet. I saw my former professor approaching. I excused myself and stepped down to meet him. He said, "John, I'm so proud of you. I've always said you were one of my favorite students." I shook his hand, looked him in the eye, and said, "Professor _____, you've had a big impact on my life."

Until I taught Leadership Principles and Practices I didn't share with many people my story and the impact one professor had on me. However, when I shared it with the leadership students, I said they could let adversity define them or they could use adversity as motivation. I said they should not become victims. They should learn from adversity and move on.

ABILITY

Many would make ability the first Key to an A. However, I believe leadership ability is overemphasized. When I addressed entering freshmen and their parents at Georgia Tech in 1976 through 1980, I provided an abbreviated set of Keys to As. At the time, I had only three keys on my key ring: attitude, attendance, and ability.

I said that every student admitted to Georgia Tech had the ability to excel, but those who would perform the best were those with the best attitudes and those who went to class. Then, I said, "If you show up, go to class, and pay attention, you'll be fine. However, if you conclude you're so bright you don't have to go to class, you won't have to worry about it very long, because you won't be here." In closing, I said, "If you have a bad attitude and don't want to be here, you, too, won't have to worry about it very long, because you, too, won't be here. It's up to you. Have a positive attitude; believe you'll succeed. Go to class. You'll be successful, because you have the ability."

While on Georgia Tech's faculty, I received a letter from the mother of one of the freshmen in the audience when I shared my three Keys to As. She thanked me for doing so, because her son didn't have a high SAT score and was concerned about how successful he would be at Tech. He decided to attend every class with the attitude he would be successful. Bottom line: He excelled, graduated high in his class, and was very happy with his employment situation. Attitude and attendance trumped ability.

John Wooden noted, "Ability may get you to the top, but it takes character to keep you there." The philosopher Virgil claimed, "They are able because they think they are able." I am reminded of something Henry T. Ford said, "Whether you think you can or whether you think you can't, you're right!" It all comes down to attitude—the first leadership key.

CHAPTER 14

Final Reflections

During the eighteen months I devoted to writing this book, COVID-19 changed the world significantly. The changes brought greater challenges and exposed the lack of leadership skills among many leaders. It was challenging to distance myself from what was happening and focus on what leadership *should be*, rather than what leadership *was* for so many whose responsibilities were to lead. I didn't succeed, but I tried.

MY LEADERSHIP JOURNEY

In reflecting on my leadership journey, some days stick out more than others. I remember well my first day on the job as instructor at Virginia Tech, as assistant director of the National Science Foundation, as dean of engineering at Georgia Tech, and as chancellor at the University of Arkansas. All are memorable, but the latter is particularly so because of the role Arkansas governor Mike Huckabee played.

During the summer of 1997, he visited numerous state agencies, including colleges and universities, and worked for a day in some area of the organization. On July 1, 1997, he was on UA's campus, working in the Office of the Registrar. Because it would be my first day as chancellor, he greeted me at 8:00 a.m. with a copy of my student transcript. Fortunately, it was in a sealed envelope, and I was glad he hadn't opened it. If he had, he probably would have wondered about the wisdom of my selection to be chancellor.

After brief greetings and a photo op, I asked if he would join me for a private moment in my office. Governor Huckabee and I had met during the interview process and seemed to resonate. Knowing he had served as a minister prior to serving as lieutenant governor and governor, I asked if he would pray for my service as UA's chancellor. We kneeled in my office, and he prayed for me to have the wisdom, courage, humility, and strength to serve the State of Arkansas as UA's chancellor. I couldn't have asked for a better way to begin my leadership journey. Many times over the following eleven years, I recalled his prayer.

My leadership journey has been filled with numerous ups and downs. At times, I've felt like I had more than my share of disappointments, been lied to, been misled, and experienced more betrayals than was reasonable. Despite the heartaches and loneliness accompanying leadership, I stayed the course and plowed ahead, determined to be successful in achieving my goal of making a difference.

When asked by a leadership student what he'd change if he could do it over, Chris Lofgren responded he wouldn't change anything because his journey brought him to where he was. I share his feelings. Sure, there're many things I'd do differently. I made many mistakes, but they weren't life-changing or career-shaping things.

What grades would I assign myself as a leader? My leadership service at Georgia Tech and NSF, on corporate boards, on advisory boards, and in professional societies would receive grades of A– or better. However, my grades as chancellor would vary significantly, depending on the stakeholder. I believe my report card, based on eleven years serving as UA's chancellor, would be as follows:

- Alumni (A)

- Business leaders (A)

- Elected federal leaders (A–)

- Elected state leaders (C+)

- Faculty members (B+)

- Leaders of other colleges and universities (A)

- Media and press representatives (C–)

- Staff members (B+)

- Students (A–)

- Trustees (B+)

- University administrators (A–)

My biggest challenges, obviously, were dealing with the press and state legislators. The only reason my grade is a C+ with elected state leaders is my grade with governors, lieutenant governors, attorneys general, and heads of agencies was an A; otherwise, it'd probably be a C– or D+. The B+ grades from faculty members, staff members, and trustees, I believe, is the result of misaligned expectations of what a chancellor can accomplish; specifically, I don't believe they understood or appreciated the breadth of responsibilities of the CEO for a large public research university.

In general, I was fortunate to be governed by supportive trustees. The ten trustees who hired me were aligned with my goal of elevating the perception (and reality) of the University of Arkansas being a nationally competitive, student-centered, research university serving Arkansas and the world. Because trustees have ten-year terms, each year a new trustee joined the governing board. Consequently, when I was in my eleventh year as chancellor, not a single trustee had been involved in hiring me. Frankly, if they'd been trustees in 1997, I doubt a majority would have voted for me to be hired.

To illustrate the challenges I faced, I'll share two conversations I had with trustees appointed after I was hired. One said he didn't understand why we were awarding scholarships to the top students in the state instead of giving them to B and C students. He said the top students would leave the state following graduation, but the B and C students would remain in the state. I said the trustees who hired me wanted me to create opportunities within the state for A students to remain following graduation and, together with B and C students, create a brighter future for all Arkansans. I said what he was asking of me was akin to a football coach asking a pro-style, drop-back passing quarterback to run a wishbone offense. I said, if that's what they wanted, the trustees should hire a wishbone quarterback. His response was, "Maybe we should."

Another trustee appointed about halfway through my tenure as chancellor said he didn't understand why I continued to promote UA as a research university. He said we should focus on being an undergraduate university because "It was good enough for me, and it would be good enough for mine." Rendered speechless by his comment, it took a few minutes for me to say we'd have to agree to disagree because I was hired to strengthen UA as a research university, and I would continue doing so.

Zell Miller was Georgia's governor when I was appointed to be Georgia Tech's engineering dean. His Hope Scholarship Program and his priority to elevate the state's research universities provided resources for us to make significant strides in improving the quality and reputation of the College of Engineering.

While serving as UA's chancellor, I had strong support from Mike Huckabee and Mike Beebe, Arkansas's governors. (Beebe, while serving in the State Senate, chaired the 2010 Commission.) Importantly, during my eleven years, the state's economy was strong. My successors didn't benefit from a strong economy.

In retrospect, I should've worked with state legislators more effectively. Lewis Epley, chair of UA's trustees when I was hired, pointed out something in me I hadn't recognized. He said, "You don't suffer fools gladly." When I asked what he meant, he said I had difficulty listening to people who didn't have my education and experience when they were telling me how to do my job. He was correct. He likened my situation to a highly trained, specialized medical doctor who was told by a patient how to diagnose the patient's medical problem. I should've done a better job of listening, learning, loving, and leading.

Over my career, the chancellor position was the most challenging leadership position I held. Based on conversations with peers, I'm not the only one who believes leading a public university isn't a task for someone not committed fully to withstanding attacks and criticism from all quarters. However, many went into the position better prepared than I. The move from engineering dean to chancellor was almost a bridge too far. Through the support of Mary Lib, family members, my leadership team, President Sugg, Lewis Epley, fraternity brothers from my undergraduate years, and numerous prayer warriors, I was able to stay the course. Being an alumnus made all the difference. If I hadn't had such strong feelings about Arkansas and my alma mater, I would've shaken the dust off my shoes and moved on.

Perry Adkisson, former Texas A&M chancellor, contacted me several times, trying to persuade me to consider leaving Arkansas and joining him. Finally, I told him that even if he was authorized by the regents to offer me the position and I could name my price, no amount of money would cause me to leave Arkansas and go to Texas A&M. I assured him it had nothing to do with him or Texas A&M. I left Georgia Tech to return home. Were Arkansas not home, I would have remained at Georgia Tech. I told him I wasn't looking for a job. Being chancellor wasn't a job, it was a calling and I hadn't finished what I was called home to do. Adkisson thanked me and said he understood and wouldn't bother me again. True to his word, he didn't.

After two years in the job, John J. Jarvis, a former colleague from Georgia Tech, asked how I was faring. I said, "I don't have a very good handle on my job. What I thought would be hard has turned out to be easy and what I thought would be easy has turned out to be hard." When asked to explain, I responded, "I thought it'd be hard to recruit high-ability students in large numbers, but we spun that on a dime." Then, I said, "Actually, it was several million dollars." I continued, "What I thought would be easy was obtaining the support of state officials for our academic and research goals. It happened in other states: Arizona, California, Georgia, Massachusetts, Michigan, North Carolina, Texas, and Virginia. Convincing Arkansas legislators to place a high priority on achieving excellence in higher education has been really tough."

Unfortunately, it didn't get any easier over the remaining nine years. And it didn't get any easier for my successors; in fact, it was harder for them than for me. The trustees who hired me were far more supportive of what I came home to do than my successors' trustees, who appeared to not understand that their responsibilities did not include managing the university.

Frankly, I couldn't have played the hands my successors were dealt nearly as well as they did. In a battle between an irresistible force and an immovable object, the immovable object won—I believe to the detriment of the state.

Despite not being able to receive state support at levels required, we achieved more than I anticipated and transformed the University of Arkansas into a nationally competitive, student-centered research university serving Arkansas and the world. We exceeded others' expectations, and we exceeded mine. Remember, I'm often pleased, but never satisfied. But when I handed the reins to my successor in 2008, I knew the University of Arkansas was much stronger than it was in 1997.

My leadership journey has been a roller coaster ride. Just as Bob Buford described in *Halftime: Moving from Success to Significance*, while I was in my fifties, I stopped thinking about what I could do for me and started thinking about what I could do for others. I recall sitting in my office, knowing I'd achieved every professional goal I had for my career and wondering, "What's next?" I thought, "Isn't there more to life than winning awards?"

The change wasn't instantaneous, but I gradually came to realize what I wanted my legacy to be. Instead of my net worth being measured in dollars, I wanted it to be measured in the number of lives I impacted positively. I recognized I was in the business of changing lives. And I concluded the best way to have the greatest impact was through leadership and teaching. I also realized leadership and teaching are redundant: Teachers are leaders, and leaders are teachers.

My faith plays a dominant role in my life. I committed to strive every day to practice Proverbs 3:5–6: "Trust in the Lord with all your heart and lean not on your own understanding. In all your ways, acknowledge Him and He shall direct your paths." Career and leadership decisions, thereafter, were made after prayerfully seeking God's will.

When UA's president, Alan Sugg, contacted me in 1996, I genuinely didn't want to leave Georgia Tech and become UA's chancellor. In fact, my position on the matter didn't change until the evening following the first day of my interview on campus. That afternoon, a reception was held for Mary Lib and me at the Bank of Fayetteville. During the reception, a woman approached me and handed me a card on which the Easter services for University Baptist Church (UBC) were listed. After inviting me to visit UBC, she said thirteen women had been praying that God would bring a Christian to be UA's chancellor. She said they believed I was the answer to their prayer. I thanked her and said fifty people in Atlanta were praying I'd remain at Georgia Tech and be active in teaching their Sunday school class. I said all I wanted to do was what God wanted me to do and, laughing, I said I'd like for Him to make it very plain by writing it on a wall.

That evening, in the hotel, Mary Lib was in bed reading. I was standing in another room looking out the window. In the still of the night, I heard, "All your life has been preparing you for this job. This is what I want you to do."

I broke out in a cold sweat. It wasn't a whisper. The words were as loud as they'd be if you were standing next to me and repeated them. I went into the bedroom and asked Mary Lib, "Did you hear that?" She sat up in bed and asked, "What?" After I told her what I heard, I said we should consider UA's chancellor position differently during the second day of the interview. We did, and, as described elsewhere in the book, subsequent events led to my selection. A new journey began.

Many times, especially during the first three years of my chancellorship, I wondered if I'd heard correctly what the not-so-still voice said. So I followed Gideon's example in Judges 6:36–40 and laid out fleece twice for God to confirm what I should do. That "fleece" was in the form of job interviews at two universities. I asked God to make it clear what He wanted me to do. In both cases, I wasn't into the interview more than five minutes before realizing, "This isn't for me." Then, I notified the search consultant I was no longer interested in considering other positions.

Knowing I was supposed to finish the race, I engaged fully in pursuing UA's goals. When resistance occurred, I wasn't dissuaded. When obstacles appeared, we found a way around or over them. I was blessed to have a strong wife and leadership team, a supportive president, and unmatched friends and supporters during the balance of my chancellorship.

During the ups and downs of my leadership journey, countless times I wondered, "Is it worth it?" The sacrifices made and the demands of leadership exacted a high price. During my first three years as UA's chancellor, in the privacy of my closet, I shed more tears than I'd shed in previous or subsequent years of leading. But after reflecting on the entirety of the experience, I concluded I'd do it all over again—but better, much better.

Mary Lib's wisdom won the day. She was right when she said I would have regretted not becoming a candidate, and I don't regret doing so—not for a moment. The joys of the journey more than offset the pains. What an impact we had. Few are given the opportunity to make a difference in the lives of so many people. Following advice from the French theologian Hyacinthe Loyson, we planted trees whose shade we'll never sit in, but thousands will.

TIME WILL TELL

Time will tell how effective I've been as a leader. Judgments regarding my effectiveness will be made, not only by people I've led and people who observed my leadership but also by people not yet born. Such judgments are being made today about the nation's founding fathers. Their stances on the issue of slavery have raised questions regarding the legitimacy of their inclusion in the nation's Leadership Hall of Fame. Similar questions have been raised regarding past leaders because of their positions on civil rights.

Senator J. William Fulbright's legacy, defined by the Fulbright Scholars Program, his opposition to budget appropriations for Senator Joe McCarthy's communist witch-hunting committee, and his opposition to the Vietnam War are being questioned because he didn't exert leadership regarding civil rights. He signed the Southern Manifesto in 1956 denouncing the US Supreme Court's 1954 and 1955 school desegregation decisions. He filibustered against and voted against the landmark Civil Rights Act of 1964 and opposed the Voting Rights Act of 1965.

Among things carrying Fulbright's name at the University of Arkansas are the College of Arts and Sciences, named for him in 1981;

a forty-one-foot peace fountain dedicated in 1998; and a seven-foot bronze sculpture of Fulbright dedicated in 2002. I played a role with the peace fountain and statue, recommending the UA Board of Trustees approve their creation and placement on campus.

When President Clinton and I dedicated the Fulbright statue on October 21, 2002, I didn't anticipate that, eighteen years later, the statue would become controversial. Clinton, a Fulbright Scholar, was mentored by Fulbright. As president, Clinton awarded him the Presidential Medal of Freedom in 1993 and delivered the eulogy at his funeral two years later. "We owe a lot to Bill Fulbright, some of us more than others," Clinton said. "Let us all remember the life he lived and the example he set."

In the middle of the turmoil of 2020, protests on the UA campus focused on the College of Arts and Sciences being named for Fulbright and the statue. A UA campus committee appointed in September of 2020 by Chancellor Steinmetz recommended the statue be removed from campus and Fulbright's name stripped from the college. On May 27, 2021, Steinmetz recommended moving the statue to another location on campus and retaining Fulbright's name with the college. On July 28, 2021, following a recommendation by UA System President Donald Bobbitt, UA's board of trustees decided to keep the statue where it is.

On July 31, 2021, an editorial in the *Arkansas Democrat-Gazette* included the following: "Like most people of his era, or any era, [Fulbright] wasn't always right. And was found wanting as history unfolded. Which is something that'll probably be said about us all in the coming generations.

"'I think we ought to also remember that he was not only a complex man, but he was living in extremely difficult times,' said one board member. Which doesn't excuse J. William Fulbright's faults—or shouldn't. But better would be to explain the faults of those times."

This brings us back around to polarities which the world struggles in dealing with. In the US, the pandemic introduced the following: wear masks versus don't wear masks and be vaccinated versus do not be vaccinated. Just as repercussions of slavery have continued to live on in the US, it is likely repercussions of polarities manifested by the COVID-19 pandemic will live on for many years.

In perhaps the not-too-distant future, my role in approving the erection of the Fulbright Peace Fountain and the Fulbright statue on UA's campus could result in removal of my name from John A. White Jr. Engineering Hall. Given the swings of the pendulum, we cannot be sure where history will come down on naming buildings, statues, and cities for individuals who were all imperfect and simply striving to do the right thing at the time. Leadership is highly situational and contingent. Polarities are among the contingencies leaders face.

Where will history come down on today's leaders who took hard-line positions on either side of polarities associated with wearing masks and getting vaccinations? Time will tell!

If you're presented an opportunity to lead, remember Mary Lib's words: Have no regrets. Also, remember General Marty Steele's words: "Carpe diem! Seize the day!" Are the rewards of leadership worth its price? Lencioni notes in *The Advantage*, "At the end of the day, at the end of our careers, when we look back at the many initiatives that we poured ourselves into, few other activities will seem more worthy of our efforts and more impactful on the lives of others, than making our organizations healthy."

Heifetz and Linsky close *Leadership on the Line* with "Opportunities for leadership are available to you, and to us, every day. We believe the work has nobility and the benefits, for you and for those around you, are beyond measure. But putting yourself on the line is difficult work, for the dangers are real. . . . May you enjoy with a full heart the fruits of your labor. The world needs you." I can't state it better, so I won't try.

In reflecting on my leadership journey, I'm reminded of a Vince Lombardi quote, "After all the cheers have died down and the stadium is empty, after the headlines have been written, and after you are back in the quiet of your room and the championship ring has been placed on the dresser and after all the pomp and fanfare have faded, the endur-ing thing that is left is the dedication to doing with our lives the very best we can to make the world a better place in which to live."

If you haven't read *Halftime: Moving from Success to Significance*, I encourage you to do so. Not only did I receive and read the first edition, which has a foreword written by Peter Drucker, but also I received and read the second edition, which has a second foreword written by Jim Collins.

The preface to *Why It Matters* began with a Dilbert cartoon, so it seems only fitting to bring to closure our present discussion with another of Scott Adams' cartoons. This one depicts what leadership is not.

DILBERT © 2009 Scott Adams, Inc. Used by permission of Andrews McMeel Syndication. All rights reserved.

The students often said the leadership course was the most demanding and the best course they had taken and that it had changed their lives. My final offering of the course during fall semester of 2018 produced a different response from one student. He agreed it was the most demanding and best course he'd taken, but he claimed it didn't change his life. It *saved* it!

My purpose statement is taken from Paul's second letter to Timothy: "I have fought the good fight, I have finished the race, I have kept the faith." To it, I add, "I have made a difference." In assessing my leadership journey, I believe I've made a difference for organizations I've led. More importantly, I believe I've made a difference in the lives of people I've served and students I've taught.

Who could ask for or hope for more?

ADDITIONAL THOUGHTS

In reading *Why It Matters: Reflections on Practical Leadership*, you learned I love to read. Among the books I've enjoyed reading are what Steven Sample calls supertexts—those written more than four hundred years ago and are still being read. I enjoy reflecting on how writings that are hundreds of years old are applicable for today's leaders. At JohnAWhiteJr.com/ WhyItMatters, I share reflections on practical leadership principles provided in Sun Tzu's *The Art of War*, Xenophon's *The Education of Cyrus* and *The Expedition of Cyrus*, Machiavelli's *The Prince*, and eight plays by Shakespeare: *Hamlet, Othello, Julius Caesar, Henry V, Richard III, King Lear, Much Ado about Nothing*, and *All's Well that Ends Well*.

Finally, drawing on my experiences being governed by and serving on governing boards, on my website I share reflections on leadership challenges and responsibilities of governing boards for publicly traded corporations, higher education institutions, and nonprofit organizations.

Thank you for purchasing a copy of *Why It Matters*. Head over to my website (johnawhitejr. com/WhyItMatters/) and use the password "LeadershipMattersMore" to access exclusive content and bonus material such as leadership lessons provided by Sun Tzu, Xenophon, Machiavelli, and Shakespeare, my thoughts about challenges and responsibilities for governing boards, and much more.

From top to bottom:
Sun Tzu, Xenophon,
Machiavelli, Shakespeare.

Acknowledgments

Where to begin in acknowledging those who brought this book to fruition? At the beginning—with my parents, who modeled servant leadership for my sister and me, as well as everyone who worked with and knew them. As family members, friends, neighbors, and teachers, they served and led. They shaped me and molded me in ways I neither recognized nor appreciated until I left the nest and discovered I could fly.

Who could top that? Mary Elizabeth Quarles. Convincing her to marry me on April 13, 1963, is my greatest achievement. My best friend and the leader of our family, Mary Lib taught me much about servant leadership, always placing others before self—she models *selfless* leadership. Our children and grandchildren are evidence of her effectiveness.

If I listed all who shaped my views of leadership, it would more than double the book's length. Many are mentioned in it and in supplementary documents located on the website: https://JohnAWhiteJr. com/WhyItMatters. Fellow board members at Eastman Chemical, J. B. Hunt Transport Services, Logility, Motorola, Motorola Solutions, and Russell contributed significantly to my leadership journey; I benefited from working alongside outstanding leaders. To them I add people I worked with in churches and professional associations, because leading a nonprofit organization prepared me to lead leaders, especially faculty members. In addition to individuals who shaped my views of and equipped me for leadership, I call special attention to colleagues and members of my leadership team and support staff at Virginia Tech, Ohio State, Georgia Tech, SysteCon, the National

Science Foundation, and the University of Arkansas, whose support contributed significantly to my leadership journey.

I am also indebted to the thousands of individuals I led; these include people in administrative roles as well as students. I taught more than 4,000 students and learned much from them, but I call special attention to those enrolled in "Leadership Principles and Practices," the course that is the foundation for *Why It Matters: Reflections on Practical Leadership*. Without their encouragement and our shared learnings about leadership, the book would not have been written.

Dusty Higgins made significant contributions to the book. When I was UA's chancellor, he was an illustrator for *The Arkansas Traveler*, the student newspaper, and drew several cartoons featuring me. Now an art professor at the University of Arkansas at Little Rock, Dusty provided the beginning-of-chapter illustrations and the caricatures in the book and on my website.

Finally, the book. Greenleaf Book Group provided tremendous support and assistance. Writing engineering textbooks and professional papers is unlike writing a book like this. The support Greenleaf professionals provided was, in a word, *superb*. Specifically, I am indebted to Stephanie Bouchard, Jen Glynn, Amanda Marquette, Jessica Reyes, Daniel Sandoval, Lindsay Starr, and Aaron Teel for their expertise, experience, and patience.

Notes

CHAPTER 1

1. Joyce E. A. Russell, "Great Leaders Don't Pass the Buck," *Forbes*, September 26, 2020, https://www.forbes.com/sites/joyceearussell/2020/09/26/great-leaders-dont-pass-the-buck/?sh=41dc56a050f2.

2. Lee Iacocca, *Where Have All the Leaders Gone?* (Simon & Schuster, 2008), 137–145.

3. Herbert A. Simon, "Rational Decision Making in Business Organizations," *The American Economic Review*, vol. 69, no. 4, 1979, pp. 493–513.

CHAPTER 2

1. History.com, "David Farragut," A&E Television Networks, August 21, 2018, https://www.history.com/topics/american-civil-war/david-farragut.

CHAPTER 3

1. Ty Kiisel, "Without It, No Real Success Is Possible," *Forbes*, February 5, 2013, https://www.forbes.com/sites/tykiisel/2013/02/05/without-it-no-real-success-is-possible/?sh=1b91e907e491.

2. "Famous Quotes by Vince Lombardi," VinceLombardi.com, http://www.vincelombardi.com/quotes.html.

3. Stephen J. Adler, Jeff Mason, and Steve Holland, "Exclusive: Trump Says He Thought Being President Would Be Easier than His Old Life," *Reuters*, April 27, 2017.

CHAPTER 4

1. "James 1:19," *Holy Bible*, New International Version.

2. Jennifer Aaker, Victoria Chang, "Obama and the Power of Social Media and Technology," Stanford Business case study no. M321, 2009, https://www.gsb.stanford.edu/faculty-research/case-studies/obama-power-social-media-technology.

3. *LeadershipWWEB,* https://soundcloud.com/user-561194034/.

CHAPTER 5

1. Barton Swaim, "'Trust, but Verify': An Untrustworthy Political Phrase," *Washington Post,* March 11, 2016, https://www.washingtonpost.com/opinions/trust-but-verify-an-untrustworthy-political-phrase/2016/03/11/da32fb08-db3b-11e5-891a-4ed04f4213e8_story.html.

2. Frank Armstrong III, "Trust but Verify," *Forbes,* October 12, 2019, https://www.forbes.com/sites/frankarmstrong/2019/10/21/trust-but-verify/#3e4b384a5873.

3. Gardiner Morse, "Trust, but Verify," *Harvard Business Review,* May 2005, https://hbr.org/2005/05/trust-but-verify.

4. Geoff Colvin and Ryan Derousseau, "Tyson CEO's $3 Billion Decision," *Fortune,* November 22, 2016, https://fortune.com/2016/11/22/tyson-ceos-3-billion-decision.

5. Reed Hastings and Erin Meyer, *No Rules Rules: Netflix and the Culture of Reinvention* (Penguin Press, 2020).

6. Cyd King, "Always Raising the Bar: John Austin White Jr," *Arkansas Democrat-Gazette,* Sunday, October 28, 2001, pp. 1D, 4D.

7. Scott Dewing, "Just the Facts, Ma'am," Jefferson Public Radio, April 1, 2015, https://www.ijpr.org/science-technology/2015-04-01/just-the-facts-maam.

8. "Elementary, My Dear Watson," Quote Investigator, https://quoteinvestigator.com/2016/07/14/watson.

9. Arthur Conan Doyle, *The Sign of Four* (Spencer Blackett, 1890).

10. Arthur Conan Doyle, "The Boscombe Valley Mystery," *Strand Magazine,* October 1891.

CHAPTER 6

1. Thomas J. DeLong and Michael Kernish, "Alex Montana at ESH Manufacturing Co.," Harvard Business School Case 405–106, June 2005, revised May 2006.

2. Kendra Cherry, "The 6 Types of Basic Emotions and Their Effect on Human Behavior," Verywell Mind, https://www.verywellmind.com/an-overview-of-the-types-of-emotions -4163976#citation-11.

3. A. S. Cowen and D. Keltner, "Self-Report Captures 27 Distinct Categories of Emotion Bridged by Continuous Gradients," *Proceedings of the National*

Academy of Sciences, 2017, 114(38): E7900–E7909, https://doi.org/10.1073/pnas.1702247114, and Y. Anwar, "Emoji Fans Take Heart: Scientists Pinpoint 27 States of Emotion," *Berkeley News,* September 6, 2017.

4. Jason Aten, "Should You Be More Like Bezos?" *Inc.,* March–April 2021.

5. Seth Blomeley, "White Asks Panel to Forgive Remarks: Comments on Funding Were One of His Flaws, UA Chancellor Says," *Arkansas Democrat-Gazette,* August 11, 2000.

6. Maylon T. Rice, "Raising the Standards: UA Board of Trustees Approves New Academic Admission Policies," *Northwest Arkansas Times,* November 22, 1997.

CHAPTER 7

1. Charles Phillips, *Leadership in 100 Quotes* (Metro Books, 2018).

CHAPTER 9

1. Tim Layden, "Hog Fight: The Feud between Arkansas and Former Coach Nolan Richardson Is Personal—and Racial," *Sports Illustrated,* February 24, 2003, https://vault.si.com/vault/2003/02/24/hog-fight-the-feud-between-arkansas-and-former-coach-nolan-richardson-is-personaland-racial.

2. Associated Press, "Richardson Is Bought Out at Arkansas," *New York Times,* March 2, 2002, https://www.nytimes.com/2002/03/02/sports/college-basketball-richardson-is-bought-out-at-arkansas.html.

CHAPTER 11

1. Susan Moore, "Focus on Moments that Really Matter to Employees," Gartner, August 6, 2019, https://www.gartner.com/smarterwithgartner/focus-on-moments-that-really-matter-to-employees.

2. Minda Zetlin, "Amazon's New CEO Andy Jassy Says this 4 Word Lesson Is the Most Important He's Learned," *Inc.,* February 8, 2021.

CHAPTER 13

1. "Difference Between Ambition and Aspiration," DifferenceBetween.com, https://www.differencebetween.com/difference-between-ambition-and-vs-aspiration/.

2. Daniel Goleman, "What Makes a Leader," *Harvard Business Review,* vol. 82, 2004, pp. 82–91.

Index

About the Author

Over his career, John A. White Jr. held leadership positions in business, government, nonprofit organizations, and academia. The chancellor emeritus of the University of Arkansas and former dean of engineering at the Georgia Institute of Technology cofounded and led his own logistics consulting firm, SysteCon, Inc., which was acquired by Coopers & Lybrand, and held leadership positions on the boards of directors for Eastman Chemical Company, J. B. Hunt Transport Services, Logility, Motorola, Motorola Solutions, Russell, and the National Collegiate Athletic Association.

Elected to membership in the National Academy of Engineering in 1987, John was appointed by President Clinton to serve two six-year terms on the National Science Board, the governing board for the National Science Foundation, where he spent three years leading the Engineering Directorate.

He served as president of the Institute of Industrial Engineers, chairman of the American Association of Engineering Societies, president of the Foundation for the Malcolm Baldrige National Quality Award, president of the National GEM Consortium, chairman of the Council of Presidents of the Southeastern Universities Research Association, and president of the Southeastern Conference, among others.

He was awarded bachelor's, master's, and doctoral degrees from the University of Arkansas, Virginia Tech, and The Ohio State University, respectively, and holds honorary doctorates from George Washington University and Katholieke Universiteit of Leuven in Belgium.

In addition to *Why It Matters: Reflections on Practical Leadership*, he is the co-author of six engineering textbooks (three of which won book-of-the-year awards) and is author or co-author of hundreds of articles. Included in numerous Who's Who publications, John is also listed by Ranker.com as the seventh "most famous" industrial engineer.

The recipient of numerous awards for teaching, research, and service from the Institute of Industrial and Systems Engineers, the American Society for Engineering Education, the Society of Women Engineers, and other professional associations, John also received the National Science Foundation's Distinguished Service Award, university-level teaching awards from Georgia Tech and the University of Arkansas, and distinguished alumnus awards from his alma maters.

John and Mary Lib, parents of Kimberly Brakmann and John III, and grandparents of Charlotte and Sara Brakmann and Austin and Emma White, have residences in Arkansas and South Carolina.